PRAISE FOR *WHEN GOD MAKES LEMONADE*

"My friend Don Jacobson has always been an amazing storyteller, with the ability to see and capture powerful truths in the events of our lives. And now in this book you can experience this gift for yourself. The heart-touching stories he shares are wonderful reminders that God is fully with us at all times, including when we have the hardest time seeing it. The encouragement Don shares reminds us that we can see beyond the hardships of this life and be showered with the hope and grace that ultimately come only from a heavenly Father who adores us always."

—SHAUNTI FELDHAHN, AUTHOR OF *FOR WOMEN ONLY*

"We all need hope, and this book offers just that—a tall glass of refreshing hope. Whether you take in these stories sip by sip or in one big gulp, you'll be sweetly encouraged, and your faith in God's sovereign goodness will be renewed."

—ROBIN JONES GUNN, AUTHOR OF *VICTIM OF GRACE* AND *PRAYING FOR YOUR FUTURE HUSBAND*

"Don Jacobson weaves together dramatic stories from the lives of everyday Christians to remind the rest of us to look for His touch on our lives. This book will encourage you and give you hope when you're wondering why He doesn't show up in the way you want Him to."

—ED UNDERWOOD, PASTOR OF CHURCH OF THE OPEN DOOR AND AUTHOR OF *WHEN GOD BREAKS YOUR HEART*

"*When God Makes Lemonade* is an uplifting journey for anyone who's been through something tough. Having recently lost both of my parents, I found that these stories brought me hope and encouragement."

—JANICE CANTORE, AUTHOR OF *THE PACIFIC COAST JUSTICE SERIES*

"I have been blessed with the pleasure of knowing Don through his personal journey of developing and refining what he calls *a theology of hope*. This isn't just an inspirational 'gift book,' but Don's heartbeat and belief that although bad things can happen to good people, God still makes lemonade and never wastes a hurt. Whether for a friend, relative, or yourself, *When God Makes Lemonade* could be the most life-changing and encouraging book you buy this year."

—KEN WYTSMA, AUTHOR OF *PURSUING JUSTICE: THE CALL TO LIVE AND DIE FOR BIGGER THINGS* AND LEAD PASTOR OF ANTIOCH CHURCH IN BEND, OREGON

"I love these lemonade stories! It's where life is lived out authentically in the midst of the miraculous. Truly amazing! Truly divine!"

—KEN RUETTGERS, FORMER NFL LINEMAN FOR THE GREEN BAY PACKERS AND AUTHOR OF *THE HOME FIELD ADVANTAGE: A DAD'S GUIDE TO THE POWER OF ROLE MODELING*

"From the moment I opened *When God Makes Lemonade,* I was captivated. What great stories! Weaving throughout each true story, the reader will discover a personalized gift just for them, the gift of hope and assurance that God is with you, always!"

—TRUDY BEYAK, AN AWARD-WINNING INVESTIGATIVE JOURNALIST AND AUTHOR OF *THE MOTHER HEART OF GOD*

"Don Jacobson has spent most of his life pushing others into the spotlight. In this book he uses his incredible gift of storytelling to remind us that God consistently uses the things that go wrong as a platform to demonstrate his goodness. *When God Makes Lemonade* is a great gift to a hurting culture that needs a fresh drink of hope."

—REGGIE JOINER, FOUNDER OF THE reTHINK GROUP AND AUTHOR OF *THINK ORANGE: IMAGINE THE IMPACT WHEN CHURCH AND FAMILY COLLIDE*

"*When God Makes Lemonade* is not a book about how all our pain gets neatly transformed into a package with an oversized bow; rather, it is a collection of glimpses into God's goodness and surprising blessings in the midst of our suffering and often wayward choices. For those needing some lemon drop-sized encouragements, these stories will prove sweet."

—KELLY MINTER, SPEAKER AND AUTHOR OF
NEHEMIAH: A HEART THAT CAN BREAK

"Our world is fraught with darkness and brokenness. These stories remind us that the light has not been overcome, and that there is, in fact, hope. And hope, I believe, is something we all need."

—DANAE YANKOSKI, COWRITER WITH FRANCIS
CHAN OF *CRAZY LOVE* AND *FORGOTTEN GOD*

"This collection of stories is all about the amazing redemptive love of our God. Joshua received this command from the Lord: 'Be strong and courageous. Do not be frightened, and do not be dismayed, for the LORD your God is with you wherever you go' (Josh. 1:9 ESV). Reading these compelling stories of how God works even in the darkest moments is an inspiring reminder that God is, in fact, with us, and He will always make a way."

—DAVE BURCHETT, AUTHOR OF *WHEN BAD
CHRISTIANS HAPPEN TO GOOD PEOPLE*

"Sometimes life gives us lemons, but *When God Makes Lemonade* opens our eyes to the beautiful way God uses our hardships, our toughest moments, and our lemons to bring hope and light into the world. Reading this book is an encouraging reminder that God is with us, and He's for us, even in our desperation."

—LINDSEY NOBLES, DIRECTOR OF SPEAKERS & STRATEGIC
PARTNERSHIPS, FOOD FOR THE HUNGRY

WHEN GOD
MAKES
LEMONADE

WHEN GOD MAKES LEMONADE

True Stories That Amaze & Encourage

CREATED BY
DON JACOBSON

THOMAS NELSON
Since 1798

NASHVILLE   DALLAS   MEXICO CITY   RIO DE JANEIRO

Published in Nashville, Tennessee, by Thomas Nelson. Thomas Nelson is a registered trademark of Thomas Nelson, Inc.

Thomas Nelson, Inc. titles may be purchased in bulk for educational, business, fund-raising, or sales promotional use. For information, please e-mail SpecialMarkets@ThomasNelson.com.

**The Library of Congress Cataloging-in-Publication
data is on file with the Library of Congress and available upon request.**

ISBN 978-0-8499-6470-1

Printed in the United States of America

13 14 15 16 17 RRD 5 4 3 2 1

When God Makes Lemonade *is dedicated to single moms and their kids:*
you need encouragement more than anyone,
and your faithfulness encourages us.
Thank you.

CONTENTS

Acknowledgments xvii

Introduction xviii

1 Roslyn Lake 1
   Don Jacobson

2 Plain Old Ted 15
   Michelle Close Mills

3 Katie's Gift 21
   Dave Burchett

4 God's Punch 27
   Ron Fazio Jr.

5 Forever Changed 32
   Kasey Van Norman

6 *Freunde* 36
   Dixie Phillips

7 Steps to Forgiveness 42
      Jay Cookingham

8 Death of Our Son 46
      Jean Matthew Hall

9 A Light to Follow 50
      JoAnne Potter

10 Mommy and Me 54
      Tracy Healy

11 Courting Through Cancer 59
      Mary Potter Kenyon

12 Colliding with the Unknown 63
      Evan Osgood

13 Six Months to Life 70
      Dave Gist

14 But Now I See 75
      Gina Graham

15 KC Can't Skate 80
      Ross Gale

16 Angels with Chain Saws 84
      Mariane Holbrook

17 Sent Away for Good 89
      Bertha Raz

18 Truth Remembered 93
      Kim Anthony

19 Timing Is Everything 99
      Veta Shepherd

20 The Peppy Saint 103
    Matt Hart

21 Third Time's the Charm 108
    LaTosha Brown

22 A Block of Cheese 114
    Stephen Clover

23 The Woman Across the Hall 119
    Judy Cocoris

24 The Stolen Radio. 124
    Melanie Elliott

25 Ever After 128
    John Shepherd

26 Death of a Dream Car 132
    Cammy Scholz

27 Unexpected Laughter. 137
    Jody McComas

28 One Saturday Morning. 142
    Rick Wages

29 Tattooed on My Heart 147
    Angel Chung Cutno

30 Kyle's Legacy 152
    Penny Whipps

31 Covered by Love 157
    Yamaris Rosa

32 Can I Call You Mom? 161
    Carla Wicks

33 *Tout Begay Bien* 167
    Susan Rickey

34 The Letters of War 171
    Ray and Betty Whipps

35 Accidental Ministry 189
    Jaclyn Miller

36 Ayden the Trouper 193
    Caryn Rich

37 The Parking Lot Predicament 198
    Todd Gorton

38 The Perfect Fit 203
    Kimberly Sutton

39 Road to Recovery 208
    April LaLand

40 The Final Days 212
    Marybeth McCullum

41 Grandma's Love 216
    Kathleen Kohler

42 Santo Domingo Sunrise 220
    Terri Elders

43 Unexpected Family 225
    Kim McKinney

44 Surviving Suicide 230
    Lisa Lane

45 Balm for Burnout 234
    Lois Hudson

46 Room 234 239
   Gina Graham

47 Twin Chances 244
   Alisa Wagner

48 The Night You Were Born 249
   Carolyn Hill

49 The Education of a Jobless Teacher 254
   Derek Smith

50 Up, Up, Up 259
   Kevin Kalman

51 Fatherless 263
   Robyn Davis

52 Sink or Swim 268
   Wyndee Phillips

53 A Tough Break 272
   Matt McGoldrick

54 The Surprise Child 277
   Connie Cook

55 A Grandma's Heart 281
   Anne Forline

56 Falling into Grace 286
   David Waterman

57 The Little Biker That Could 291
   Karen Hessen

58 Behind Bars 294
   Danielle Barrett

59 Swept Away 297
        Erika Hoffman

60 Penniless but Not Broke 301
        Diane Williams

61 A Long, Rough Ride 306
        Jim Coon

62 Empty Coke Bottles 310
        Luke Beling

63 Ten Days in Dallas 315
        Donna Matthews

64 Marked by Love 320
        Sharie Robbins

65 A Divine Hair Appointment 325
        Amy von Borstel

66 Connection. 331
        Anonymous

67 A New Song 336
        Jay Cookingham

68 Friday Night Lights 340
        Becky Alexander

Afterword 345

About the Author 347

ACKNOWLEDGMENTS

My name's on the cover of this book, but the truth is that my behind-the-scenes team made this project possible. A huge *thank you* is in order for the following folks:

to the wonderful folks at Thomas Nelson who caught the vision,

to Marty Raz for doing everything and then some these past twenty-three years,

to Matt Smith for helping our authors tell their stories in heartfelt ways,

to Danae Yankosi for her amazing editing skills,

to David Jacobsen and Steffany Woolsey, who were there at the beginning,

to Brenda for being my partner and inspiration on this journey,

and to everyone who shared a true story of hope and inspiration with the *God Makes Lemonade* community . . . this is your book as well, and your honesty and encouragement are changing people's lives.

Don Jacobson

INTRODUCTION

The stories in *When God Makes Lemonade* are from everyday people who are surprised by unexpected sweetness in the midst of sour life circumstances. Why true stories? Because they give us hope, and in these difficult times, most of us don't need to be told to work harder—we're already working as hard as we can! What we need most is to be reminded that God is here working all things together for good.

So if you're struggling beneath the weight of unemployment, depression, broken relationships, an unexpected death, or any of life's other difficulties, don't give up!

Though the settings, names, and outcomes are unique in each lemonade story, they all say the same thing—you're not alone!

Yes, *stuff* happens in life, but so does lemonade, and when it does, it's as refreshing as a cold drink on a hot August day. May you find that kind of refreshment in the stories you're about to read, and may God bless you with the courage you need to hold on.

1

ROSLYN LAKE

DON JACOBSON

It's a chilly day in late November, and the clouds are hanging low over the Cascade Mountains. The woods where I am hunting around Roslyn Lake are thick and wild, just like the forest in Canada, where I grew up.

Trekking around the boundary of the water, I think back to the endless hours I spent fishing, hunting, and camping as a kid. Some of my friends wanted to fly into space, others dreamed of catching touchdowns in the Super Bowl, but I just wanted to be outside, breathing fresh air, living with a little dirt beneath my nails. I was captivated with the outdoors, so after high school I joined a logging crew. Then I got into construction. The specifics of the job didn't really matter; as long as I had the sun on my skin, I was a happy man.

I circle the lake, making sure to keep quiet. I don't want to scare the ducks, but Big Boy, my rambunctious black Lab, whines behind me and plunges into the water.

"Big Boy, quiet!" I whisper sharply. He splashes out of the lake and shakes his fur dry. A few more steps and I hear a pair of mallards on the shore, behind a thicket of weeds. I freeze. Big Boy stops behind me and whines; the ducks fall silent.

He keeps whimpering, and I know he will scare the ducks away, so I grip the barrel of my shotgun like a tennis racket and swing behind me.

"Quiet," I say, as the butt of my gun whacks Big Boy's flank.

Suddenly a deafening burst shatters the stillness, and I'm violently spun around. I tumble into the water and crash, face-first, into the shallows of the lake.

Desperately I gasp for air and try to sit up, but an intense burst of pain thrusts me back into the water. I roll over onto my back and spit the water out of my mouth.

Breathe, breathe, breathe, I say to myself, my ears ringing and my mind scattered.

What was that? There was a noise. Something hit me. I'm hurt.

I look up into the dark, gray clouds, and the unthinkable hovers over me.

God, I shot myself.

"Don!" I hear my buddy shout my name.

I lean over, lay the Sheetrock against the wall, and turn around.

"Phone!" he says, holding it up into the air. "It's your wife!"

I walk across the dusty floor and pull the glove from my hand one finger at a time.

"Hey, babe. How are you?" I ask, pressing the phone up to my ear.

"Doing great. How's work today?"

"Not bad. We're moving along really well. Should finish on schedule."

"That's great," she says. "I just wanted to remind you that Eric and Jeri will be here at six-thirty."

"Yep. Can't wait. Need me to pick anything up at the store?"

"Nope. We're all set. I'll see you soon?"

"Yep. I love you."

"I love you too."

"Oh wait," I hear her say, loudly, as I lower the phone. I raise it back up.

"Yeah?"

"I almost forgot. The gunsmith called, and he said your shotgun is ready and you can pick it up anytime."

"Really? That's great. I'll stop and get it on the way home."

"Just don't be late!"

I smile, picturing her shouting the words into the phone.

"Don't worry; I'll be there!"

A few hours later I take off early from work and run by the gunsmith. I tuck the stock up firm against my shoulder, look down the barrel, and follow a pair of imaginary ducks across the room.

"Feels good."

The gunsmith leans on the counter, nodding in agreement. I pay him his fee, jump in my car, and head home.

When I pull into the driveway, I check my watch.

I have a few hours until Eric and Jeri show up. Brenda is out running errands. *Maybe I have time to try out the gun?*

I check my watch one more time, think it through, and head into the garage. I stuff my pockets with shotgun shells, grab a coat, and whistle for Big Boy to jump into the car.

Should I leave a note for Brenda? I ask myself as I pull out of the driveway. *Ah, it's okay. I'll be home in time.*

I run my trembling hand up my right leg and stop when I reach a large, numb knot over my hip. The pain presses deeper into my side, through my gut, and down to my spine.

Oh, Lord, I pray, feeling the damage with my fingers, *I'm going to need your help on this one.*

I look back to the shore and see the stock of my gun resting in the water. Reaching out, I pull it back, close to my chest, and realize the stock is dangling from the double barrel.

Something malfunctioned. It's broken, I think to myself, sure that I've never seen a gun come apart like this.

I examine the damage and discover if I'm going to fire an SOS shot, I'll have to rip the stock from the barrels; so I grab the barrels in my right hand, the stock in the left, and snap it apart like a twig. The stock comes off easily, and I drop it into the water. Then I spread my fingers into my pockets, fish the shells from my wet jeans, and lay them on my stomach.

Holding the twin barrels in my left hand, I aim them to the sky and rest the bottom on a tree stump coming out of the water. I reach over with my right hand, load each barrel, and then rest my right index finger on the triggers.

Three shots for an SOS call, I remind myself. Then I count:

One, two, fire.

Boom!

One, two, fire.

Boom!

I quickly reach back to my chest with my right hand and grab another shell, but already I know I'm moving too slowly to fire a third shot in rhythm. Still, I fumble the shell into the barrel, and fire.

I listen for a moment, hoping for footsteps, or someone shouting, but there is nothing. I reload the gun and perform the same agonizing task.

Please, I pray, each time I reload, *please let there be someone nearby.*

I fire sixteen shots and run out of shells. The forest is still quiet, empty. I drop the gun back into the water.

"Help!" I shout as loud as I can. "Can anybody hear me?"

I yell so loudly I lose my breath. I'm light-headed.

"Help! I'm hurt. Help!"

My voice echoes off the water into the woods. I try to remember if I passed any cars parked along the road on the way up or if there were any homes nearby, but I can't. I'm alone, and I know it—no one can hear me, and nobody knows where I am. The fog resting over the treetops might as well descend and hide me forever.

My mind is hazy, losing hope, and slowly stumbling toward my only option.

If no one is coming, I have to get out of here by myself. Get to the car.

I slowly roll onto my abdomen and brace my hands beneath me. Drawing my knees up one at a time, I push up and find my balance.

Okay, good, I encourage myself, wobbly with pain. *Get going.*

Gripping my wound with both hands, I shuffle my left foot forward through the water. Next I pull my right foot up, but a searing pain paralyzes my leg, and I stumble back into the lake.

I hesitate to try again, but the command compels me: *get to the*

ROSLYN LAKE · 5

car. I roll over and brace myself on the muddy lake bottom. The pain stabs at my side, but with a deep breath I inch my hands forward, then follow with my knees. Another deep breath, and I crawl an inch farther.

Ten minutes later I'm out of the water, crawling on hands and knees down the path toward my car, when an intense surge of pain explodes in my chest. It pumps through my heart, burns down into my lungs, and causes my stomach to turn over with nausea. I collapse, moaning, on the path.

God, I plead, *if you're going to take me home, do it quickly, because it hurts.*

Instantly the fire cools and relief washes through my body. I draw in a long breath, and my muscles relax.

Thank you, God, thank you! I continue to breathe, thanking God with each exhalation, sensing him near, telling me, *If you make it until morning, you'll live.*

The light is fading from the sky, and the clouds are reaching down, hiding the forest in fog. I try once more to crawl to the car, but after fifty feet I simply stop moving. I am utterly exhausted and losing blood. I simply cannot go on.

As the day's last light leaks from the clouds, Big Boy prances up to me with a stick in his mouth and pokes me in the side. He whines, begging me for a game of fetch. I don't react, and he keeps pushing the stick into my wound.

God, he is going to kill me.

"Big Boy," I manage to say, "no, boy. Lie down."

Surprisingly, he obeys, and nestles up next to my cold body. I immediately feel the warmth from his body and once again sense God's presence.

If you make it until morning, you'll live.

Dusk slowly fades to black, and the woods grow ever quieter, tucked beneath a blanket of thick Oregon fog.

I start waiting, eyes open, for the break of dawn.

At 6:30 p.m. Eric and Jeri pull into our driveway as scheduled, and Brenda welcomes them by herself, excusing me for being late.

Eric, my longtime friend, asks Brenda where I am.

"I'm not sure, but if he doesn't get here soon, he isn't going to find out who shot J. R.!" replies Brenda, half joking, half concerned.

They eat, clear the dishes, and turn on the TV, but I still haven't arrived.

"I'm going to call my dad," Brenda says right before *Dallas* starts. "Maybe he's heard from Don."

"No, sorry. Haven't heard from him," her father, John, says, "but I wouldn't be too worried. He has some old tires on that car. Maybe one went flat."

"I don't know, Dad. I'm worried. I want to call the police," Brenda says.

"No, that won't help. They can't do anything now. Just wait until after the show. If he's still not home, call me back."

"Okay," Brenda relents. "Thanks, Dad."

After *Dallas* is over, Brenda gets back on the phone.

"Dad, he still isn't home. I have a bad feeling."

"I don't know what to tell you. The police still can't help because he's only been missing a few hours. I'll call if I hear anything."

They hang up, and Brenda sits back down with Eric and Jeri.

"I don't know what to do," she confesses. "Where is he?"

Anxious hours pass, and finally, just after 11:00 p.m., the phone rings. Brenda rushes to the receiver and picks it up.

"Hello? Don?"

"No, sweetheart, it's me." Her father is calling back. "Your brother just got home and said Don called him this afternoon about hunting."

"Hunting?" Brenda asks.

"Yeah, he said Don called and wanted to go try the new stock on his gun. We are going to look for him now. You stay home and wait by the phone."

"Dad, I can't stay home. I have to look too."

He sighs, and Brenda can hear him thinking on the other end of the line.

Where do I send her? John wonders to himself. He knows it's important to have as many people out searching as possible, but he can't send his daughter into the woods with the risk of finding her dead husband. The trauma would be too great.

"Okay," he finally says, deciding to send Brenda to the least likely hunting spot he can imagine. "You go with Eric and Jeri up to Roslyn Lake; he might be up there."

"I don't know why we are looking here. It feels like we are wasting time," Brenda laments. They have been driving around for over an hour, taking wrong turns, getting lost in the fog, growing frustrated. It is long past midnight, and they have yet to reach Roslyn Lake.

Slowly, Eric steers the car around a bend in the asphalt road and sees something glimmer in the darkness. He slams on the brakes and shouts, "What is that?" as he looks intently in the rearview mirror.

Brenda turns and recognizes it instantly. "It's Don's car! The fog is so thick we drove right past it!"

They leap out into the cold and check my car.

"He hasn't been here recently," Eric says, feeling his hand to the cold hood. Together, they walk out onto the man-made dike at the end of the lake.

"Don!" Eric shouts. "Can you hear me?"

I open my eyes. Big Boy's warm body is still against me, keeping me warm, and his ears are up. He whimpers, looking into the dark.

I can hear something.

"Don!"

It's faint, but I hear it. *Is it real? Am I dreaming?* I close my eyes and lean forward. I try to listen to every sound in the forest.

"Don!"

I snap my eyes open and turn my head toward the scream.

They found me.

"I'm here!" I try to shout, but my voice is too dry to speak. I swallow, but my tongue sticks to the roof of my mouth.

Water! Find water!

I look to the lake. *Can I crawl down and drink in time?* I keep looking, desperate, and see the glimmer of dew on my parka sleeve. Quickly I suck the moisture from the fabric and shout, "I'm here!" I gasp and swallow. "I'm here!"

Eric throws his hands up. "Wait! Did you hear that?"

Brenda and Jeri shake their heads.

"Listen," Eric whispers. A quiet moment passes. "There!" he erupts. "Did you hear that?"

"No!" Brenda says. "What is it?"

"Go wait in the car. I'm going to check it out." Eric runs down the dike and turns into the forest.

I hear someone coming through the woods, and Big Boy starts barking. Again I feebly try to shout, "I'm here!"

Please, Lord, please let him see me.

On cue Eric steps through the mist and kneels down beside me. "Oh, thank God! Don, what did you do?"

"Eric? Is that you?" I ask, my voice scratchy.

"Yes, Don, it's me. What are you doing here?" He kneels down next to me. "What happened?"

"I shot myself. It was an accident. How did you find me?"

"Everyone is out driving around."

"Brenda," I stammer, "is she here?"

"She is in the car . . . You stay here, and I'll go get help." He stands to run back to the car, but I stop him.

"No, Eric, I can walk. Get me up."

He helps me to my feet. Leaning heavily on his shoulder, I try to step, but everything starts spinning. I collapse, and without hesitating, Eric dashes off into the dark.

"Don't move! I'll get help!" he says as he disappears.

Brenda and Jeri are startled when Eric opens the car door.

"What happened?" cries Brenda.

"I found Don. He's okay, but he shot himself. We have to find a phone."

Rushing up to the first farmhouse they find, Eric and Brenda pound on the door. A light flickers on, and a young man shuffles to the door.

"Sorry to bother you, sir," Eric greets him, "but we need to call an ambulance."

Within the hour I'm surrounded by several members of the Sandy, Oregon, volunteer fire department. The paramedics check my vitals and discover my heart rate and body temperature are dangerously low.

I am nearly hypothermic, and my veins have collapsed, keeping the medics from inserting an IV.

They call in another ambulance, equipped with inflatable pants, and when they arrive, they strap the pants on my legs, fill them with air, and push the blood back up into my vital organs. Finally, they are able to insert an IV and transport me, but they don't load me into the ambulance. Instead, they call dispatch and request a medevac.

"Stupid idea calling in the helicopter," Brenda overhears a police officer say. "They'll never land it in this fog."

But a few minutes later, with the air ambulance on its way, the fog pushes back just enough to reveal the night sky. The chop of the rotors starts echoing through the dark surrounding hills, and the helicopter sets down safely.

Eight minutes later, just before we arrive at the hospital in Gresham, the fog once again peels away for the pilot to land gently on the helipad. As soon as I am wheeled from the helicopter, the fog rolls back in and grounds the flight crew for several hours.

As I'm being pushed down the hospital hallway, the fluorescent lights blurry overhead, a nurse leans down.

"Don, I have some good news for you. Dr. Brose is on call tonight. He's one of the best trauma surgeons in the city."

I force a faint smile, and they wheel me to the emergency operating room. People are everywhere, rushing around me, rolling machines across the room, prepping me for surgery.

I survived the three-hour-long operation, but Dr. Brose was worried about gas gangrene, so he moved me to a hyperbaric chamber at

Providence Portland Medical Center. He told Brenda I'd never walk again, and if I lived, I'd have a colostomy for the rest of my life.

On my eighth day of recovery, Eric came to visit me. His face was long and sad, but we exchanged tired smiles.

"How are you liking ICU?" he asked.

"What do you mean?" I replied, looking at him, confused. "I'm in ICU?"

The smile faded from his face. "You've been in critical condition for eight days. You didn't know?"

"No." I tried to shake my head. "I just thought I was in the hospital."

I thought, quietly, for a moment, but my mind was still hazy and scattered. "Are people worried about me?"

He nodded slowly, up and down, and his lips barely parted. "Everyone."

"Don't," I told him confidently. "God showed me the night I was shot that if I lived until morning, I'd make it. Tell everyone I'll be okay."

The very next day I was moved from the ICU to a regular hospital room. As the slow, painful days of recovery turned to weeks and months, it became clear I not only was going to live but would enjoy a full recovery.

Thirty-two years later I'm not only walking without a colostomy; I'm still hiking the hills of central Oregon, wrestling with my kids, and whipping friends at table tennis.

I can say confidently I would not be here if not for Dr. Brose. Because of his unique training in central Africa, treating trauma victims, he was equipped to save my life. I can also say my rambunctious dog saved my life, lying down beside me, giving me his warmth. My wife's intuition to call her dad and demand to join the search also saved my life—as did Eric's keen eyes and ears and the water on the sleeve of my jacket. Paramedics, pilots, a farmer—they all saved my life.

Even the gunshot saved my life. Despite the close range, the blast failed to create an exit wound; and a month after I was discharged from the hospital, the doctor pulled sixteen pellets from my back, millimeters from the surface of my skin. Had even one BB escaped during the incident, I would have bled to death in the forest. Instead, the mass of lead stuck in my abdomen, tore away muscles, nicked one kidney, and damaged my liver. I later discovered that the intense pain in my chest as I crawled to my car was caused by a BB flowing through the chambers of my heart before depositing in my left lung.

I have often wondered, what stopped the shotgun blast from killing me instantly? And what blew back the fog at the exact right time for the helicopter to land? And whose voice spoke Big Boy into obedience? Who could have planned such an elaborate rescue?

Was it the hand of God? The breath of God? The voice of God? The rescue of God?

I believe so, and not just because I survived, but because I was transformed.

The accident didn't just cause the physical pain of a gunshot, traumatic surgery, and slow recovery. It also wounded my soul.

After the accident I spent many sleepless nights, asking God how I was supposed to provide for my family with a crippled body. And if I really couldn't work doing manual labor, what job would ever give me the satisfaction of working outside with my hands?

I was disoriented and depressed, thankful to be alive yet confused as to what my life was all about. I'd always been the strong guy with calloused hands and flannel shirts. It wasn't just a job, working as a commercial carpenter; it was who I was—my very identity. I couldn't imagine being anyone else. As I grappled with the emotional loss, my father-in-law came to visit.

"Don, all your life you've used your body," he said. "Now God is giving you the opportunity to use your mind."

Initially I felt his timing to be insensitive, and I was offended that he would trivialize my desire to make a living with my hands. But with time and prayer, I came to see he was right—God had forcefully yet tenderly cleared a new path for me to walk.

I returned to school at Multnomah Bible College, and after graduation I took a job in the publishing industry, where over the past two and a half decades I have experienced the unexpected joy of working with some of the wisest, most encouraging authors in the world. Their friendships have blessed me, given me hope, and taught me to believe in the miraculous power of story—even my own.

All those years ago at Roslyn Lake, I never would have asked for a cross-threaded screw in my gun, but it is the story I was given, and I now can thank God for that malfunction. It started me on a journey that has led me here, to *When God Makes Lemonade*, to share the truth I've learned over and over. God can, and does, use life's worst moments to invite us into life's greatest blessings.

It is the truth written into my story, the real-life stories collected in this edition, and the greatest story of all: God's. My prayer is that with a little hope, courage, and time, you, too, will begin to sense God at work, crafting your life into a beautiful story of redemption.

2

PLAIN OLD TED

MICHELLE CLOSE MILLS

The neat, winding paths of the cemetery near my home in Florida were peaceful and serene. Although my father and grandmother had been laid to rest last year a thousand miles away in Indiana, walking through the memorial garden helped me feel connected to them.

Ever since they passed away within one month of each other, I'd felt isolated and adrift, like a boat whose moorings had been cut. I couldn't seem to move past the one question burning in my heart: Why had they been taken from me so suddenly?

I walked the path every day, alone, looking for answers, praying, crying, and grieving. I looked out over the cemetery landscape as if I were surveying my own soul: empty, lifeless, and full of a thousand buried memories. How many more memories would I have to lay to rest before I moved on? Could I move on?

One Friday morning, as I crested a small hill, I discovered a well-dressed, elderly gentleman sitting on a bench overlooking a monument. He was reading aloud from a book, and next to him I could see a Styrofoam cup and a red rose.

I found the gentleman there again the next Friday, and the Friday after that. Each week he sat, reading aloud next to a white cup and a red rose. I was too curious to pass by for a fourth time, so I stopped and introduced myself.

"How do you do, Michelle?" he said politely, shaking my hand. "I'm Ted Henderson."

"Nice to meet you, Mr. Henderson. Who are you visiting?"

He smiled. "Please, call me Ted. I'm spending time with my wife, Margie," he said, nodding toward the gravestone with the red rose and the Styrofoam cup. "Every Friday you'll find me here, rain or shine."

I was definitely intrigued. "Are Fridays significant somehow?"

Ted nodded. "Friday evening was date night for Margie and me. We'd go to supper, see a movie, or play cards with our neighbors— that kind of thing. It gave us a few hours together away from the kids."

Ted looked from me to the monument, took a breath, and continued.

"When Margie got sick and went to a nursing home, we still had date night. It was something we both looked forward to. I'd bring her a red rose and a chocolate shake. Then I'd read to her—the newspaper, a book, or a chapter from the Bible. Forty-nine years . . . that was a lot of Friday night dates."

Ted sighed. "I figure just because I can't see her anymore, it's no reason to cancel our date night. And maybe she can see and hear me still."

My approach to grief suddenly seemed so flawed. I was walking around crying, bitter at the world, but Ted was on a date with his sweetheart of fifty years. How did he do it? Could he teach me?

"May I join you?" I asked.

Ted smiled. "Sure. I'd like that."

For a while we sat in companionable silence. Then I asked, "Would you tell me more about Margie?"

It was as if a jolt of energy raced through Ted. He sat up a little straighter and rubbed the palms of his hands on the knees of his slacks. "Margie was the prettiest girl I ever saw—deep blue eyes, cheeks the color of peaches, and long curly hair as red as a fire truck. And spunky! I fell in love with her on the spot."

I smiled encouragingly—not that Ted needed any encouragement to talk about his true love. "She was crazy about me, too, though I never understood why. I mean"—he said, shaking his head slightly—"I'm just plain old Ted."

He chuckled, but then out of his fond memories grew a melancholy shoot. "Margie passed on eleven years ago." His voice slowed slightly. "It seems like only yesterday we were newlyweds weeding the garden together. When the weather was hot, we'd squirt each other with the hose."

Ted paused and then continued, as if he'd made a decision. "Folks at church keep trying to fix me up with widows," he said. "I tell them no thanks. There's only one lady for me."

"She must have been very special," I said, feeling my words inadequate.

Ted took my comment in stride. "Margie loved people. She visited sick folks, knit booties for new babies, gave away most of our home-grown vegetables to the needy, and taught the kindergarten Sunday school class. Little ones were crazy about her."

"How many kids do you have?"

Ted gazed into the distance. "We had twin boys: Theodore Jr. and Andrew. Teddy played football, and Andy was our scholar. Both were as handsome as movie stars, but they couldn't have been more different. It's funny how that works. After college . . ."

Ted stopped, but I could tell that he wanted to finish his story, so I waited.

"After college, they enlisted in the army. We lost them in Vietnam. They died seven months apart."

Ted's voice grew husky. "After that, a light went out in Margie. Children aren't supposed to go first, you know?"

We were both crying now, but Ted lifted his chin resolutely. "Our boys were proud to serve their country. They were where they wanted to be."

Feeling guilty, I started to apologize. "Please forgive me for stirring up painful memories."

Ted looked surprised. "Young lady, I believe the Almighty sent you to me so I'd have a chance to talk about my family. Nobody asks about them anymore. I miss them like crazy, but since they left, God has never stopped giving me a million reasons to get up each day. I have wonderful friends and a beautiful granddaughter who spoils the heck out of me, and my needs are met. What more could I want?"

When he said it that way, the answer was obvious: nothing. So why was it so difficult for me to answer that same question for myself? I realized Ted must know something I didn't.

"How did you find peace after all you've suffered?" I asked.

"When Margie died, I was devastated. I moped around for months. Then one day I imagined what she'd say if she saw me sitting around in my pajamas at one thirty in the afternoon, my hair looking like shredded wheat. She'd holler, 'Ted, quit bawling, get off your lazy behind, and find something to do!'"

We laughed, and he continued. "So I got out of my chair and started moving. It was hard, and there were still days when grief got the better of me. But I kept pushing forward through the pain—for Margie and for me. Of course, I make an exception on Fridays . . . but otherwise, I'm a go-getter!"

The sun was setting, and Ted looked at his watch. "Mercy, look at the time! Margie always said I talked too much." We laughed again, and then he studied my face intently. "Young lady, next time I want to hear about you. There's a world of hurt in those green eyes."

I smiled and wiped away the last trace of tears. He patted my shoulder, then bid me farewell: "You know where I am every Friday."

The next week Ted wasn't sitting in his customary spot, nor was he there the week after that. The following week I read his obituary in the newspaper.

Even though we had shared only one conversation in our lives, it felt right to attend his memorial service. I'm glad I did, because it was the best party I'd been to in years. The hall was packed with friends and family laughing, sharing stories, and listening to Ted's favorite music from the stereo.

I met his granddaughter, Sharon, and she gave me a tour of his photo album. It turns out plain old Ted wasn't very plain at all. He was a World War II pilot, a POW, an MIT grad, a NASA team member, a loving husband, a caring father, and a committed grandfather.

On the drive home I marveled at the fullness of Ted's life and remembered something he had said: *I kept pushing forward through the pain—for Margie and for me.* I knew with certainty that Daddy and Grandma would want me to do the same—before I ended up in my pajamas at one thirty in the afternoon, with hair like shredded wheat!

That week I enrolled in grief counseling, and as time passed, the sharp wounds of my grief began to dull and heal. Soon after my last session, I began meeting with individuals looking for help and healing. Before I met Ted I would have had nothing to offer them. But now, God uses my darkness to light the way for others, and I have Ted to thank for that: "Plain old Ted," who taught me how to grieve, but most important, taught me also how to live.

MICHELLE CLOSE MILLS is a freelance writer from central Florida, but her most rewarding job is proud wife and mother of two grown children. She is also "cat mom" to fur-kids Simon and Maggie. Michelle maintains there is a special place in heaven for those who rescue fuzzy buddies from animal shelters. She enjoys singing and coffee dates with loved ones, and she often has her nose in a book.

3

KATIE'S GIFT

DAVE BURCHETT

In 1985, Kathryn Alice Burchett was born into our family. We were overjoyed to welcome our first daughter into a home with two boys. My wife, Joni, and I had both secretly wanted a girl, and Katie's arrival thrilled us. She would be Daddy's special girl and Mommy's little partner.

We anticipated that she would light up our lives. What we couldn't know was that Katie's life would be both more tragic and more incredible than we could imagine.

The way the doctor announced Katie's birth to us told us something was very wrong. Whispered orders and urgent instructions flew around the delivery room. Moments later our happiness was shattered when we received the news about our baby girl's condition.

Katie had a terminal neural tube birth defect. Her condition, known as anencephaly, meant that her brain had not developed normally in the womb. A large portion of her brain was simply missing, and she was not expected to live beyond a few days. The delivery room doctor summed up Katie's condition in cold terminology: "Her condition is not compatible with life."

Not compatible with life? His words didn't make sense to us. The daughter we'd dreamed about was right there with us, alive.

Our shock and grief were as deep as they were sudden. Katie would never enjoy a normal life, even for the tiny number of days she was expected to live. There was no cure, no hope for even modest improvement. I still recall nearly every agonizing word I choked out as I relayed Katie's condition to our friends, our family, and—most painfully of all—our two young sons. The day she was born, we had to start thinking about her death.

Katie would never open her eyes. She couldn't smile. She lacked the ability to regulate her own body temperature, so her room temperature had to be monitored constantly. Part of Katie's condition was an area of exposed tissue at the back of her skull that never healed and had to be covered regularly with sterile dressing.

Despite all this, Katie confounded the doctors by living. She refused to let go of life.

Joni's devotion to Katie shone like a beacon in those dark days. She insisted that we bring Katie home with us. I worried about the effect that caring for Katie at home might have on the boys. Truthfully, I was probably more concerned about the effect on *me*. But Joni would have it no other way, so I showed husbandly wisdom by agreeing to bring our daughter home.

Soon, little Katie had established her place in our family's routine. She responded to her mother's touch and learned to drink from a bottle. She even grew a little. We took her on a family camping trip. For one precious summer, Katie was a faithful fan at her older brothers' baseball games.

A lot of people, including some close friends and family, thought our decision to bring Katie home was a mistake. Some made hurtful remarks. A kid at school taunted our oldest son by saying his sister didn't "have a brain" (no doubt something the classmate had heard at home).

One time we dressed up the troops and went to have family pictures taken, only to have the photographer insist that Katie open her eyes. Even when we explained that she physically could not open her eyes, he refused to take our picture; he argued that the lab would not develop any pictures in which eyes were closed.

One Sunday morning a friend called to tell us that Katie wasn't welcome in the church nursery. The other moms feared that Katie might die in their care and traumatize a volunteer worker. They also worried that the opening at the back of Katie's skull might generate a staph infection. If they had come to us with their concerns, we might have been able to allay some of their fears. But the decision was made without our input, and we could no longer take our baby daughter to church.

When Katie was three months old, Joni decided she wanted to have another baby. I wasn't sure. What if the same birth defect manifested itself again? Even so, we decided to trust God, and soon Joni became pregnant. We celebrated Katie's first birthday at the end of Joni's second trimester, and just three months later a healthy baby boy joined our family. Katie couldn't see Brett, but she could feel his soft newborn skin.

Life grew even more hectic. My work as a television director required me to travel, and Joni was at home with Katie and three boys aged eight, five, and brand-new.

One evening in May 1986, Joni and I made plans to get away for an evening. We had a nurse come stay with Katie and Brett, and we took the older boys to a friend's house.

Late that night, after picking up the boys, we pulled into our garage and started to get out of the car. Suddenly two men wearing black masks and brandishing guns burst into the garage, screaming at us not to move.

They forced us into the house. One of the gunmen held the boys, Joni, and the nurse at gunpoint. As Joni prayed fervently in the living room, I experienced a supernatural calm—believe me; it was not of my own doing. The leader walked me around the house and threatened to harm my family if I didn't reveal where things were stashed. He demanded cash and grew angry when I told him that all our money went to pay Katie's medical bills.

Our oldest son, Matt, heard the exchange. "Mr. Robber," he said, "you can have my piggy bank." They actually took it.

All the while, Katie slept quietly in her room. Both intruders seemed to be terrified of her. Perhaps they thought she had something contagious, since we had a nurse in the house. Whatever the reason, they steered a wide path around her room and never threatened her.

Before they left, the robbers forced us into a bedroom and jammed the door shut from the outside. But the bedroom those rocket scientists locked us in shared a common bathroom with Katie's room. As soon as they left, I went through Katie's room and outside to my car phone (they had cut our phone lines) to call the police.

Soon the ordeal was over, and we began to regain some of the calm that Katie never lost. Some of our possessions had been taken, but the things that matter most to a family—our lives, our love, and our hope—remained beyond the grasp of the thieves. Aside from some tough talk and waving pistols, they didn't harm us in any way. It was as if they were operating under a "steal but do not assault or maim" directive. We found out later that the two gunmen did far worse things, including sexual assault, to other victims before they were caught. We were the exception, and I'm convinced that Katie's presence spared our family those terrors.

Some people wonder about Katie's purpose in living fourteen months, especially since every medical opinion maintained she would die within a few days of birth. In my heart I'm persuaded that there are many reasons our baby girl stayed with us for so long, reasons beyond what I will ever comprehend.

But I will always be convinced that Katie lived as long as she did for at least two particular reasons. First, so that her brother Brett could join us and for a season we could be a whole family. Even though it was short, we will treasure that time for as long as we live. And second, to be our guardian angel during that robbery. Katie's severe physical abnormality, coupled with her almost otherworldly serenity, so unnerved the robbers that they abandoned their hyperviolent pattern of behavior.

Just weeks after the robbery, Katie's heart began to fail. On June 4, 1986, on a warm spring morning, Katie died with her family at her side.

From the time she was born, Katie could never smile; her only facial expressions were a tiny frown or grimace. But when Katie's life began to ebb away, a feeling of peace entered the room like a comforting breeze. As her courageous spirit finally left her tiny body, a wide smile lit her face for the first time. I will always believe her smile was a response to the heavenly escort whispering, "Well done, little one. It's time to come home."

DAVE BURCHETT is an Emmy Award–winning sports television director. Dave and his wife, Joni, faced the heartbreak of finding out that their daughter's life would be very brief. That tragic news was compounded by the hurtful actions of their church.

That incident began a journey that resulted in Dave's first book, *When Bad Christians Happen to Good People*. But Katie's story is ultimately a story of hope and amazing grace. You can follow Dave's blog at daveburchett.com or at crosswalk.com.

4

GOD'S PUNCH

RON FAZIO JR.

When I heard the shouting, I knew there was going to be trouble.

"Here we go," I sighed to myself, pushing through the crowd toward the altercation brewing on the other side of the club.

I stepped up onto a small platform between two groups of guys, each swearing at the top of his lungs. "What seems to be the problem, gentlemen?" I asked, hoping we could settle things without a fight.

I'd been working as a bouncer for a while, and I'd learned a few tricks along the way. Never lose your patience. Never punch first. Never try to reason with a group of drunken guys. And these guys were definitely drunk. As I tried to get some space between them, a glass was thrown and shattered against the wall. The fight erupted immediately.

My security team and I almost had them under control, but then a sucker punch struck me square on my jaw. That isn't allowed. You don't punch the bouncer. I turned around and landed a quick jab on the guy's mouth, and he went down. I turned my back on him and helped a coworker corral some other troublemakers.

After picking himself up off the floor, the guy I punched wobbled his way over to a phone and called the police. A few minutes later the scene was bright with flashing sirens, and the guy I punched tried to accuse me of assault. Thankfully, as soon as the cops smelled alcohol on his breath, they closed the case.

"Man, what a night," a coworker said as we watched the police drive away.

"Seriously, I'm getting tired of these guys who think that—"

"Wow," he interrupted me, looking at my hand. "You better get that looked at."

I lifted up my right hand and turned my palm to the ground. Blood was pooling around a small white sliver in my right index finger, and I winced as I yanked the sliver from the cut. I held it up to the streetlight, and my friend stepped in for a closer look.

"It's a piece of a tooth," I said.

"Like I said." My friend patted me on the back. "You better get that looked at."

After my shift was over a few hours later, the doctor in the emergency room cleaned out the cut but refused to stitch it up.

"Human bite wounds can easily get infected," he explained, "and sewing it closed can trap the germs inside."

"So is that it? I just leave it open?" I asked.

"I'll dress the wound with some gauze and send you home with some antibiotics and painkillers. We will also need to schedule an appointment with a surgeon to reattach the severed tendon."

I went home, popped some painkillers, and fell asleep.

Two days later, when I woke up, I rubbed the sleep out of my eyes and discovered red streaks on my hand and arm.

Is that the infection the emergency room doctor told me about? I wondered.

Just to be safe, I went back to the hospital and was quickly admitted. They hooked me up to intravenous antibiotics and told me I'd be staying until the infection disappeared completely.

Great, I thought. *How in the world am I going to pay for an extended hospital stay?*

After two days of being trapped in my hospital room, I was growing antsy. My arm was still infected and showed no signs of recovery. I moped around the room.

What am I doing? I asked myself. *Is this really what I'm doing with my life?*

I didn't move to New York to be a bouncer. Though I enjoyed the job and the A-list company, it wasn't my passion. I was an actor, trying to make it big in the big city. The bouncing job paid the bills and left my schedule open during the days for casting calls and auditions. I got paid to use my six-foot-four, 250-pound frame for security, but my real job was working out, staying in shape, and mailing headshots and cover letters to producers.

Since I'd landed the lead in *Toxic Avenger 2* and *Toxic Avenger 3*, things had been a little slow. I loved making movies, but I had to be honest with myself.

I have a college degree, and I'm punching drunk guys to pay my rent.

For the first time since moving to New York, I thought it might be time for a new dream. But what? How often do opportunities walk through the door in New York City?

"Mr. Fazio, good to see you today." I turned away from the window and watched the surgical team enter my room. The doctor was speaking. "How are you feeling?"

"Good, thanks." I looked to my arm. "Doesn't look like there is much to report."

"Let's just go ahead and take a look."

I sat down on the bed, and everyone crowded around me. With my arm in his hands and his eyes inspecting the infection, the doctor introduced me to his team. There was a hand specialist, a nurse, and a woman he said was a physician's assistant.

"A physician's assistant: What is that?" I asked, hoping it didn't sound too rude.

"I get that a lot." She smiled. "A PA works as an extension of the doctor. We specialize in different fields and even assist in surgery."

The next day I asked the PA a few more questions. I was surprised to discover it only takes two years to complete the training, and their services are in high demand all across the country. Suddenly I remembered my childhood dream of being a dentist or working in a hospital, and I wondered, *Could I be a PA? It sounds like a great job, the steady paycheck would be great, and I could really help a lot of people!*

After a week in the hospital and a successful operation to reattach my severed tendon, I was discharged without a bill—by God's grace the nightclub picked up the tab! My arm was healthy, and I had a decision to make. Go back to bouncing and try to land some more acting jobs, or maybe, just maybe, become a PA?

I researched some schools and found a great PA program at Bayley Seton Hospital in Staten Island.

It's nearby. It's affordable. It's a rewarding job. It pays consistently.

I could see no reason not to apply.

Dropping the application in the mail, I remembered the hundreds of times I had sent out my headshots and bio. I had no idea what to expect this time, but I knew it felt right. Two months later the director of the program called and invited me to the hospital for an interview. I showed up a thousand times more nervous than I had been for any casting call. Would they like me? Was I a good fit? Would they accept me?

The interview went great, I was accepted, and two years later I graduated with honors.

Today I have a wonderful wife, three beautiful daughters, and the rare blessing of loving what I do. I get to help people heal, which is a tremendous gift. I also get to answer the question I asked so many years ago: "What is a PA?" I tell the story of how I was a wannabe actor in New York when opportunity walked right through my door. I laugh and say, "Some people think fate is the hand of God, but in my case, it was the punch of God!"

RON FAZIO JR. grew up near Philadelphia and attended the University of Maryland, where he played football. After a brief stint in the NFL, Ron moved to New York in 1988 to pursue an acting career. After becoming a PA, Ron continued to work in New York. He now lives in North Carolina, where he attends St. Michael the Archangel Catholic Church and enjoys life with his wife and three daughters.

LEMON DROP

Ron Fazio Jr. wasn't looking for a career change when he took a sucker punch to the face, but he was open to God's plan, and a visit to the hospital was all God needed to reveal himself. It's not easy to see God's hand at work when we are hurting—pain too rarely makes us praise God. Yet Ron's story is a good reminder that God doesn't waste our pain, and if we are listening, it will invite us into a world of blessings.

—Don

5

FOREVER CHANGED

KASEY VAN NORMAN

At the tender age of fifteen, I had never been kissed. So when the older, handsome, most popular boy in my small, country high school gazed into my eyes and whispered, "I love you," I was beyond smitten. It was only our first date, but I was certain that his attention was a gift from God, a "Thank you, Kasey" from the hand of the Almighty himself for being such a good girl. Despite my troubled home life, I'd managed to make the honor roll, sing in the choir, go to youth group, and even wear a WWJD bracelet. Finally God was repaying me for my effort.

Later that night, as I fell asleep, I couldn't stop smiling. For the first time in my life, a male was taking interest in me; the fact that he was the cutest, most desired boy in town made it all the sweeter. I drifted off to sleep, certain no dream could compare to the bliss of my reality.

A few hours later I was startled awake by a sharp pain in my throat. Someone was on top of me, pushing down into my chest and my wrists; and when I managed to sit up, I discovered it was him, my date. He had snuck into the house and crawled on top of me.

"What are you doing?" I choked. But the pain didn't stop; instead, it quickly spread through my body. I begged and pleaded over and over for him to stop and get off of me, but my frightened words and ample tears were powerless to stop him. *Why is he doing this?* I screamed inside. Four hours earlier he was laughing and joking with me over a late-night snack of Cheerios and Cheetos. Now he was a ravenous, angry, hormone-driven animal taking what he wanted. What happened to "I love you"?

Later that night, even the scalding hot water pouring into the bathtub couldn't keep me from shaking. I was hot, sweating, and trembling from betrayal. I hugged my legs close to my chest and fixed my senses on the water—watching it flow from the faucet, listening to the flood, feeling the heat warm my legs. I filled my lungs with the dense, moist air and exhaled. I imagined the water as a pure mountain spring, coming from the earth to wash away the pain. But it couldn't.

Just as I was powerless to stop the rape, I was powerless to stop the pain. It consumed me. Day after day it raged within, compromising my self-worth, wounding my spirit, and destroying my identity. Before long I was acting only out of pain. I ran to promiscuous relationships, developed an eating disorder, and began cutting myself. Every time I pulled a razor blade from the drawer and placed it to my arm, I welcomed the pain. It was gruesome, but I preferred the physical suffering to the deep, dark, terrifying truth that ruled within me.

Surprisingly, despite my destructive behavior, I was able to maintain a presentable and popular appearance. All throughout high school, from freshman to senior year, I was the consummate actress, fooling everyone all of the time. But when I was alone, hunched over the toilet, placing the cold blade to my arm, I begged God to take the pain out of me. Four years passed, and I never spoke a word about the rape. I was hospitalized for anorexia and admitted to therapy for cutting, but no one knew the source of my problems.

Then, toward the end of my senior year of high school, I was invited to attend a church camp in the mountains of New Mexico. On the last night of camp, a sun-kissed, scripture-quoting college girl dragged me and nine other girls up a mountain at 10:00 p.m. When we reached the top, she circled us up and said, "Okay girls, I would like for us to go around the circle and tell how the Lord has spoken to us this week." Immediately my pulse raced, and a wave of hot terror rushed through me. *What now, Kasey?* I thought to myself, panicking as my turn grew closer. *Come on; think of something! You're a good actress—make something up! Quote John 3:16 or something else. Don't break down. Keep it together.*

Then suddenly, the group was silent, and all eyes were on me. I opened my mouth, but nothing came out. Instead, I began to cry. The wounds festering beneath my polished, color-coordinated shell escaped. I was broken, and for the first time in a long, long time, I sensed God's loving presence invading me from the inside out. Where I had felt darkness for so long, there was now light. Where there was bitterness, forgiveness flowed.

Finally, after four long years of defining myself as the girl who was raped, God blessed me with a new identity. His was the love that would never betray me, always nourish me, and eternally cherish me. At last I knew I would not lose my life to pain, bitterness, and anger. My darkness would become my ministry—and the tremendous pain I endured would be the very thing I needed to help other women heal.

Since that week in the mountains of New Mexico, I have desired—more than life itself—to show others the merciful, restorative healing that Jesus offers to the most unlikely and unworthy of lives. I live to tell others what true healing looks like. Through God's grace I have experienced true worth, value, and security that will never fade. In fact, it is a light so bright, it is able to banish any hint of shadow or sadness.

KASEY VAN NORMAN is the founder and president of Kasey Van Norman Ministries, located in College Station, Texas, where she lives with her husband, Justin, and her two children, Emma Grace (seven) and Lake (four). Kasey received her degrees in public speaking, psychology, and biblical studies, and is a certified counselor. Kasey's breakout series, *Named by God*, was released May 2012 by Tyndale House Publishers, and includes her memoir as well as a six-week Bible study and DVD teaching series. Kasey will be joining the national Extraordinary Women Tour for 2013 as a speaker. To learn more about her ministry, check out kaseyvannorman.com.

6 ===

FREUNDE

DIXIE PHILLIPS

The motor on the landing craft whined and gurgled, and the platoon leader shouted over the sounds of war:

"Go! Go! Go!"

Orville Willard Phillips Sr. splashed down into the water and hustled toward the bloodstained beach. He looked up to the dunes cast against the bleak morning sky and shivered. D-Day was as grim as they had said. The shells raining down, the endless spray of German bullets, and the lifeless bodies floating facedown in the water—it was all true.

Still, the Allied troops that stormed the beaches of Normandy two days earlier had made headway. The German front was breaking, and Orville was one of several hundred thousand soldiers called in to reinforce the invasion.

"To the right, push up to the hill, and hold!"

Orville fell in step with his unit and obeyed the order.

He was a prince of a man, a true Southern gentleman, born and raised in Pine Bluff, Arkansas. Four years ago he had never heard of Hitler, or the Third Reich, or Normandy. He was home in the South, raising two young sons with his darling wife, Heula Mae Insley. Then news of a European tyrant took hold of his small town, and soon enough he was called by his country to fight in General Patton's army.

Thoughts of Pine Bluff marched with him everywhere he went, and as he hunkered down on the coast of France, he couldn't help but think of Heula Mae and the boys.

A few miles inland on their third night in harm's way, his platoon was pinned by a German company. They radioed for help, but the Allied army was spread thinly across the countryside. Their options were to surrender or die—they chose to surrender.

Orville was marched at gunpoint to a railroad station with his fellow soldiers and crammed into a cattle car. As the train lurched forward, a friend whispered to Orville, "Where are they taking us?"

"I don't know," he answered, looking at the dirty, worried faces crowding around him.

Hour after hour they rolled along the European countryside, standing shoulder to shoulder with no room to sit, food to eat, water to drink, fresh air to breathe, or corner of privacy to relieve themselves.

Twenty-four hours later the train squealed to a stop and the doors slid open. Sunlight poured into the cattle car, and fresh air filled their lungs. German guards banged on the car with their guns and shouted, "Out! Hurry! Hurry!"

The weary soldiers lumbered from the car and lined up in the dust. As their eyes adjusted to the painful afternoon light, the landscape came into focus.

"It's a prison camp," Orville whispered to his friend.

"Yeah, and it will take a miracle to get out of here," he answered, shaking his head as they marched toward the gates under close guard.

They were locked into a wooden barrack called 11B and each assigned a wooden bunk with no mattress. Square shapes were cut into the weathered walls for windows, but they held no glass. Orville looked through the opening and surveyed the surroundings. Barbwire fences stretched around the perimeter. Towers of wood and razor wire constructed at the corners of the camp housed guards, spotlights, and machine guns.

After a few days all talk of escape and rescue fell quiet. The camp was too isolated and well guarded for the soldiers to imagine a prison break. They knew they would die trying to escape, and as the days turned into weeks, weeks turned into months, and summer gave way to cold autumn nights, they slowly realized they would die before rescue would find them.

Lying on his wooden bunk, lice scouring his body, hunger stabbing his stomach, Orville passed the nights praying.

"Lord, if you spare my life, I promise to go home and teach my boys right from wrong and take them to church every Sunday."

A few months after arriving at the prison camp, a group of German officers barged into their barrack and asked for twenty-five volunteers to work the farm.

Orville quickly raised his hand. When he was a boy, he had helped his dad on the family farm, and the thought of pulling food out of the ground sounded better than the labor camp. Twenty-four other prisoners raised their hands, and they were quickly whisked away to the farm.

Their job was to pull potatoes from the field, and the work was never ending. From sunrise to sundown they hunched over the roots and yanked them from the hard German soil. At night they rested their weary bodies on beds of straw thrown down on the floor of a rat-infested barn.

One night, as Orville lay listening to the rats scratch around the floor, he pulled his picture of Orville Jr. and Dennis out of his pocket and held it up to the moonlight. Their smiles glowed in the soft blue light.

How long has it been since I've seen them? How old are they now?

Orville started counting. Suddenly a guard burst into the barn. Orville tried to stuff the picture into his pocket, but the beam of the guard's flashlight washed over him.

"What is that in your hand?" the guard asked as he stepped up to him.

Orville's heart skipped a beat. He couldn't lose the photo. It was his way home, his only hope. He hesitated to turn it over into the light.

"What is that?" the guard asked again.

"My two sons," Orville answered, holding the picture up with two fingers.

The guard squinted his eyes and leaned forward to the picture. Quickly he looked back over his shoulder and then reached for his back pocket.

A tiny smile parted his face. "*Meine Söhne,*" he said, showing Orville a picture of two young boys.

Orville stared at the picture, stunned. "Our boys look to be the same age," he said softly, a lump rising in his throat.

"Yeah," said the guard, "we are not very different." Then the guard paused, and began again with a lowered voice. "No winners in this war. Maybe when it is over, your boys and my boys will be friends."

He tucked the photo back into his pocket and reached his hand down to Orville. For the length of a handshake, the two men were *freunde* . . . friends.

Several months later, on February 18, 1945, the same guard approached Orville and a group of prisoners doing daily chores in the barn.

"Well, boys," he shouted, "the war is over! You are free!"

Orville and the other prisoners leapt into the air.

"We're going home!" one prisoner shouted, as they all hugged and celebrated. Orville and the guard, for the second time, shook hands and smiled.

The next day six hundred POWs marched toward Stople, Germany, to a Red Cross camp. When they arrived, they were fed, treated, and given three parcels, one being a new journal to record their experiences. Orville took his to the guard, his friend, the father of two boys, and asked him to sign it.

"Yes, of course," he said, and then he wrote:

> **WHEN THE WAR IS OVER,**
> **AND WE ALL GO HOME,**
> **WE WILL ALWAYS REMEMBER OUR FRIENDSHIP.**
> **GEFR. PATBERG***
> **MARIENFELDE, GERMANY**

**Gefr.* is the German military equivalent of *Pvt.*

His first Sunday back in Pine Bluff, Orville ushered his wife and boys to the front row at the local church for Sunday worship. Throughout the years, no matter the season, or how busy they grew raising four boys, the Phillips family was always there, listening to the Word of God, learning right from wrong.

Though Orville could never share the trauma of war with his wife and children, he did tell them of the German guard who extended his hand in friendship. He showed them the inscription in his journal, and when they prayed together as a family, they prayed for Gefr. Patberg and his two sons.

Up until the day he died on August 7, 1998, fifty years after his release, Orville still thanked God for the unlikely friendship that saved his life that night on a German potato farm. It gave him the hope he needed to endure the hell of war, and indeed, gave him the faith to lead him home to heaven.

DIXIE PHILLIPS and her husband, Paul, have been honored to serve the Gospel Lighthouse Church in Floyd, Iowa, for thirty years. They have four grown children, three grandboys, and one granddaughter. Dixie loves Southern gospel music and throwing tea parties with her girlfriends. If you'd like to read more about Dixie's writings, go to floydslighthouse.com.

7

STEPS TO FORGIVENESS

JAY COOKINGHAM

The first time I heard the voice, I was sitting in the forest with a blade to my arm. I was fifteen years old and miles away from home, in a secluded spot where I was certain no one would find me. I'd left a recorded message on my desk for my mom, saying goodbye. I knew when she listened to it, she would be upset, but I hoped she would understand. The abuse was too much. His fists were too strong. His words were too destructive. I couldn't face him. Or ignore him. I could only escape him.

So I started pressing the cold steel into my skin, and that's when I heard it.

No!

The voice echoed through the woods, and I jumped to my feet. I turned around and around, looking in every direction, but I was alone. Too startled to continue with my plan, I sheathed the knife and ran home to destroy the tape.

The second time I heard the voice, I was in a cabin, looking up at the log roof. My friends had dragged me there from the forest, where we had been drinking beers and goofing off. They bet me I couldn't shotgun six cans in a row, so I did and then fell flat on my face. They thought I was passed out, but I wasn't; I was dying.

I could feel death crawling through my body, starting at my feet, running up my legs, pressing into my chest.

"This is it," I said to myself. "My life is over." I waited for death to cover my eyes, but then I heard a voice:

Is this the way you want it to end?

I waited for one of my friends to lean over me, expecting an answer. But they were all asleep, snoring on the cabin floor.

It was the voice from the forest from years before. I cried out, "No! Father, no!"

Then everything went black. The next morning I packed up my sleeping bag, stepped over my friends, and never looked back.

The third time I heard the voice, I was about to kill my father. I was eighteen, on my way to church, when I heard my mother scream from the house. I ran back inside and found my father berating her. I knew as soon as I opened my mouth, he would leave her alone and come at me, and I was ready.

I shouted at him, and he instantly stormed toward me. I absorbed several punches and then deflected the next few. Surprised I was still standing, my father unleashed another torrent of punches, but I blocked them all.

For the first time in my life, I was big enough to fight back, and we both realized it at the same time.

"You can't hurt me anymore!" I shouted, with newfound confidence.

I turned and started up the stairs to see if my mother was okay, and he followed me, shouting a verbal attack, trying to cut me down with his words.

"You're worthless! Do you hear me?" he barked continuously. "Nothing but a piece of trash, a worthless nobody!"

I'd heard it all before, but it still made me furious. Every word that left his mouth fueled my desire for revenge. I tightened my fists.

"One more word and you're done!" I shouted, reaching the top of the stairs, but he didn't quit. His words kept coming.

"You're good for nothing, you worthless . . . You are a—"

"That's it," I erupted. In a flash I turned around and planted my foot. I cocked back my right fist and picked my target. His arms were down, and his chest was open, so I aimed for his heart, thinking if I hit him hard enough, he would fly down the staircase and break his neck.

I thrust my weight forward and then heard the voice gently say, *Forgive him.*

Instantly I released the tightness in my body and my hand fell harmlessly to my side. I looked into my father's eyes.

"I forgive you," I said, shocked by my own words. "And God loves you."

He shook his head and turned to head down the stairs, muttering insults beneath his breath as he went.

I wish I could tell you that my father and I reconciled after that encounter on the stairs thirty-eight years ago. The truth is we never did. Losing him was painful, and the pain taught me that while reconciliation requires two people, forgiveness takes only one. That day I was miraculously given a second chance at life—a chance to leave victimhood behind forever. My father didn't *deserve* to be forgiven, but my lack of forgiveness would forever imprison me.

The choice to forgive my father unlocked my chains—the same chains that almost dragged me to my death as a teenager—and set me free to hear my true name. I was no longer—am no longer—named by the insults of my father, but by the loving eternal Father, whose grace and forgiveness have shaped my true identity as a husband, a father, and a man with a hopeful future.

JAY COOKINGHAM is a freelance writer/poet as well as a graphic artist. He writes a blog (soulfari.blogspot.com) geared toward men and their role as fathers and husbands. He has been published in the following books: *God's Way for Fathers*, *God's Ways for Teachers*, *God's Way for Christmas*, *Smiles for Dads*, *Soul Matters for Men*, *The Rainy Day Book*, and *A Man of Honor*. A father of seven, Jay has been happily married to his wife, Christine, for twenty-nine years.

LEMON DROP

Suicide, abuse, pain . . . Jay's story is far from pretty, yet it's similar to many stories from Scripture. Whenever I talk with someone who thinks his or her story is beyond the reach of God, I point to the stories of Job, the woman at the well, and the wounded beggar waiting for the good Samaritan. God didn't leave or forsake them, Jay, or me, and he won't leave or forsake you.

—Don

8

DEATH OF OUR SON

JEAN MATTHEW HALL

When he was thirty, my son's heart stopped beating.

He was in his small, peaceful house, perched on the side of a Kentucky mountain, when he took and exhaled his last breath. His friend performed CPR while his girlfriend called 9-1-1, but there was no saving him. The ER physician pronounced him dead on arrival.

Stephen wasn't rich or famous or living all his dreams come true. He was a hardworking, dependable, long-haul trucker, faithfully crossing the country with his cargo. He was a somewhat rebellious loner, drawn to the solitary lifestyle of trucking, and he was also a caring son and loving brother.

When his sister, Tabitha, was born, twelve-year-old Stephen instantly became possessive of her. He loved to play games with her and race across the lawn, but he also took time to cuddle and tickle her. Stephen and Tabitha were close as they grew older. He teased her, of course, and loved to scare the dickens out of her, but he adored his little sister.

As Tabitha entered middle school, Stephen began encouraging her to think about college. He had learned a thing or two about life in the real world and wanted his sister to find a career that did more than keep her financially secure. Stephen wanted Tabitha to make a difference in the world and find fulfillment in her work.

"Don't settle," he told her over and over. "Do something important with your life."

Tabitha took Stephen's pep talks seriously, and during her senior year, she applied to a school of health sciences to fulfill her dream of becoming a nurse.

As soon as she was accepted, she started applying for every sort of grant and scholarship available to her. We'd decided, as a family, to avoid going into debt for her schooling, so student loans weren't an option. We knew they would leave her living paycheck to paycheck after graduation, and our own finances were precarious. My husband had been out of work for several years, and the combination of his social security checks and my tiny salary meant we were living below the poverty line.

God had always provided enough to meet our needs, but we had to be frugal. My husband and I talked through the issue from every angle and prayed for wisdom. It seemed as if Tabitha was meant to become a nurse, but how could we afford her dream?

As graduation approached, Tabitha was awarded several grants, which, along with some disability money my husband received from Veterans Affairs, covered the cost of her books and nursing uniforms. The much larger, daunting cost of tuition remained unpaid.

Then Stephen died, and instead of looking forward to a future of school and nursing, we looked back, painfully remembering Stephen's place in our family. We struggled through the process of planning the funeral and memorial service and endured the long nights of loss.

Sorting through the details of Stephen's life was excruciating. We had boxes of papers on our kitchen table, each one a weight of grief that pressed down into us. One by one we pulled them from the file and remembered the mark left by the one we'd lost; then we'd file it away for good or throw it in the pile to be forgotten—not that Stephen could ever be forgotten.

One day, as we read through his financial documents, I pulled his life insurance policy from the filing cabinet. I silently passed it to my husband, and we began to weep together, struggling to understand how our beautiful son's life could be reduced to dollar signs.

In that moment we began praying, and over the next few days, as we talked, prayed, and wept, it became clear that nothing would please Stephen more than to help his little sister achieve her dream of becoming a nurse. We gave the money to Tabitha, and sure enough, it was the exact amount she needed for school.

Two years later Tabitha walked across the graduation stage to receive her nursing degree, resplendent in cap and gown and beaming with pride. My husband and I watched through our tears, our hearts filled to bursting with a mix of grief and amazement and gratitude.

Stephen died more than a decade ago, and there is no denying that the pain of his passing has dramatically shaped our lives. The process of mourning taught us some valuable lessons about life and family and love. The grief brought us closer together, and even though we can talk about Stephen now without being overwhelmed by grief, we know the wound will never heal completely.

Nothing will bring Stephen back, but I also believe nothing can take away what Stephen has given. When he was alive, he would have sacrificed his life for his little sister without a second thought. In a way that's exactly what he did—and now she gives her life for others as a NICU nurse, caring for premature and critically ill newborn babies.

She's told me that each time she sends a healthy baby home with grateful parents, she thanks her brother Stephen in her heart. Stephen somehow lives not only in heaven but also in the work Tabitha does day after day. And that makes living with Stephen's death a little easier for all of us to bear.

It may seem a little odd or insensitive to say something good came out of losing one we loved, but that is also the hard-earned lesson of losing our son. Death is not the end of life. God is working with a resurrection power, and even after death, even *through* death, he brings life to others.

JEAN MATTHEW HALL lives in beautiful North Carolina with her husband, Jerry. She enjoys spending time with her children and grandchildren, leading a ladies' Bible class at her church, reading, gardening, and writing. Jean is also the chairperson for the nonprofit organization Write2Ignite!

9

A LIGHT TO FOLLOW

JOANNE POTTER

E nough sitting around," Dad announced, pushing himself off the couch. "Let's do something!" It was the summer of 2003. Our family had gathered in Reno to celebrate Dad's eightieth birthday, and we were in the mood to indulge him. "We're going to raft the Truckee!" he declared. "I know just the place!" Without waiting for anyone to agree, he went to look for his khaki shorts and deck shoes. Clearly, he didn't see anything odd about an elderly man with limited agility and failing vision who was starting the ninth decade of his life, clinging to the inside of a raft. But then, he wouldn't.

Maggie, my stepmother, eyes shining with customary delight, exclaimed, "Oh John, what fun!" If Dad wanted to go rafting, she did too. Maggie orbited his bright glow like Europa around Jupiter—constant and beautiful in his reflection. We never understood why she loved our eccentric father, but she did. Oh, she absolutely did. My brother, Frank, and I watched, skeptical, as the two of them twittered about the proposed adventure. "But the Truckee is full of rapids,

Dad!" Frank reminded him. Dad, still searching for his shoes, called over his shoulder, "I'm eighty. I'm not dead!"

Three generations piled into the raft that afternoon. My son, Bryan, a strapping college boy, would do most of the steering from the back while Frank helped paddle and I stayed within arm's reach of the geriatric thrill-seekers in the front. We three younger shipmates pushed off from shore with trepidation, but Dad and Maggie jittered with excitement.

At first, alpine terrain slid serenely by—stately pines towered over the water, rock strata recalled bygone ages, and birds called in chirps and squawks. We dragged our fingertips in the water, leaving widening ripples in their wake as a long, lazy hour passed. It looked as if Dad was right. This had turned out to be a lovely afternoon.

Then Bryan frowned and leaned in toward the center of the raft. "Listen," he said. A low rumble, like distant traffic, grew into a roar as we rounded the next bend. The river, so placid before, boiled into a froth, exposing rocks it had hidden earlier. Our raft picked up speed. Bryan and Frank stiffened and gripped their paddles in earnest. I wedged my feet into the footholds, but Dad turned his head, right next to Maggie's, into the wind, their expectant grins looking like a pair of dogs leaning out of an open car window.

We surged into the rapids. Frank's and Bryan's best steering efforts couldn't avoid the rocks, and we careened over some, lurching left, then right, then left again. "Look out!" cried Frank, as we crested a big one, raising up the front end for a second into midair, then bringing it down with a crash. As the boat fell, so did Maggie, landing faceup in the bottom of the boat. With all the pitching, I couldn't reach her, and she couldn't sit up.

"Hold on, Maggie!" I shouted over the roar of the river. "Don't be afraid!"

"Oh, I'm all right!" she shouted back. Then she threw back her head and laughed with childlike abandon. "This is fun!"

The following year Dad was diagnosed with dementia. Months, then years passed, and he gradually dimmed, but Maggie, his adoring moon, kept her shining orbit.

While Dad drifted deeper into his dementia, his care absorbed more and more of Maggie, step by gradual step. She first began forgetting to apply her lipstick; then her beloved garden grew over with weeds. Eventually she neglected to eat regular meals, and her clothes began hanging unnaturally loose.

"Maggie, can we talk?" I asked her one day, taking her soft hands in mine. "You seem so tired. How are you doing? Are you okay?"

"Well, of course I am," she responded with a smile.

"No, I mean *really* okay. Do you know what's happening here?"

She smiled, heartbreaking and beautiful. "Yes, darlin'. This is part of life. Death comes to everyone—and until it does, I'm spending as much time with your dad as I can." She paused, but her gaze did not waver. "As much time as we're given. I wouldn't miss this for anything. I don't ever want to be anywhere else."

Dad died in April 2009, just as spring was taking root. Two months later, in June, my husband was diagnosed with cancer. Almost overnight my life began to resemble Maggie's while she cared for Dad: doctors demanded decisions in the face of suffering, brave words belied pain and nighttime tears, and constant duty taxed what I feared was my inconstant heart. We could do nothing but put one foot in front of another down a long, dark tunnel, accelerating as helplessly as we had that day on the Truckee rapids, no sure end in sight. *Can I love well enough for this? Will he die? Will I fail? Do you really have a plan, God?*

Then I remembered Maggie, bravely facing her own uncertainty and darkness, and understood that she had traced a faithful orbit for me to follow. Through my own doubt, the sweet light of her love for my father lit a clear path. By its light I followed her lead into that unknown place.

After two long years and three surgeries, my husband recovered, but I know that someday he and I will walk to the end of our path together, just like Maggie and Dad. Until then I thank God for our journey into the darkness and uncertainty of near death. It forged a bond between us stronger than sunshine ever could, and thanks to Maggie's faithful glow, I know what love looks like, even when it's shining in the darkness.

After writing and publishing creative nonfiction in newspapers and magazines for more than twenty-five years, JoAnne Potter retired from teaching in 2009. She now relishes the company of her husband, Dave, makes wine, blogs, and works on her first novel amid the improbable hills of southwestern Wisconsin. Visit her online at joannempotter. blogspot.com and joannepotter.weebly.com.

10

MOMMY AND ME

TRACY HEALY

One day when I was a baby, I cried to tell my parents that I was hungry. For some reason this made them mad. Instead of picking me up and giving me milk, they picked me up and shook me. A lot. I was scared and hurt, and I screamed even louder to tell them to stop. But they didn't.

I don't think my first parents knew how to love me.

Then some people came and took me to live in a different house. The adults there were called foster parents, and they picked me up all the time, but never to shake me. They just wanted to hug me, sing to me, carry me around, and help me eat food through a tube.

The doctors told my foster parents I had something called massive head trauma. They said that when my first parents shook me, it gave me lots of problems, and I was lucky to be alive. The doctors also said I would never roll over or sit up or stand on my own.

I had five operations and lots of trips to the doctor. That's a lot for a baby, and I was scared, but I always got to come home to my foster parents afterward. I didn't have to worry about any more shaking.

I really liked my foster parents, but my favorite person was my special babysitter. She watched me all the time. I loved when she got me ready for sleep: she would wrap me in a soft blanket, rock me gently, and sing to me and pray with me. I felt safe with her.

One night she was rocking me before bed. She told me we could make a deal. If I prayed for her to have a husband, she would pray for me to have new parents. She said maybe she could be my mom, but it would be hard without a husband. I didn't know a lot about praying, but she prayed all the time, so I did it like her.

"God, please let my special babysitter become my mommy. I love her. You can even give her a husband if it helps."

When I was two years old, some people said I needed to go live somewhere called an *institution* since no one would want to be my mom anymore.

I knew *that* wasn't true! Mommy was already taking care of me all the time, even though everyone else called her my babysitter. When Mommy heard that I was going to have to go away, she got really upset, but not at me. "They can't do that to my son! They can't take him away!" Even though she was yelling, it didn't scare me. Her loud voice was full of love.

The next day she had a meeting with the people who wanted to send me away. She told them a lot of things, and afterward they said it would be good if she kept me all by herself.

I wondered why it took everyone else so long to figure that out.

Four months later I went to live full-time with Mommy, even

though I still got to see my old foster parents all the time. It was awesome. Her smile was the first thing I saw every morning when I woke up, and every night I fell asleep in her arms, listening to her sing. We did everything together.

A few years later Mommy told me something: she said she was now officially my mom. I guess it meant that everyone else could call her that now. I thought it was funny because Mommy and me already knew that!

The doctors found out lots of things that were wrong with me. They told Mommy I had cerebral palsy, seizure disorder, and cortical vision impairment. They also said I had developmental delays, speech delays, and severe gastrointestinal problems. I didn't know what all those things meant. But I did know it was hard to do some of my most fun things with Mommy, like catching a beanbag or holding a Popsicle.

Whenever we left the hospital, Mommy always took me right home to play. We sure played a lot! We played with toys and letters and cups. We read stories and played peekaboo and tasted new flavors. And you know what? I kept doing things that made her so proud—and my old foster parents too. I used to drink my food through a big tube that went inside me, but now I don't even need it. I'm a spoon guy now!

Every day it gets easier to understand Mommy's words. I always know what her face is saying, like when she smiles at me or kisses my cheek.

But now when she says words like, "We're going to the park—I'll bring a blanket, and you can eat Cheerios," I understand what to get excited about!

Remember how my doctors told Mommy I would never roll over, sit up, or stand? Doctors can sure be silly. Mommy taught me to do *all* that stuff. That's why we didn't worry when the doctors said I would never understand anything. It takes grown-ups a while to see what Mommy and me already know.

Oh, I forgot to tell you one other thing my doctors said. They told Mommy, "Your son will never walk."

That would have been okay. Lots of my friends can't walk, and Mommy and me can go everywhere we want in my special chair. But she always wants me to try out new stuff, so she got me my very own walker. It had tiny wheels, and Mommy put my favorite stickers all over it. I just grabbed the handles and started going—and before long my legs got so strong that now I can walk by myself!

Walking is pretty tricky, for sure. But I feel so happy when I make it across the room with Mommy cheering me on. Sometimes I lose my balance and fall over, but I don't mind. When I'm falling, I can already see Mommy running over to pick me up and help me try again. Now I can walk at my special kindergarten class too. School is kind of scary, but Mommy says I'll do great!

It's so weird that I almost didn't meet her, because Mommy told me I'm the greatest gift God has ever given her. I thought that was crazy because she is the best gift anyone has ever given me!

TRACY HEALY graduated from Westmont College in 1999. When she met Brandon, the little guy featured in her story, Tracy was working for ACT (the Autism Center for Treatment in Moorpark, California: autismcenterfortreatment.com), a job that helped prepare her for all of Brandon's special needs. Now she works part-time at Simi Covenant Church in the children's ministry department and is a full-time mommy— the best job of all.

LEMON DROP

Remember how Brandon's doctors gave Tracy a long list of things he would "never" be able to do? Well, riding a bike was on that list, but we just heard from Tracy that Brandon is cruising up and down the street on his tricycle. God continues to reveal himself in Brandon's story, and it is cool that his mom isn't shy about who should get the credit. It isn't just Tracy's committed parenting; it's the love of God making all things possible.

—Don

11

COURTING THROUGH CANCER

MARY POTTER KENYON

This isn't what I wanted!" I wept to myself. I had just absorbed another explosive outburst from my husband before he slammed the door and barged out of the room.

Behind me my two youngest children were silenced with fear.

There has to be more to marriage than this, I told myself. *Or is this as good as it gets?*

I could hardly believe I was thinking such things, but then again, I could hardly believe my husband. Twenty-five years before, we had been starry-eyed lovers starting out on a beautiful journey. We were best friends, allies, husband and wife; but shortly after we were married, I discovered his hair-trigger temper.

Ten months after our wedding, we had our first child, and what I expected to be the greatest blessing in our life turned out to be a constant source of frustration for my husband.

It was hard to say what would set David off. Loud music. A spilled glass at dinner. A slammed door. A missing remote control. I slowly learned the best way to keep the peace in our house was to keep our children away from David. In small and big ways I absorbed the energy of our eight children, even going so far as to take a baby with me to my college courses at night to save David some stress.

Of course, it all was his fault; I didn't doubt that. Who screams at his wife? Or slams the door in her face? Or leaves his children weeping with terror?

I thought I was a martyr, stoically holding our family together at the seams. Even when David began to see a counselor and began making visible signs of progress, I refused to share any of the family stress with him. I inadvertently encouraged disrespect for him in the kids. I'd lived so long under the tyranny of his anger, I didn't acknowledge his progress. I believed that he deserved my disdain.

For twenty-seven years we survived as husband and wife. Then David was diagnosed with a cancerous tumor at the base of his tongue.

On the way home from the hospital, looking at him from the passenger seat and sensing his deep fear, I knew without a doubt I would care for him. Despite my deep resentment and our failing relationship, I would be faithful to him in this time of need.

Less than two weeks after his diagnosis, David had an invasive surgery to remove the cancerous tumor. Sitting at his bedside days after the operation, a nurse handed him a dry-erase board and a marker.

"You won't be able to speak for a while with the tracheotomy," she said kindly. "In the meantime you can use this to communicate with your wife."

Slowly, his hand shaking with effort, I watched as David labored to construct his first question letter by letter.

How are the kids?

I took his hand. "They are doing fine." I smiled. "They are actually having fun with the babysitters, but they miss you." I paused. "And I miss you too."

David smiled and erased the message. Putting the pen back to the board, he began scribbling the next question.

For days after his surgery, I sat by the bedside of my mute husband. Away from the busyness of bills and children, I gradually stopped seeing him in terms of adjectives such as *angry*, *selfish*, and *unsupportive*.

Through his voiceless pain I once again saw the man I married. David. My love. In the silence created by cancer, I could no longer hear his angry words—and he no longer heard my resentment.

One morning as I readied myself to go visit David alone in his hospital room, I caught myself anticipating his loving gaze. Tossing aside my usual casual attire, I put on a flattering outfit and sprayed on David's favorite perfume. Looking at myself in the full-length mirror, I couldn't help but laugh at the thought: *I'm courting my husband!*

It was true, and day after day, month after month, my gentle ministrations in caring for him during his treatment rekindled the flame of our first love. I changed his bloody dressings, cleaned his wounds, and set up the liquid nutrition feedings with his feeding tube. We gazed into each other's eyes, held hands, smiled, kissed, and truly cared for each other. For the first time in our marriage, I knelt down in front of my husband and rubbed his tired feet. For the first time in a long time, David felt cherished. And I felt free from the bile of bitterness I'd been swallowing for so long.

We were forming a real, lasting relationship, but when David first came home, I worried our children would once again trigger David's anger. Thankfully it was an unnecessary fear. Throughout his recovery he was like a man seeing his family for the first time, looking lovingly at his children, who in turn looked lovingly at their father. Even three-year-old Abby sensed what he needed, spending hours at his feet, quietly turning the pages of her books as her daddy watched and smiled.

We shared nearly six years of a renewed relationship before a heart attack unexpectedly took my beloved from me. In those darkest of days since his death, I have taken great comfort in the knowledge that David and I found real love at last. Some people never experience it in their lifetimes. I will always be grateful for the *bonus* years we experienced after cancer.

MARY POTTER KENYON lives in Manchester, Iowa. Her writing has been featured in magazines, newspapers, and anthologies. She blogs about motherhood, writing, and saving money at marypotterkenyon.wordpress.com.

12 ═══

COLLIDING WITH THE UNKNOWN

EVAN OSGOOD

When I stepped out of the house, I looked up into the flat, dreary clouds and felt the cold rain on my face. I jumped into my old pickup truck, cranked the engine, pulled out onto the storm-soaked highway, and shivered as the cab slowly filled with warm air.

The frayed windshield wipers cranked back and forth, streaking water across my view of the road as I leaned forward to see through the haze. Just before I reached my high school parking lot, I came to the bridge crossing the creek. As I hit the puddled concrete, my truck suddenly felt weightless beneath me.

I quickly pumped the brakes and jerked the wheel, but the truck didn't respond. I hydroplaned across the median, sliding into the lane of oncoming traffic.

"Oh no!" I shouted, fighting the wheel for control.

I looked up, and for one heartbeat the moment slowed. I could feel the water carrying me forward; see the lights of the oncoming truck; see the whites of the driver's eyes. Then there was the terrible sound of metal on metal, like a thousand soda cans suddenly crushed underfoot.

My unbuckled body flew forward, and my face smashed into the windshield, then slammed into the dash. The steering column snapped downward and pinned my left leg to the door. The mangled radio casing jutted out into my right leg, thrashing into my muscle, and the gearshift jammed into my hip. My Nissan truck bent around me in an L shape, and the cab was pushed back into the bed. The glove compartment and the passenger seat fused together. Only twelve inches of breathable space separated my body from the dash.

The combined speed of 120 miles per hour spun my truck around and pounded the back bumper into the guardrails. The twisted metal from the guardrail caught the frayed corners of my truck and kept me from careening off the overhang.

Suddenly nothing was moving. I blinked, over and over, but my right eye wouldn't open. Through my left eye I could see, just barely, the steel coffin of my cab.

This is it, I knew, scanning the destruction, feeling the pain pushing into my body. I coughed, and blood spattered on the dash.

Get help, or you're going to die.

I gasped in and out and tried to shout, but my voice was hardly a whisper.

"Help, please . . ."

I heard footsteps and clanging in the bed of the truck, and then there was a voice.

"Evan! Evan! Are you okay?" It was my neighbor, reaching through the wreckage.

"Help," I whispered.

"Help is coming; just stay still," he said as he reached a towel up to my face and held it to my wound.

"My face . . . it hurts. Is it bad?"

"You just have a few scratches. Don't worry. You're going to be okay."

Why does it hurt so bad? I wondered. *A few scratches shouldn't hurt this bad.*

Thirty minutes later the emergency responders were still trying to get me out of the truck, and my dad had arrived on the scene. He called my name, reached through a hole in the door, and grabbed my hand.

"Dad . . . I wrecked the truck. I'm sorry."

"I don't care about that. All that matters is you're still alive. All that matters is that we can make you better." He held my hand as they continued to pry the truck away from my body.

When they finally freed me from the wreckage, an ambulance rushed me to the local hospital, where I was stabilized before being loaded back into the ambulance and taken an hour west to a larger hospital. As they prepped me for emergency surgery, people frantically ran around the ER, and I knew something was wrong.

CAT scans, X-rays, ambulance rides, and now this? I thought to myself. *For only a few scratches?*

The anesthesia pumped into my veins, my eyelids grew heavy, and the room went dark.

The next morning I woke up in the hospital bed and felt an itch on my face. I reached up to scratch my cheek, but a thick layer of dressing was wrapped around my head.

A nurse walked into the room and asked me how I felt.

"What happened to my face?" I asked, still feeling the bandage surrounding my head. "When do I get to go home?"

She didn't say a word. She just sat me up in bed, gently unwrapped the dressing, pointed to the mirror, and quietly left the room.

I looked at the reflection for a long time without moving. The reflection looked back at me. Finally I tilted my head, and the reflection did the same.

A few scratches, a few scratches . . . My mind raced. For the first time I could see what everyone had seen since the accident. A maze of bloody stitches was holding my face together, piece by piece. I looked like Frankenstein's creation, a monster from a twisted imagination. I was not me.

Over the next few days, I learned from the doctors and my parents how bad the damage really was. I had lost the right side of my face when I hit the windshield. Paramedics had found pieces of my skin in the truck, and the surgeons sewed them back on. My nose had shattered into hundreds of fragments and was meticulously wired back together. My right eye suffered considerable damage, and there was a question as to how soon I'd be able to walk again.

As the details emerged, I sensed my future growing dark. I wouldn't be able to play sports anymore. I might be blind in one eye. I might not walk again. I would look like a freak for the rest of my life.

Why would you do this to me, God? I asked, wondering if I was being punished. Then I began to wonder, *Do I even believe in God?*

I didn't know.

Alone with the pain, looking into the reflection in the mirror, I thought of how I could finish what the wreck had failed to do—end my life. I didn't want to recover and live a wounded life. I didn't want to be a scarred victim. I wanted to die.

I thought of ways to kill myself. I worked on a plan through muddled thoughts, but then a new fear gripped me as I realized, *I didn't die. I almost died. What if I had died? Would the things I hoped in have helped me?*

I knew instantly that the answer wasn't to end my life. The answer was to find a new hope in something bigger than myself, so I prayed out loud in my room:

"God, I don't know why you let me live. I should have died, but I believe you let me live for a reason. I do believe you have a plan to redeem this. So I'm in. Whatever you want me to do with this, I'm there, no matter what it means."

Over the next few days, the darkness around me began to turn to light. I felt at peace, and when I thought back to the accident, I didn't remember the wreckage or the pain. Instead I remembered my dad's words: "All that matters is you're still alive. All that matters is that we can make you better."

I believed him now, and I sensed that he had been a mouthpiece for God, saying exactly what I needed to hear. Even as a parade of doctors consulted with me and my parents about surgeries, grafts, and plates, I was at peace. I didn't care. Even when they told me 90 percent of my face would die, my nerves would never recover, and my eye condition was still bleak, I didn't care. It didn't matter what happened; it was part of my story.

After a couple of days in the hospital, I was released into my mom's care and sent home. As I recovered, I was reminded that my church was sponsoring a speaker at our upcoming school assembly. I hadn't been out of the house or hospital since the wreck, and I hadn't really seen anyone from school, so I convinced my dad to take me to the assembly.

As my dad helped me down the hall, my principal spotted us, and he welcomed me back.

"Do you want to introduce the speaker today?" he asked me, to my surprise. "Everyone wants to see you. What do you think?"

Five minutes later I was standing in front of the entire student body, my teachers, and the school board, with a microphone in my hand. As I looked up at the rows of faces, I knew they were looking at mine: still stitched up, covered in cream, my right eye bloodshot. I could see the shock in their eyes, and the auditorium was quiet and somber.

"It's good to be back," I said, my voice echoing through the sound system.

Then I felt it wash over me just like it did in the hospital. The peace was back, and I knew I was doing exactly what I was supposed to be doing.

I began speaking again. "I'm sorry if I'm violating any religious rules here, but I want to tell you my story, and it is a story about Jesus coming to save that which was lost."

I told them about my life before the wreck, the pain of the accident, and the prayer of hope I desperately spoke in the hospital room.

I've been telling the same story for seventeen years as a youth pastor, and every time I point to the scars on my face as the evidence of God's grace. I tell students that despite the urging of several doctors, I decided to forgo plastic surgery to remove the scars. I didn't, and still don't, ever want to forget the worst day of my life because, thanks to God, it is now my greatest memory. God crashed into me at 120 miles an hour and left me a marked man. Like Jacob, I wrestled with God through the pain and found God's blessing—true life.

EVAN OSGOOD is originally from Parsons, Kansas, where his story takes place. He became a student minister five years later and has been ministering to students for the last fourteen years. Evan currently serves at Wildwood Christian Church just outside of St. Louis, Missouri. Married with two boys, he loves the outdoors, is an avid cyclist, and has the best job in the world.

13

SIX MONTHS TO LIFE

DAVE GIST

I know what I'm gonna do," I say to my friends, my words falling sideways out of my mouth. "I'm gonna go in there and get us some beer!"

It's just past midnight on New Year's Eve, and the entire town is lit up. Everyone is out having a good time, but my friends and I are out of beer and money. I stumble, drunk, toward the gas station and hear them cheering me on from behind.

I stroll down the beer aisle and yank the cold door open. I pick up a six-pack of cheap beer and turn to walk out of the store, but the cashier is looking at me. I walk up to the counter and hold the beer up into the air.

"I'm taking this beer," I slur, and I look down to a pack of cigarettes on the counter. I quickly grab them and look at the woman in line. "These too!" I declare.

"Those are my cigarettes," I hear the lady say, behind me, as I walk out the door.

"Hey! I'm talking to you," she says, louder. "Those are my cigarettes!"

I turn around, and she is outside, a few feet behind me. I shove the pack into my pocket and pull out my knife.

"Back off, lady! Now they are mine!" I yell.

She steps back, cautiously, fear flashing in her eyes, and I leave the parking lot to join my friends and enjoy the fruit of my labor.

A few minutes later a squad car pulls up in front of our little New Year's Eve celebration. The turning sirens color the city street red and blue as a policeman walks toward us.

"Those are cute little shorts, Mr. Police Officer," I say, trying to have some fun, but he is not in the mood. Five minutes later he puts me in the car, handcuffed, and drives me to the station.

I slump down into the chair and glance up at the judge. He is looking down at the papers on the bench, over the rims of his glasses, and I know that he is reading my rap sheet: my forty-three arrests, my numerous convictions, and my seven years in jail. He looks up and thinks for a second.

"Mr. Gist, it says here you are being charged with two felony counts of armed robbery and one count of assault with a deadly weapon."

I stole ten dollars' worth of beer and cigarettes, and they have me up for felony charges. I can't believe it.

"I am finding you guilty on all charges, Mr. Gist. You could face up to six years in jail for these crimes, but I'm ordering you to serve six months in state prison. I want you to use the time wisely and think about your life."

He reaches over and picks up the gavel.

"Case closed."

It's nothing, I tell myself, laughing. *Six months is easy.*

When we reach the prison, I'm processed, given new clothes, and escorted to a large dormitory by a guard. I remember the smell of this place from previous stays—the cold concrete, the iron bars, the old mattress on the bunk. I don't mind being back in here; it's not all bad. Drugs are easy to find. The fistfights are fun.

On my first day I'm assigned to dishwashing duty. I have to work a few hours after every meal; then I get to sleep, sit around, pick fights, whatever I want to do to kill the time.

On my third morning a deputy sheriff appears in front of me.

"Prisoner Gist, get up."

"Why?"

"You're being moved." He looks up from his clipboard. "You are infected with hepatitis and are highly contagious. We are moving you to an isolated area."

An isolated area meant a desk in the front of the jail. Alone.

The deputy hands me a handwritten list of each prisoner who had entered or exited the prison that day. Then he nods at the old manual typewriter on the desk.

"Type."

I laugh out loud. "Are you serious? I don't type!"

"You do now," he says.

Great, I think, looking at the list. I turn the page, and the next page, and the next . . . *This will take all day.*

I scoot the chair up to the table and put the list down next to the typewriter. I look at the first letter in the first name. *S.* My eyes scan the keyboard. *S, S, S, S, ah, there it is.* I punch the key, and it thwacks off the paper.

Okay, now M. M, M, M, M; there is no M on here. Then I see it and strike it with my pointer finger.

Over the next few days, I lose count of how many times I curse at the old typewriter. The keys are too small, and I hit the wrong ones; then I have to pull out the paper, white-out the mistake, and roll it back in.

"Can't you find someone else to do this?" I beg the guard.

"Nope," is all he says, without looking up from the newspaper.

"Great," I mumble to myself. "Where is the stupid *L*?"

After four months of sitting at that desk, hunched over the typewriter, hunting, pecking, typing name after name, I know how to type. I am no secretary, but I can do it. A page that used to take me an hour only takes ten minutes now.

When I work, I hear the judge's voice in my head. *Use the time wisely and think about your life.* It's not my favorite thing, looking back. I was adopted by an abusive family and learned at an early age how to run away. I took off from home, school, summer camp, juvenile hall, a mental hospital, and even jail. Running was the only thing I knew how to do.

But now I know how to type. For the first time in my life I can do something useful. I figure when my six months are up, I'll get my hands on an old typewriter and start writing. I've always had stories in my head but no way to get them out. Now I have what I call "the gift from the deputy." He was trying to stop a hepatitis outbreak and knock out some of his busywork, but in the process he gave me the first real skill of my life.

As it turned out, all my time typing kept me out of trouble, and I was released two months early for good behavior. It's been thirty years since I sat down behind that beat-up typewriter, and it was the last time I ever set foot in a jail. I've been too busy making a living as a screenwriter to get in any trouble. Now I get paid to type all day, and nearly fifty of my screenplays have become television shows or movies.

It's hard to imagine a guy like me, with my background, from my neighborhood, living the life of a screenwriter. Most of the guys I grew up with are spending their lives behind bars. My old buddy Bam-Bam is serving a double life sentence. Preacher is in for life without parole. Kay-Kay has a life sentence. Butterfield has double life, and Dirtdog is in with a death sentence.

Those guys never made it out, but by God's grace I did. I thank him every day that I went to jail, got hepatitis, and had a lazy deputy sheriff who didn't want to type.

DAVE GIST is a screenwriter living in North Hollywood, California.

14 ══

BUT NOW I SEE

GINA GRAHAM

Life sometimes provides the opportunity to give up something we think we need in exchange for something we truly need. True, it seems like a simple concept, but it took me a great deal of time, and a little bit of pain, to discover the thing I needed to surrender in order to be blessed.

It started as a young woman when I first embraced the joy of the creative process. Freshly mixed paint, charcoal on canvas, pencil shavings on the desk, pastels rubbed into my apron—the medium didn't matter. I loved making art. I used the canvas to communicate my emotions, thoughts, and questions, and people were moved by my expressions. My teachers praised me. My pieces sold. I won competitions and impressed judges. I found great purpose in creating new pieces and decided I would always, first and foremost, be an artist.

Yet a few years and kids later, I found myself teaching art to bored middle school students. It was a far cry from my dream of being a working artist, but my husband and I both agreed it would be nice to have some extra income for our family. I had my hands full at home with the kids, and the part-time teaching job was a good fit for my schedule.

It's not your dream, I told myself, *but someday you will get to be a real artist. Maybe when the kids leave home or graduate college. Maybe once you get a degree.*

I thought about someday a lot but secretly wondered if it would ever come. Would I ever have enough time? Would I ever have the courage to take the risk? Was I good enough to cut it as a professional? The fear of someday quietly stalked me, and then one night it hit me right in the face.

I was tucking my son into bed when he saw our dog in the hallway. Impulsively, he grabbed a small plastic toy from his side and tried to throw it for a game of fetch. As his arm came forward, the toy slipped from his hand and flew straight into my eye.

It was so unexpected, so close, I barely had time to close my eyes. Instantly an explosion of pain seared my eye, and I doubled over on his bed. All I could see were multicolored sparks firing on a black background.

What is happening to my eye? I shouted internally, as the colors danced and mingled in the darkness. My stomach became nauseous, and I stumbled out into the hallway. I called for my husband and then found my way to our bed.

"What happened?" my husband asked, quickly coming to my side.

"My eye. I don't know what's happening. All I can see are sparks, and my stomach is in knots."

My husband called his father, an optometrist, and he rushed over. As he helped me out to his truck, I could hear my husband comforting our children in the background.

"Mommy will be okay; she just has to go with Grandpa for a little while."

On the way across town, I sat hunched over with my head between my knees and told my father-in-law about the sparks.

"Then you better sit up," he told me. "You might be losing your retina."

After an examination at his office, he decided my eye would be okay for the night, so he called a colleague and scheduled a follow-up appointment the next morning.

After a short night of sleep and a lot of worry, my husband drove me to the appointment and listened with me as the doctor explained my injury.

"You've suffered damage to your retina." His voice was cold and frank, free of emotion or sympathy, as if he had told a thousand patients the exact same news.

"Okay, well, how long will it take to get better?" I asked, hoping for no more than a week.

"That is the thing about retinal damage," he answered flatly. "There is no guarantee it will heal. Sometimes they heal totally; other times, not at all. It can also partly heal. It's hard to say, and it's out of our control. All we can do is wait."

Wait. Is there anything harder than waiting?

I quit my teaching job so I could stay home and rest. But the time seemed far from restful. As hard as I tried, I couldn't figure out how God was going to work in the situation. Still, I believed he was with me, so I did what I was ordered to do and waited.

In the midst of my waiting, I realized I had been waiting for *someday* to come for a long time, and suddenly it had arrived. Almost as though a divine hand were leading me, I dusted off my old easel, unboxed my pencils, and started to draw. At first I was cautious, faintly touching the page, watching the lead strokes fill the white space with my one good eye. I turned to a clean sheet and filled it with sketches. Another sheet, more sketches. Soon, I was drawing in long, looping arcs and short bursts of tight shading. Amazingly, as I waited for my eye to recover, I rediscovered my passion for art. In a season of half-darkness I saw more clearly than ever before that God had given me a love and talent for creating.

I decided, once and for all, that I would never let my talent and passion be removed. It can be seen and appreciated only when it is used here and now, not someday soon or somewhere else.

Over time my eye and art both improved slowly. Learning to work with limited vision taught me to create at a slower pace, which in turn helped me pay more attention to detail and ultimately led to the best artwork of my life.

My joy was back, and surprisingly, others started taking notice. I was asked to illustrate an original curriculum for a church's summer children's program. I partnered with a master painter to create a massive mural celebrating creation. I launched an online resource center for churches and parents who need illustrated children's material. I even returned to teaching, freshly inspired by the artistic discoveries I was making.

Years after the accident, my right eye still has a blind spot the size of a pencil eraser, directly in the center of my vision. When I look at what I'm typing with just my bad eye open, I can't see the exact word I'm trying to focus on—but I can see all the surrounding words with my peripheral vision. When I paint and illustrate and draw, I've learned to take a second, third, and fourth look, and in the looking again I see more clearly than ever before.

Sometimes I close my good eye to be reminded of the little vision I have lost because it also reminds me of the passion God allowed me to rediscover. He used an innocent accident and a small blind spot to teach me that today, not someday, is the right time to start following our dreams.

GINA GRAHAM and her husband live in the sunny South. Her most important job is keeping her three teenage boys happy, fed, and productive. Visit Gina at ginagraham.com. She hides a heart symbol in all of her art and often draws a Scottie dog in her illustrations.

LEMON DROP

A successful visual artist with trouble seeing? Only in *When God Makes Lemonade*! When I spoke with Gina, her eye was doing better than ever, though she'll always notice a tiny spot there. She was working on an ambitious series of six Easter paintings for her own home—and without the injury she never would have taken the time for it. Her less-than-perfect vision will always remind her of what God took away, and gave, to bring her passion back to life.

—Don

15

KC CAN'T SKATE

ROSS GALE

When my older brother, KC, was three years old, he walked around with a plastic yellow baseball bat longer than his body. He would wait all day for my dad to get home from teaching and coaching at the high school. When Dad finally got home, he'd take KC outside into the grass and pitch him Wiffle balls. Swing after swing, KC sent the balls whistling over the fence into the neighbor's yard. "Can't believe a three-year-old can hit that far!" our neighbor would say; then he'd toss the balls back to my dad.

On the weekends when Dad coached his team, KC would watch the game from the bleachers until he grew bored; then he'd join in a pickup game with other kids twice his age. He loved sports, especially baseball, and the Seattle Mariners were his absolute favorite team. Even though they played on Astroturf in the Kingdome and finished dead last in the American League West, KC was their biggest fan.

One day in September, KC broke into his piggy bank and ran up to my dad with the money in his hand. "Is this enough for two tickets, Dad? Can we go, please?" My dad counted up the change and smiled. "Sure is!"

When they arrived at the stadium, they began hiking up the left-field steps to their seats, but KC tripped, and quickly rolled underneath a railing. My dad turned around just in time to see him disappear over the ledge of a drop-off. Dad shouted for him and jogged back down a few steps; but when he leaned over the railing, KC was twenty feet below, motionless on the concrete, lying in a pool of blood. My dad screamed for help and scrambled to find a way down to him, but he had to run all the way outside the stadium to find the way to KC's broken body.

The surgeons reassembled his skull one piece at a time, and later they likened the operation to putting "Humpty Dumpty back together again." After three months in a coma, he woke up and started all over: walking, talking, tying his shoes. He had to learn how to do everything again. He began in a wheelchair, progressed to a walker, and then graduated to leg braces. All along he suffered seizures and took medicine. After a full year of physical and speech therapy at Seattle Children's Hospital, he was released to come home.

It was different with KC home again—he was different. He couldn't run around anymore with his yellow Wiffle bat or jump down the stairs like a kangaroo. He couldn't play catch with Dad and could hardly lift a spoonful of cereal to his mouth. He wanted to; he just couldn't. It didn't make sense to him that things were different, and when my parents signed me and my other brother up for hockey lessons, he expected to be there with us, skates laced up, sliding around the ice.

I remember watching from the hallway as my parents told KC he couldn't skate because of his disability. He just cried and cried in my dad's arms.

My brother and I continued our baseball and hockey careers

through high school, and not surprisingly, KC was there for every game. Even though he couldn't play, he found ways to be involved. One year he was the water boy for my hockey team. He'd show up wearing the team jersey and hang up his homemade banner behind our bench.

We also had a journalism class together, and even though he didn't write a single article, he got involved through photography. He started using the school's camera to photograph sporting events, and he practiced developing film in the darkroom. His eyesight had been poor since the accident, so most of his pictures turned out blurry. He also had a hard time seeing in the dim, red light of the darkroom, so one time he opened the door to see what he was doing and ruined his classmates' photos. I remember listening to my parents tenderly encouraging KC to keep searching for a hobby he would be good at, but this didn't deter him.

He saved his money, bought an expensive digital camera and several large lenses, and kept practicing. He'd come out to my baseball games and aim his lens toward the action. Over time, shutter by shutter, he improved. The spring before he finished high school, four years since he'd started photography, a national baseball magazine published one of his photos. He was so excited, he bought extra copies of the magazine and hand-delivered them to all of his friends. He had done something that no one thought he could do! The even more remarkable thing is this: he's still doing it today as a professional freelance photographer for a baseball magazine.

Nobody would have guessed a kid with his disabilities would be doing what he's doing, but that is what makes KC who he is. He's too stubborn to quit and too courageous not to try. It's the reason he survived a headfirst fall and painful recovery; he doesn't know how to do anything but make the most of everything.

My family calls the day KC fell "Grace Day." It's our reminder that KC easily could have died in the Kingdome that day, and he just as easily could have been unharmed. Yet God's grace changed him into the young man who has changed us all. The young man who doesn't give up or lose hope. The young man who reminds us that every day is grace day.

ROSS GALE is a writer and editor. His work is featured in *Burnside Writers Collective*, *Antler*, *Relief Journal*, and *Archipelago*, and he contributes to MagicalTeaching.com. He earned his MFA in creative writing from Seattle Pacific University. He lives in Oregon with his wife. Connect with him at rcgale.com.

16 ═══

ANGELS WITH CHAIN SAWS

MARIANE HOLBROOK

Eighty-eight-year-old Edna stood alone looking into the darkness. Outside, the wind of a midwinter storm was ravaging her North Carolina farmhouse without mercy. She had listened to the weatherman in the morning, but this storm looked and sounded stronger than forecast. With the power already out and the night just beginning, she wondered if she would make it to morning. A heavy sigh escaped her lips, and her breath fogged on the windowpane.

Placing a few logs in the fireplace, she struck a match and placed it to the crumbled newspaper. Quickly the kindling was crackling with heat. A warm glow filled the room, and in the flicker of the firelight, she saw the old frame over the mantel. In the picture she stood, younger, holding hands with her husband. She smiled faintly.

"I wish you were here."

She turned, grabbed another blanket, and sat to rest in her chair. Again she looked to the window and gave attention to the storm.

She heard a pine tree, heavy with ice and weak from the relentless wind, snap and slam to the ground. Ice crystals pelted the siding. She listened to the storm unleash its fury and began to speak softly: "Oh, God, protect me from this storm."

When the lonely hours of night finally faded into morning, Edna rose from her chair and stepped back to the window. The destruction was devastating. Large, splintered branches lay stacked upon one another, frozen in the grip of ice. Small saplings were uprooted and thrown across the lawn. Drifts of snow climbed the side of the house. Power lines had blown to the ground and were tangled in the mess of debris.

"Where will I ever find the money to clean up this mess?" she whispered to herself.

It was a particularly bad season for unexpected expenses. Edna's monthly Social Security check was hardly enough to get her from month to month, not to mention the furnace she just replaced or the leaky oil tank she recently had fixed. It hadn't been easy for her in the old house since her husband passed away. Little things broke and stayed broken. Leaky pipes dripped and just kept dripping. It was a lot of work to keep up with the day-to-day chores, but she couldn't stand the thought of leaving. It was home.

She considered calling her grandson to come over and help clear the mess. It would save her money, but it would be a tremendous burden for him due to his poor health. She thought of other options and wondered if it was even worth the money to clean it up now. What if another storm picked up? The weatherman said it might snow again. She left the phone on the hook and waited.

Thirty-six hours had passed, and still Edna had not called for help. The power was still off, she was running out of firewood, and the yard remained a disaster. Lying down by the fire, wondering whom to call, she suddenly heard several engines roar around the corner and die in her driveway. Car doors opened and slammed shut.

She shuffled over to the window.

"My goodness . . ." she remarked, surprised to see ten men unloading tools in her front yard. One of the men—tall, dressed in winter boots and a parka—stepped up onto the porch and knocked.

Cautiously, she opened the door and shivered as a cold breeze brushed her feet.

"Ma'am," the gentleman said, smiling, "my name is Joel. We live nearly a hundred miles away in South Carolina. We heard about the terrible ice storm you had up here, so several men from our church got together and decided to come up and help out."

He looked back to the other men, already firing up their chain saws, and turned back to Edna.

"We brought our tools to clean up your yard."

Edna was stunned. "But I have no money to pay you," she stammered. "I'm very appreciative of you coming all this way, but this is a very big job, and I just don't have the money."

"Ma'am," Joel kindly interrupted her, "we don't expect nor will we take any money for our labor. Our pastor received a call that you and several others in this area were in desperate need of assistance, and we've come as Christian brothers so we can help."

Joel paused, and Edna looked over his shoulder to the men in the yard, working together to move a log. Her eyes jumped back to Joel.

"I don't know what to say . . ." She shook her head, holding back her tears. "Thank you."

Edna watched from her window as the angels with chain saws cut down the large, damaged trees and sawed the limbs into manageable lengths. Despite the bitter cold, they worked all day, and when the sun softened on the horizon and disappeared behind the hills, they packed up their trucks and drove into the night.

The next morning they were back with smiles and waves. Edna waved back from her window and watched them tirelessly labor through the cold morning hours. They worked all day to clear the yard, replenish her stack of firewood, and rake the empty flower beds.

When the job was done and their tools were loaded up, Joel again knocked on the door.

"Ma'am, may we come in for a moment?"

"Of course, my goodness, of course, come in," Edna insisted.

Gently, all ten men filed into her small living room. Without hesitation Joel handed her a New Testament complete with their signatures on the inside front cover.

"This is a gift from us."

She reached out and gripped the Bible in her frail hands.

"If it is okay, we would like to pray for you."

She nodded.

Circling together, they held hands and prayed for God to protect Edna, comfort her, and bless her with a long, healthy life.

When they were finished, they exchanged hugs, handshakes, and thanks with Edna and then departed for their next assignment. Standing on the porch, wrapped in blankets, she looked at the yard and marveled—it looked better than before the storm.

She closed the door behind her and knelt by her old, worn sofa. The scent of their winter clothes still hung in the house.

"Thank you, God. I was bitter at this storm, yet you blessed me. Thank you for those men and their obedience. Bless them, Lord, and help me do likewise."

Mariane Holbrook is a retired schoolteacher who lives with her husband, John, in Kure Beach, North Carolina. She enjoys playing the piano and painting her favorite birds. She is the author of two books, *Prisms of the Heart* and *Humor Me*. To learn more, visit marianeholbrook.com.

17

SENT AWAY FOR GOOD

BERTHA RAZ

Hunger was twisting my stomach in knots, but I knew there was no food in the house, so I crept down to the creek that flowed across the west side of our land. Glancing over my shoulder to make sure I was alone, I looked into the glassy water where we refrigerated what little perishable food we had.

Just below the surface was a bottle filled with milk. I looked back one more time to be safe, then knelt down by the creek and slid my hands into the water. The bottle was cold to the touch, and as I pulled it up, water beaded down the sides. I removed the top, put my lips to the opening, and then tilted my head back. The cold milk chilled my throat as I gulped one delicious mouthful after another. When I finished, I replaced the missing milk with water from the creek, capped it, shook it, and returned it to its resting place.

Later that night my older brother pulled me out of the house and marched me down to the creek. He pulled out the glass bottle and shoved it in my face.

"Did you do this? Did you drink the family milk?"

I cowered with guilt and tried to apologize, but he lashed into me with a vicious beating.

It was 1930, a year after the stock market crash, and the Great Depression had stretched its sorrow all the way across the county into our home in Chehalis, Washington. My hardworking parents were doing their best to provide for me and my ten brothers, but jobs were few, food was scarce, and there was no national safety net to catch our fall.

We didn't have beds to sleep on, clothes to change into, or enough soap to wash our overalls more than once every few weeks. We had so little food in our house that my baby brother and I developed painful cases of rickets, a disease that softens your bones and bows your legs. It was terribly painful. Walking was hard, and no matter where I went, there was always someone ready to tease me.

The Depression felt like a trap that clamped down on our family. There was no way out and no one to help us. We just had to make do and hope things would get better.

One day, when I was about five and a half years old, a city official had a long, serious chat with my parents. I couldn't hear them talking, but I could tell by the way my father was standing that he didn't like the official's words.

When he came back into the house, he said the official couldn't offer any help to the family. Instead, he recommended that my younger brother and I be put up for adoption.

Even though we were hungry, sick, and hardly clothed, my father couldn't even think of letting his kids live with another family. His Swiss roots were still strong, and family mattered.

But the idea stuck, and not long after the official came to visit, my father called my uncle in Portland, Oregon. He asked if my brother and I could go and stay with him and his wife for a while. They didn't have kids; they lived on a farm, worked the land, and could afford to care for us. But would they want to?

Family matters, so they agreed. What I wanted, however, didn't matter. Leaving home sounded awful. I'd never really been outside of Chehalis, and even though I hated the hunger and stink of dirty clothes, I wanted to be with my parents. But the decision was made, we were going, and I cried the entire way to Portland.

At my new home a doctor came and looked at my legs. He said a healthy diet of goat milk would fix them up, so my aunt and uncle made sure there was plenty to drink in the house. They didn't have a lot of money, but they sure did have a lot of food coming in off the farm, so we never missed a meal. After one year of living in their house, helping milk the cows and collect the eggs, I discovered my rickets was gone, and both my legs were long and straight.

That is when my mother came to visit for the first time. I remember I was so scared I would have to go back home with her I ran and hid in my uncle's pasture. When my aunt found me and told me I didn't have to go back to Chehalis, that my mother was just coming to see us, I slinked back to the house.

As I grew older, I came to think of Portland as my home, and my aunt and uncle as my parents. They loved my brother and me as if we were their own children; and more than the milk nourished my body, their love nourished my soul. With their encouragement I graduated from high school, studied to become a bookkeeper, and married a handsome young man.

Now I'm almost ninety, and I can tell you that the years have been more than okay: they've been wonderful! I am thankful I have lived to a ripe old age, when the Great Depression cut so many lives tragically short. Most of all I am thankful my parents loved my brother and me enough to send us away, and that my aunt and uncle loved us enough to make us their own. Moving to Portland was a traumatic experience as a five-year-old, but it most likely saved my life. What a gift to be loved so well, and what a God to replace something I desperately wanted in order to give me what I most certainly needed.

BERTHA RAZ was born in the mid-1920s to Swiss immigrants Arnold and Elsie Blaser. At the age of five she moved to Portland, Oregon, and was raised by her aunt and uncle, Henry and Annie Tannler, on their dairy farm in southwest Portland. She graduated from Commerce High School in 1942 and married Paul Raz in 1951. They raised three children together. Her favorite memories include the many trips she and Paul took traveling around the United States and to Europe to visit relatives in Switzerland.

18

TRUTH REMEMBERED

KIM ANTHONY

The fans are filing into the seats, and I can feel the energy pulsing through the building. I look up at the sea of people and smile. I'm home. My favorite place: Pauly Pavilion on the UCLA campus, the historic site of John Wooden's record-setting ten consecutive men's basketball championships.

Today is the first big meet of my senior year, and if everything goes as planned, I'll be one step closer to defending my title. I have three consecutive NCAA national floor exercise titles in women's gymnastics, and in just three months I'll be at nationals, competing for my fourth. It's a record that has never been set and can never be broken, only repeated.

I jog out onto the floor with my team and wave at the crowd. They erupt. I hear chants, whistles, and applause. I look for my mom, sitting somewhere on the first level, blending in with all the smiling faces. She flew in from Virginia yesterday to cheer me on. She's been my biggest fan from my first front flip as a little girl. Now, thousands of jumps, twists, flips, and landings later, it all comes down to this.

Our time to warm up begins, and we head to the vault. I wait and stretch as one teammate after another sprints down the blue runway. Their hands push off the vault, and they gracefully twist high into the air. They pull out of their rotations at the last second and land feet first, squarely on the mat.

I take a deep breath. The vault is my weakest event, but this year I've trained harder than ever before—hour after hour, week after week, month after month. I've worked to add height to my hand-spring front tuck. Now the day is here, and I am ready.

I start slowly but quickly gain speed. My hands are pumping by my sides, and I'm in a dead sprint. I leap onto the springboard and thrust my hands forward. I push off, and I'm airborne, tucking, sensing my place in the air, waiting for the exact moment to release and land.

Now!

I pull out of the tuck and hit the mat beneath me with too much momentum and step forward.

You opened too late, I tell myself, walking back to the vault start. *Open sooner. Release high. Stick the landing.*

On my second practice run, off the springboard, high over the mat, I overcompensate and straighten my legs too early. My legs lock, and I hit the mat. My head snaps back, and the lights go out. I stumble off the platform and quickly sit down on the floor. Slowly the lights come back into focus. My team is moving on to the uneven bars for warm-up.

It's okay, I tell myself. *You've been here before. It's just pain. Overcome it.*

When the warm-ups finish, the announcer introduces us to the crowd.

"Three-time NCAA national floor exercise champion, Kim Hamilton!" I smile and wave as I think to myself, *Four times. It is soon to be four.*

My turn for the vault comes, and I quiet the memory of blacking out. I only remember the training. I've done this a thousand times, and I can do it now.

Ready? Go.

I stick the landing flawlessly. The crowd screams as I walk off the mat, and then the scores come in. Next I move to the uneven bars and then to the balance beam. They both go as planned, and my scores are good. Now there is just one event left: the floor exercise.

The fans are cheering as I take a warm-up pass. My double backs feel good, so I line up for my middle pass, starting with a front somersault; for more of a lift, I try the Russian front with its circular arm movement. As I take off, I hear a loud pop, and my left foot pulses. I know instantly I can't land on my foot, so in midair I cartwheel out of the pass and keep the pressure off my left foot.

Quickly I hop off to the side and sit down on the edge of the floor mat. I try to wiggle my foot and am surprised that it doesn't hurt. Still, I can't move it; my range of motion is only a few degrees.

It's just an injury. Gut it out.

I motion for the trainer. She turns my ankle around in her hands and rules out a dislocation.

"Can you stand up and put pressure on it?" she asks.

I stand up. Immediately pain shocks my system.

Oh no, oh no.

I fall back onto the floor.

The trainer bites her lip and puts her hand on my shoulder. I see her mouth moving, but I don't understand anything she is saying. She helps me over to a chair next to my teammates and leaves me sitting.

All I can feel is the fire in my foot. I try to talk myself through the pain, but I can feel the tears coming, hot behind my eyes. I look up and see the trainer coming back to me with crutches in her hand. Her face is pale, and her shoulders are slouched forward.

It's over, I tell myself, looking out over the empty floor as my championship vanishes like smoke.

Ten years later I was informed UCLA was inducting me into the UCLA Hall of Fame. When I heard the news, I instantly felt unworthy of the honor because I was one title short. And it's not as if it were a distant memory; I still carried the wound. I wanted my chance back, and every time I didn't get it, I grew more and more bitter.

At the induction ceremony I sat at my table and read through the program listing everyone's accomplishments. I found my name and was surprised to discover all the records I set during my career. Still, when I saw the phrase "First to win three consecutive NCAA national floor exercise titles," my bitter heart surged.

"It should have been four," I said under my breath.

Suddenly I had a flashback. It was my senior year again, and I was speaking with my coach shortly after hurting my foot.

"Kimmy, because of your foot injury, you're not going to be able to compete at nationals."

"I know, I know. Believe me, I know!"

"Look—there's something else you need to know . . . something the MRI revealed."

"My season's over. What else could I possibly need to know?"

"A previous MRI found something else. Something other than your foot."

"Something else?"

"It's your neck. The whiplash from your hard landings has dam-aged it."

"I know it hurts, but it'll be okay."

"No. No, it won't. If you had kept snapping it on landings . . . you would have paralyzed yourself."

"Paralyzed? Are you serious?"

"Yes—paralyzed. Or even killed."

Immediately, as the Hall of Fame induction ceremony continued around me, my memory was set straight.

How could I forget such an important conversation for an entire decade? Was I really so fixated on what I lost I couldn't remember what I gained? And why remember it then, at the Hall of Fame?

Maybe it was the UCLA camaraderie that helped me remember the truth. Maybe I had been in too much pain in the moment to appreciate my coach's words. Maybe I just needed ten years to get over the loss of something I desperately wanted.

What I do know is the pain of hurting my foot and suffering the loss of my dream saved my life. I wouldn't have chosen the injury as a senior at UCLA, but now, looking back, I wouldn't change a thing. Thanks to God's redeeming power, my greatest disappointment turned out to be my greatest blessing. I get to run with my kids in the park. We volunteer together. We travel. To think I almost missed it all reminds me of the miracle of God's grace. He knew what he was doing all along, and I can't help but be thankful, open my hands, and ask, "What's next, Lord?"

KIM ANTHONY is an author and speaker who resides in south-west Ohio with her husband and two children. She serves on staff with Athletes in Action, where she works with wives of professional athletes, coaches, and executives. To learn more, visit kimanthony.net.

LEMON DROP

Bitterness is a tough pill to swallow, no doubt about it. Kim was angry for a long time, thinking something she deserved had been taken from her. But God wasn't being cruel or unjust or unkind—he was saving her life. At times it may feel as though you are a child asking for a fish only to receive a stone from your Father, but I promise, if you're holding a stone, it's exactly what you need!

—Don

19

TIMING IS EVERYTHING

VETA SHEPHERD

The timing was ironic. My husband and I had been married for nine years and three hundred sixty-four days, one day shy of a decade. And instead of celebrating our anniversary with a weekend getaway, a romantic dinner, or a party, we finalized our divorce.

Exactly one month later my father died unexpectedly. I hardly had the money to travel to Jackson, Mississippi, for the funeral, and I couldn't help my mother cover the burial costs. I returned home exhausted, grief stricken, and nearly broke.

Three months after the funeral, a company-wide memo circulated around my office. Upper management had decided the business would be better off in another state, and they were scheduled to relocate in six weeks. People considered not vital to the success of the transition were relieved from their jobs, including me.

Three things no person ever wants to hear: "I want a divorce." "Your father passed away last night." "We have to let you go." I was heartbroken, grieving, and anxious about the bills all at once. I didn't know what to feel first: sad, mad, angry, bitter, betrayed, grieved, anxious, afraid, or doubtful? Some days I felt so full of emotion, I could burst; others, I dragged along, empty and lifeless.

I longed for someone to share the burden with me, someone like my husband. I wished I had a warm shoulder to cry on, like my father's. I wanted to wake up and go somewhere I could forget about my personal problems for a few hours, like to a job. Everything I wanted and felt I needed was gone.

That is when the house sold. I knew it was coming, I couldn't keep paying for it after the divorce, and my ex-husband insisted on splitting the proceeds as a settlement. Moving into a small apartment with my five-year-old daughter was disorienting. My place of refuge, comfort, and familiarity was gone.

Lord, what am I supposed to do? I prayed daily, lost and alone.

The first glimmer of hope was my new landlady, a kind older woman who agreed to watch my daughter whenever I went out looking for a job. Some mornings, if I needed to leave early, she would even walk her to the bus stop for school. As we got to know each other, she lowered my rent so I could afford to pay it with my unemployment checks.

I told her I'd be working soon and could pay the full rent, and I meant it. I treated every day of unemployment like a job, checking job postings, leaving résumés, going to interviews. But no one was calling back with that happy tone in his or her voice: "Congratulations! Welcome to the team! We can't wait for you to start!"

My only offer was to work a night shift at a home improvement store. The money was enough to take care of my daughter and me, but how could I say yes? I'd have to leave her with a babysitter every night. She'd already lost one parent—wouldn't this be like losing another? Yet *not* taking the job was foolish. My unemployment was set to run out in a week, and once it was spent, we wouldn't have a single penny to our names.

It doesn't matter if I'm around at night if we are homeless and hungry, I thought to myself. *I have to take the job; there is no option.*

Still, my spirit was restless, and the day before my unemployment benefits were set to run out, I hadn't accepted the home improvement job. I felt as if God was telling me to wait. Even with the final hours ticking by, I stood in faith, hoping for a miracle.

Then the phone rang.

"Mrs. Shepherd, good afternoon. I have your résumé here and think you will be a good fit for a full-time position we are looking to fill. Would you like to come in for an interview?"

"Of course!" I shouted, wishing I could leap through the phone and into the office in that moment.

The interview went well, and I was a great fit for the job, but the full-time paid position was only for three months. I shuddered at the thought of looking for work again so soon, but at least it would be twelve weeks of seeing my daughter in the evenings. I accepted the position and went to work, using every free minute to research new job openings.

I enjoyed the job, working as an entry-level secretary in the finance department of a nonprofit, and wished it could last forever, but twelve weeks came and went. Despite my best efforts, I hadn't lined up another job, and as my last day ticked by, I dreaded the five o'clock hour.

"Finance department," I said, picking up the ringing phone in front of me.

"Veta, hi." It was my supervisor. "Can you come back to my office for a moment?"

I thought it was standard procedure for a last day. She was going to have me sign some paperwork and thank me for my service, but when I sat down, she surprised me.

"Veta, we've really enjoyed having you here the past three months. You're a great addition to our team, and if you are available, we would like to have you interview for a permanent, full-time position doing data entry."

I cupped my trembling hand to my mouth. "Permanent?"

She smiled and laughed at my excitement. "Yes, Veta, permanent."

In life, timing is everything. The day before my tenth wedding anniversary, my life crumbled around me. The day before my daughter and I were set to run out of money, a great job dropped into my lap. How great? Well, I've been working full-time at that nonprofit for a while now—almost twenty years.

My daughter is now twenty-seven, and if she learned anything from growing up with me, it's this: never settle for what you think you need. Instead, wait for what you really need. And never, ever, ever forget that God has a plan to prosper us and to give us hope and a future.

VETA SHEPHERD is married to her wonderful husband, Lawrence, with four fantastic grown daughters, Sherri, Lisa, Lauren, and Jessica, and nine exceptional grandchildren. Because of her history with singing, writing, and community theater, she is able to use those gifts as head of the drama ministry at the City of Truth Covenant Church in Chicago Heights, Illinois, and has started the Love Your Neighbor Foundation, which advocates for those in need.

20

THE PEPPY SAINT

MATT HART

I n 1952, Covell and Ruth Hart—my paternal grandparents—sold all their belongings, said their good-byes, and moved from America to the Middle East.

The international move and transition weren't easy with two young sons, but they believed God had called them to open a coed orphanage in Lebanon, the first of its kind. They settled into their roles, and soon a third son joined the family.

Life in Lebanon was hectic; raising three kids, caring for thirty orphans, and dealing with the daily challenges of cross-cultural communication all contributed to the chaos. Ruth was constantly exhausted from the never-ending demands, but there was nowhere in the world she would have rather been.

"When I get to heaven, all I am going to do is *rest*," she used to say, bone tired.

On Christmas Eve 1954, the Hart family celebrated with all the children in their care. The orphan children opened small presents, and everyone shared a delicious meal before ushering in the holiday with songs sung by candlelight.

The next morning Ruth woke up to celebrate the birth of Christ with her husband and children, but as she sat up in bed, she suddenly lost control of her body and fell back onto the mattress. She lay there, motionless, until Covell walked through the room and saw her.

"Ruth, what happened? Are you okay?"

"I can't move," she said, her voice trembling with panic. Covell sat down next to her on the bed.

"What do you mean?" he asked, looking down and feeling her legs.

"I don't know. I woke up, and now I can't move. I don't understand. Is it polio?"

"Don't worry, Ruthie; you'll be okay," Covell said, picking her up.

He raced her to the hospital, she was examined, and the doctor confirmed their dreaded suspicion.

"This is terrible news, and I am very sorry." The doctor paused, took a deep breath, then continued. "But you have polio. You will be paralyzed for the rest of your life."

Within days the disease began attacking her organs, and with her diaphragm failing, she was placed inside a device called an iron lung. There was only one machine of its kind in Lebanon, and fortunately for Ruth it was freed up the previous day. She was placed inside the metal, tubelike case, with her head and neck exposed, as the airtight container increased and decreased air pressure around her abdomen, allowing Ruth's lungs to expand and contract.

She lived on her back, contained in the iron lung, for three straight months, and on her thirtieth birthday she was finally able to breathe again under her own power. Even with her improving condition, arrangements were made for her to return to the United States for further medical attention.

An ambulance dropped Ruth off at the military airstrip used by the air force, and she was loaded by forklift—still lying on her hospital bed—directly onto the cargo plane that flew her to America.

Her destination was the polio ward at the University of Michigan in Ann Arbor, where she was hooked up to all sorts of contraptions to help her move her limbs. Despite the mechanical assistance, she was completely paralyzed from the neck down, and it was a terrible position for a young mother to be in.

Once, her youngest son, Jim, was placed beside her on the bed for some snuggle time. When he woke, he rolled off the bed and fell painfully to the floor. Ruth watched, helpless, as he wailed on the ground. According to family lore, that was the only time during her decades of suffering that Ruth cried.

Ruth was a light of hope in that dark hospital. While other patients were growing bitter and cold, she remained faithful and never shied away from thanking God for his goodness.

One young, paralyzed polio patient named Pat was particularly impressed with Ruth's demeanor. One evening she listened to Ruth laugh and converse with her husband and children during a visit, and when they had gone, she couldn't help but ask, "Ruth, why don't things bother you? Your children come to see you—you can't take them in your arms and love them. When Jimmy fell off the bed, you couldn't do a thing to stop it."

"Well," Ruth replied quietly, "of course things bother me, Pat. I wouldn't be human if they didn't! But I've learned what it means to trust in the Lord Jesus Christ, not only for salvation but for grace to live each day."

Pat asked, "Why can't this happen to me?"

"It not only can but will, right now, if you'll just receive the Lord Jesus Christ as your Savior." Ruth suggested they pray together, and just as she was about to begin, Pat interrupted her.

"Wait a minute—could I pray?"

They filled the room with prayers and thanks, and later, after the lights were out, Pat whispered, "Ruthie, Ruthie! Are you still awake?"

"Yes, Pat. What is it?"

"You know, I've just been lying here thinking. I believe God allowed me to get polio and come here to be saved!"

Ruth smiled and thought of her journey to that dark polio ward. The Christmas morning, the iron lung, the long flight back home. She marveled and thanked God for the disease—the blessing—that brought her and Pat together.

As word of Pat's conversion spread around the hospital, so did hope; and other patients began asking Ruth about life in Christ. In a letter to friends back home, Covell wrote, "Several other patients in the ward have asked for gospel literature and expressed general interest in the things of Christ. Please pray for the continued working of God in the hearts of those Ruth contacts. Certainly God has made no mistake."

Indeed, it was no mistake, and Ruth kept on blessing everyone in that hospital until she was released to go home, where she spent the next twenty-nine years in bed. Through it all, she never lost her sense of humor or eternal perspective, and toward the end of her life, right before she passed, she told us, "I used to imagine how wonderful it would be to get to heaven and just *rest*, but I've had my share of resting. I've spent thirty years on my feet and thirty years on my seat!" With that she rolled her head back and let out her famous laugh, a loud chortle followed by delightful sniffs. Then she added, "Now all I want to do is get to heaven and jump up and down. When you show up and see a peppy saint, don't ask me to sit, for I've sat long enough!"*

MATT HART is married with four young children, Katie, Alex, Will, and Maddie. They live in Moline, Illinois, where Matt delivers home medical equipment. A Christian since age thirteen, Matt credits his grandmother Ruth as his hero in the Christian faith and looks forward to dancing around heaven with her one day.

---

*Parts of this story were borrowed from "The Woman Who Refuses to Quit" by Bernard DeRemer, published in *Adult Power*, vol. 21, no. 3, July–Sept. 1963.

21

THIRD TIME'S THE CHARM

LATOSHA BROWN

No, no, no, no, this can't be happening, I weep to myself.

My head is heavy in my hands, and I can smell the salt in my tears. I wipe my eyes but keep crying. The lady in the room smiles sympathetically and then leaves me alone with the news.

I don't know what to do. I'm not ready to be a mother, not even close! It isn't supposed to happen this way.

How could I be so irresponsible? I shame myself. *You know better!*

Members of my family don't have children out of wedlock; it's never been done. My grandma, mom, and aunt have always told me to do it the right way: *Get your schooling done first, find a good man, and then raise a family!*

How are they going to understand this? My senior year in college I get pregnant by a man I know I don't want to marry and face raising a kid by myself?

They won't understand—they'll kill me! I can't tell them. The loneliness sinks in, and I know what I have to do. *Just take care of it before anyone finds out!*

A few days later I throw my purse into the car and steer away from my college campus. The clinic is a few hours away in a small rectangular building by a shopping mall. I hesitate to get out of my car and cross the parking lot, but I remind myself why I'm here.

Get rid of the baby, and everything will be fine.

I unbuckle my seat belt and get out of the car. After some paperwork, a short wait, and an examination, the technician tells me my pregnancy is too far along for a normal abortion. They have to perform a more complicated procedure, and it will cost more money.

"I don't have that much right now. Can I come back in a few weeks?" I ask.

"Of course," says the lady in the white coat.

The next few weeks are a blur. I'm not studying or going to class, and I can't focus. All I can do is work, save money, and try to keep my secret safe. When the day of my second appointment finally comes, I take a shower and get dressed. On my way out the door, I can't find my purse, and suddenly I remember I didn't have it coming home the previous night. I try to retrace my steps, but nothing makes sense.

I drove home with my friend, took my shoes off, washed my face, went to sleep—where is it?

I walk around my apartment in circles, looking under every surface. After a few minutes there is nowhere left to look, so I call the clinic and reschedule. When I hang up, I stare out the window and start thinking about the money in my missing purse.

Two more weeks at work and I'll have enough again, I tell myself, defeated.

Time drags by, and I can hardly stand to talk to my family or friends. They know I'm sad and tired, but they don't know why.

"I'm working a lot," I tell them, which is true. But I'm not being honest. I want my problem fixed and my secret gone.

The morning of my third appointment comes, and I have the money in my wallet, in my hand, in the car on the way to the clinic. Almost there, I hear a small voice speak peacefully.

Exit the interstate. Pull over.

It's strange, but I flip on my blinker. As I'm driving down the off-ramp, my car suddenly shuts off, and I coast down the hill into a parking space at a restaurant.

My hands are on the wheel, and I sit quietly for a moment.

"That was weird," I say to myself out loud. I get out of the car and wander across the parking lot. I'm not thinking straight. My car just randomly shut off. I lost my purse last time. The first time I didn't have the money.

Why can't I fix this problem? Am I supposed to keep my baby?

I see a tree stump in a median of the parking lot, and I sit down.

"I just want this over with!" I shout as I start weeping. I'm so angry I can feel it crawling through my body. My fists are clenched, and I'm thinking of all the reasons I have to be mad.

I'm stupid for letting this happen! My boyfriend is stupid for not being supportive. God is stupid for not understanding! You don't know how hard this is, God! So leave me alone! I'm not having this baby!

Suddenly an old, beat-up truck comes to a stop in front of me, and an elderly man rolls down the window.

He looks at me as I cry, with my fists tightly balled in anger, and I look at him.

"Baby, get in—you need something to eat," he says, as if he knows me.

It doesn't even cross my mind that he is a stranger. I just know I want to leave this parking lot, so I climb into the passenger seat.

Across the street he pulls into a trailer park and stops in front of an aging single-wide. An older woman opens the door and waves us in.

"You can call someone to come help with your car," he says as he steps out and walks into the trailer.

For the first time it strikes me: *I don't know these people! What am I doing here?* But the old man tells me to come on, and I jump out of the truck.

After I call a friend to come pick me up, the woman tells me to sit down. Then, one plate at a time, she delivers a feast to the table in front of me.

"Come on; eat!" she says as she smiles and points to the food.

"This is so kind of you. Thank you!" I grab a fork and start tasting different dishes. They are all good, but I feel terrible. I put my fork down, and I feel it coming. I know I'm about to cry, and I can't stop it—the tears start pouring out.

The old woman doesn't miss a beat. "It's okay, sweetheart. You go on and cry. It will be okay. Trust me; God is good."

On the way back home in my friend's car, I can't stop thinking about the old woman and her husband. *How did he know my car was broken-down? Why did I trust him? Why did they have a big meal prepared? How did she know exactly what I needed to hear when I never even told her I was pregnant?*

When I broke down in the middle of the meal, they didn't judge me or react strangely. They never even asked me what was wrong. They just told stories of God's goodness and shared scriptures with me. They encouraged me to listen to what God was saying, and for the first time, I was listening. The thwarted first attempt, my lost purse, the car shutting off, and the unexpected hospitality of strangers; suddenly it all makes sense, and I know exactly what I am supposed to do.

I'm going to keep my baby!

It wasn't easy, but I told my family and friends about my pregnancy. Then I ended my dysfunctional relationship with the baby's father. Surprisingly the remainder of my pregnancy went smoothly. I got a new job as a general manger at a clothing store that provided enough money to have the baby. The money I had saved for the abortion was the exact amount I needed to furnish the nursery.

A year after my son was born, I loaded him up in the car seat and drove back to the exit where the old man found me sitting in the parking lot. I wanted to tell them the real story of why I was so upset that fateful day and introduce my baby boy.

"This is my son," I was going to say. "You saved his life."

I passed the restaurant where my car broke down and turned into the lot toward the trailer park, but something was wrong. I unbuckled my baby and carried him into the empty field, looking in every direction; the trailers were gone. I was certain I was in the right location, but there were no signs of life.

Nineteen years later and I still don't know if the trailer park was relocated, destroyed, or even there to begin with. I have never found the elderly couple who influenced the biggest decision of my life. They knew nothing about me but gave me everything I needed. To this day,

I still thank God for the angels in the trailer park, who encouraged me to receive God's greatest blessing in my life, my son.

LaTosha Brown is an aspiring writer, award-winning community organizer, professional singer/songwriter, and national philanthropic consultant working on a variety of human rights and social justice issues. She is the founder and CEO of TruthSpeaks Consulting and The Way Productions. She is the recipient of *Redbook*'s Strength and Spirit Award and the White House "Champion of Change" award for her environmental and Gulf Coast work. She is currently working on her first book, titled *The World's Systems Don't Work for Me*. She is the proud mother of one son, Keambi, who is a nineteen-year-old freshman at Morehouse College.

22

A BLOCK OF CHEESE

STEPHEN CLOVER

I don't understand why you are here," said the lady in the bulky winter sweater behind the desk. I took another deep breath and tried to explain.

"The factory where I work closes every year for the holidays. We've already cashed my last paycheck for the year, and since I am a new employee, I don't receive a Christmas bonus. We need a little help to make it through the holidays until the factory opens back up."

"Mr. Clover"—she shook her head—"we can't help you because technically you have a job. You aren't eligible for assistance."

"But my job disappears for a month, and we won't make it without some help," I reminded her. "Just a little for the month is all we're asking. I pay my taxes. I vote. We don't have the police living outside of our house. I'm not asking for you to feed my family for five years." Nothing I said could have wiped the blank look of helplessness off her face. Welfare was a dead end, and she was the brick wall standing in our way.

"Sorry," she said halfheartedly as we left. "Have a Merry Christmas." That night my wife's sister called and said she and her three boys were coming to stay with us over the Christmas break. I almost ripped out my hair.

"How are we going to afford that?"

"I don't know," my wife said, "but we'll figure it out."

My sister-in law and my three little nephews arrived on Christmas Eve. We put on some Christmas carols, played with the kids, and tried not to let money interfere with our celebration. Over the next week, as the cupboard grew more and more bare, my wife kept finding creative ways to use our few remaining ingredients. She put extra water in the stew, added extra flour in the beans, and started using honey as a sweetener when the sugar ran out. She pulled out a half-full bag of oats, from who knows how long ago, and made a wonderful breakfast. During our family devotions, we continued to pray for provision, and every day we found another bag of some long-forgotten food stuffed into the pantry.

By the grace of God, we made it through three weeks without running out of food. But then, one week before the factory was set to reopen, we were down to just flour and water. We all gathered around the kitchen table: my wife, my sister-in-law, all the kids, and me. I pulled out a pen and a piece of paper and asked my family what groceries we needed.

"Stephen," my wife said, "we don't have any money. How are we going to buy groceries?"

"God will provide for us," I replied, "so let's write down what we need and pray."

"Butter would be nice," my sister-in law said, "and bread."

"Great." I quickly scribbled them down. "What else?"

"Tomatoes, lettuce, flour," my wife chimed in.

"Good," I said. "Anything else?"

"Yeah, I want a block of cheese."

I looked at my wife, smiled, and said, "That really isn't a need."

"I know, but I don't care. I want a block of cheese," she said, looking at me with an unwavering gaze.

"Okay," I said, writing it on our list, hoping to keep the bickering to a minimum. Tensions were high enough in the house as they were, and I certainly didn't want a block of cheese to be responsible for a fight. I opened the Bible on the table, placed the list inside, and closed it. Together, we laid hands on the worn leather cover and prayed. "Father, we are grateful for the food you have provided the past few weeks. We pray now for the blessing we are about to receive. Thank you."

Three days passed with no answer. I was eagerly awaiting a mysterious knock on the door, but no one came. Angels did not suddenly appear. No anonymous donor slipped money into our mailbox. We were eating flour mixed with water, and when we grew tired of the pasty texture, we fried the flour in fat. An entire week came and went, and finally the factory was reopening. I kissed my wife before leaving for work.

"I should get paid a little bit today, at least enough to get something to eat."

After my eight-hour shift the pay clerk handed me a few measly dollars, and I folded them into my pocket. I walked out to my van with my hands in my pockets, bracing myself against the cold. I could feel the flimsy dollar bills in my hand and wondered how I'd spend them wisely.

"Stephen!" someone shouted from behind me. I turned around and saw the factory owner's secretary waving to me. I waved back, but then she motioned for me to come over. I walked back across the parking lot.

"We have some gifts for you," she said, pointing down to a few boxes full of groceries. "Just a little thank-you for all of your hard work."

"I don't know what to say." The words stumbled out of my mouth. "Thank you." She smiled and told me to take a few boxes, so I loaded them up in my van and drove home. I pulled into my parking spot and let the van run for a while as I looked at the groceries and reflected. I wondered what was inside. Could it be everything we asked for? My wife came outside and climbed into the van.

"What are you doing out here?" she asked, closing the door behind her. I pointed at the boxes in the backseat. She turned around and paused for a moment.

"Where did you get those?"

"Work. They just gave them to me as a gift." We took the boxes inside and gathered everyone around the kitchen table. My wife opened the first box and pulled out flour, bread, butter, lettuce, and tomatoes. I opened up my Bible, grabbed the grocery list, and crossed those items off. There was only one thing left. Then my wife opened up the second box, reached down into the cardboard, and pulled out a family-size block of cheese.

STEPHEN CLOVER has a diploma in freelance journalism with NZ Institute of Business Studies. He also has a blog on Orble titled *Christianity Forever*.

LEMON DROP

I was reading this story for the first time when my publisher called and caught me crying! What gets me emotional is that Stephen and his family were bold enough to ask God to provide for their needs and their wants. Did they need a block of cheese to survive? Probably not, but their faith led God to come through in an improbable way. So, Matt, now you know why I was crying!

—Don

23

THE WOMAN ACROSS THE HALL

JUDY COCORIS

It was May, and on the other side of the window in Daddy's hospital room, the Tennessee day was bright and warm. Inside, it was dark and chilly. My brother George and I didn't know all the words the doctors used when they spoke to Mama, but we knew exactly what was happening—Daddy was dying of cancer.

He had been sick for a long time, and he did his best to get by, but on that day he looked especially weak in his hospital bed. It looked as though he was shrinking, and soon there would be nothing left but the clean, white sheets.

Mama told us that we didn't go see Daddy so that we could dwell in despair. Our job was to make sure everyone inside Campbell's Clinic had hope; so whenever Daddy was tired and needed to rest, Mama would take us around to all the other rooms to say hello. If there was ever anyone new in a room, which happened a lot, she walked into the room, smiled, and said, "I'm Mrs. Eaves, and this is my daughter, Judy."

I'd always curtsy and drawl out a long, "Hi-dee-yah-doo!"

Then she introduced George, he would nod his head, and she continued on listing everyone in the family.

"I've got another one at home, Betty Jo, and there's seven more—six grown and on their own, and little Johnny in heaven."

From that point on the person in the room was no longer a stranger, and Mama called them "sweetie." I'm sure Mama knew all their names, but it didn't matter; everyone was sweetie.

Whenever a sweetie asked about my daddy, Mama didn't spend much time answering. She always said things like, "We'll make a way," or "My husband's favorite verse is, 'Seek ye first the kingdom of God.' That's what we've always done, and we're not going to stop now. We're doing what God wants us to do here, and he'll take care of us."

People didn't ask a lot of questions after an answer like that. They just enjoyed the company, compassion, and warm cookies Mama brought to share.

There was one lady my mama especially liked. No matter how much time we had at the hospital, Mama always made a point to see if she was visiting her husband in the room across the hall. My brother and I thought she dressed a little funny, but my mama said it was because she was smart and professional and rich. She had an important job at the Veterans Affairs office, and usually when she came to the hospital, she was either on her way to or from work. Mama didn't seem to mind that they were from two different worlds; she talked to her just like she was anybody else.

One day the woman across the hall asked Mama how she was going to take care of the kids if Daddy passed away in the hospital. As usual Mama didn't say much other than, "God will provide for us," but the lady wasn't very happy with the answer. I think she really liked Mama and wanted to make sure we would be okay, so she asked if my daddy ever worked in the military.

"Yes, he did," my mama answered proudly, "in World War II, but he was still in boot camp when the armistice was signed." Then she unwrapped a plate of hot cookies, let the good smells fill up the room, and changed the subject.

A few days later Daddy died. We knew it was going to happen sometime soon, but that didn't make it any less hard. Things started changing. We stopped going to the hospital. We started running out of money. It didn't really change Mama, though. Even though she was sad, she had too much faith to believe things wouldn't work out for the best. She kept on helping others.

When my sister came home with her four young children after a divorce, Mama opened up the door and welcomed them in.

"We'll make a way," she always said. "God wants me to take care of this family, and if I'm doin' what God wants me to do, then he'll take care of us."

We made a way, all right, but it wasn't easy. We lived in a small house in the poorest neighborhood around. We didn't have enough beds for everyone to sleep in or enough food for three square meals. Mama worked hard to fix up old things and stretch out the little money we had. Somehow, she managed to keep us going.

Then Mama got an unexpected visit from the woman across the hall. She showed up with a big smile and a folder holding a piece of paper.

"I have good news," she said, beaming with a smile. "Your husband qualifies for several benefits through Veterans Affairs, and you'll start receiving payments immediately!"

"My goodness!" Mama shouted. "If I didn't know God was look-ing down on us, I'd be right shocked!"

"What, Mama? What is it?" All of us kids rushed into the room, curious about the noise.

"Veterans Affairs is going to be sending us some money because your daddy was a soldier. We'll be gettin' monthly checks!"

A lot of other people thought it was a really big surprise, but Mama just threw up her hands and praised God.

"You see, if we take care of God's children and do what he wants us to do, he will take care of us!"

And he did take care of us, with a check every month for twelve years. Up until the day my little sister turned eighteen, my mother had all the money she needed to take care of our family.

Mama died after a long, beautiful life of eighty-three years. Through the decades she never tired of telling her children and grandchildren about the woman across the hall and their providential conversation. I, for one, never tired of hearing her tell it.

Her faith seemed like a miracle to a lot of people, but to us kids, we knew it was as natural as the air she breathed. Even while her hus-band was dying of cancer, she found a way to be a blessing to every other hurting soul in that small hospital. That is what Mama did with pain; she took it into her heart and transformed it into a gift of encouragement, like a batch of fresh cookies that she served to every sweetie, with a smile and a prayer.

JUDY COCORIS grew up one of ten children in Chattanooga, Tennessee. She attended Tennessee Temple College, majoring

College, majoring in music. Judy serves as executive administrator at Church of the Open Door in Glendora, California. She loves to travel, read, and sing. Judy has three children and nine grandchildren, whom she adores.

24

THE STOLEN RADIO

MELANIE ELLIOTT

I t was hard to believe. My '92 Grand Am wasn't that old, and it seemed to be running fine. It didn't make any funny noises or refuse to start. But the estimate was in my hand and the mechanic was staring right at me.

"So it will really be that much?" I asked, hoping it was a mistake. His bid was for three thousand dollars, and I was fairly confident the car wasn't even worth that much.

"Afraid so," he answered, chewing his gum, grease stains streaking his coveralls.

"And there is no way to leave it be for now? It has to be fixed?"

He shook his head from side to side. "You'll pay to have it fixed either now or later. The longer you wait, the worse it gets."

His answers felt rehearsed, as if he'd used that line a million times. I was annoyed and couldn't help from letting him know.

"It's just not a good time to be spending this much money. My

husband just got out of the military and is taking college courses—"
I stopped suddenly.

Why am I telling him all of this? I quickly asked myself. The
mechanic was looking at me blankly.

"Sorry. I'll just take it home now and think about it. Thanks."

A few days went by, and the problem didn't seem to be getting
any worse, but it didn't keep me from worrying about the car breaking down at any moment. I would have left it at home, but it was
my only way to work, so I motored along, begging the engine not to
explode.

I pulled into the parking lot of the school where I teach and
turned the key. As I stepped out of the car, I couldn't ignore the feelings of discouragement. I had no idea how many more days the car
would get me to work or where we were going to get three thousand
dollars to get it fixed. I couldn't think of a solution, yet the problem
plagued me like an impossible, maddening riddle.

I walked to my classroom and flipped on the lights. I loved looking out across the neat rows of desks in the morning quiet. In a few
minutes the room would be exploding with energy, but now it was a
peaceful little sanctuary. I dropped my bags at my desk and checked
my watch. I had five minutes before the students arrived.

Maybe some classical music, I thought. *That sounds like a good way
to start the day.*

I turned to the bookshelf where I kept the stereo, and for a few
seconds my mind went blank. Something wasn't right, but I couldn't
figure out what. The books were there, the CDs were there, the empty
space between the books was . . . *the empty space!*

"Oh no!" I whined out loud, feeling small and defeated. The stereo was gone. Stolen. Immediately I thought of my car and the repair
bill and our tight finances, and my hands flew up into the air.

"Not now!" I shouted. "I don't want to buy a new stereo!"

Usually I take little things in stride; it's just part of the job. But the timing was too much, and my anxiety was too high. I looked out the window and couldn't help but wonder, *Is this the second thing in a chain of bad luck? What's next?*

I didn't have long to think. The first bell rang, and kids started filing into the classroom. During my lunch break, I wove my way through the hallways to the principal's office to report the theft.

"You don't happen to have a picture of the stereo, do you?" he asked, filling out the paperwork.

"I don't think so," I said, shaking my head. "Oh, wait; yeah, I have the user manual at home. I'll bring it in tomorrow."

It didn't take me long to find the stereo manual in my filing cabinet that night. I pulled it out, leafed through the pages, and saw a great diagram of the make and model.

"This will work," I said and tossed it on the desk to grab in the morning.

I turned back to the filing cabinet and randomly started flipping through the files. Taxes. House. School. Car. Family. Health.

I stopped. Car?

I thumbed back to the file and pulled it out. Inside was a non-descript letter addressed to me. I remembered reading it years ago but had forgotten why I kept it.

Dear Mrs. Elliott,

TECHNICAL SERVICE BULLETIN #57-61-267

Due to a technical difficulty with the cylinder head near the exhaust manifold, your automobile is eligible for immediate repair.

Suddenly I remembered. When I received the letter, my car wasn't having the problem listed in the recall notice, so I filed it away just in case.

"Yes!" I shouted and ran into the other room.

"Look!" I put the letter down in front of my husband. "They are going to fix the car for free! It's a faulty part! We don't have to pay a thing!"

I gave him a big hug.

He looked over the letter and asked, "Where did you find this?"

"It was filed away. I was looking for the manual to my stolen stereo, and I just stumbled across it. Isn't that great?"

"Wow," he marveled. "Thank God someone stole your stereo!"

He was right, and we did thank God, a lot, because even with little things like car repairs and stolen stereos, he loves to work all things together for good.

MELANIE ELLIOTT lives in Bentonville, Arkansas, with her husband, Rob, and their kids, Cade and Hollie. She was a public school teacher for eight years and has been a full-time wife and mom for eleven years. She is also the author of the book *Why Am I Conservative? 24 Topics for Kids or Anyone.*

25

EVER AFTER

JOHN SHEPHERD

Some people think fairy tales are only for children and happily ever after never actually happens in real life. I used to think the same thing. Then one spring, while flowers and trees bloomed across the city, my wife invited our two grown sons to meet us at home with our fifteen-year-old daughter.

Once everyone was gathered in the living room, she wasted little time.

"I think getting married was a mistake," she said, "and I'm not happy. So I'm moving on."

My sons were shocked, and I was in disbelief.

Twenty-five years of marriage and she is leaving? I asked myself.

My sons asked questions and protested the decision. My daughter cried. Yet my wife offered few reasons for her decision. She was leaving, and it was final. The next day she drove away, and I was unexpectedly and painfully alone, suffering the sting of betrayal.

What did I do? I wondered. *What didn't I do?* But there weren't any answers. We had managed to work through every problem that came our way during our marriage, until this one.

Why now? What happened?

Months passed. The dark season of grief carried me from spring to summer, and I was randomly struck with the nostalgic desire to reconnect with friends from high school. Were they doing well? Raising kids? Married? Divorced? Was anyone hurting like me?

I logged onto Facebook and started typing in names of old friends. I looked at some photos, left some messages, and then saw a face I remembered instantly. Her green eyes, red hair, and beaming smile took me back to my senior year at Ukarumpa High School in Papua New Guinea. My parents had been missionaries in the South Pacific since I started high school, and during my senior year, I met a girl named Joni. She moved to the island with her parents and joined my class halfway through the year.

Green eyes, red hair, and beaming smile Joni—it was her! Looking at her picture, I wondered how long it had been since we had seen each other or spoken a word.

Twenty-five years? No, thirty years. An entire lifetime of jobs, spouses, kids!

I wondered how she was doing, so I opened a new message and reintroduced myself.

It would be fun to hear from her, I told myself, not expecting much, but I did check my in-box every few hours to see if she had replied. It didn't take long, and when she did reply, I was captivated. The little information she shared about her life was eerily similar to mine. She had grown children, and her husband had left her the previous spring, leading her to ask many of the same questions I had. *Why now? Did our marriage matter at all? Will I ever find love again?*

I felt it was too much of a coincidence to ignore, so I opened up an e-mail and drafted a longer reply. When I clicked Send, I had a feeling I'd be hearing from her soon, and I was right. That first e-mail led to more—longer, personal letters, conversations on the phone, and Skype dates. Two months and hundreds of hours of talking later, we both expressed the same clear, unambiguous conviction: we were meant to spend the rest of our lives together.

There was only one thing left I needed to do, so I boarded a plane to meet her face-to-face in Denver. She was waiting on the concourse for me, and when I saw her, I knew I was looking at my future wife. We hugged and kissed, and then I knelt down on one knee and asked her to marry me.

Was it too soon? Yes, that is what some people said. I had never expressed a desire to remarry, especially so soon after my divorce, so friends and family were concerned about my sudden revelation and decision. How could I want to spend the rest of my life with a woman I met thirty years ago and had just reconnected with on Facebook?

Those were good questions, and I didn't know the answers. But I did know this: the Author of our story had been planning this final chapter of our lives all along.

We were meant to meet when we were teenagers, follow different paths, and reconnect three decades later. We were meant to fall in love and live happily ever after.

And that's exactly what Joni and I are doing—living happily ever after. We now reside in Oregon, where we run a program that helps men and women recovering from addiction find stable employment and safe housing. We watch tragic stories being rewritten every day, but not one ever surprises us. We know the Author of the universe is crafting the greatest love story of all for his children. Didn't he come like a prince to a castle to rescue his beloved? Isn't he a king preparing a great feast for the return of his bride? Aren't we all living proof that God is good and fairy tales do come true? We believe so, and we enjoy telling our Cinderella story as encouragement to God's children everywhere.

JOHN SHEPHERD and his wife, Joni, are the cofounders of Shepherd's House Community, and John is the founder of M25 Ventures, Inc., both of which work together to help recovered addicts become business owners and productive employees, living in safe, Christian community. For more information, visit m25ventures.com or shepherdshousecommunity.wordpress.com.

26

DEATH OF A DREAM CAR

CAMMY SCHOLZ

When my good friends called me to go float the river, I was eager to accept. It was a hot summer afternoon in the high desert of central Oregon, and I had nothing better to do. Relaxing on the water sounded just about right.

An hour later I was enjoying life, laughing with my friends, and soaking up the sun, with my toes dangling in the refreshing Deschutes River. Back home my little brother, Cavan, was running late for a conference across town. He knew that his archaic Honda Accord was low on gas, so he asked my mom if he could borrow my car. She said no and that he should put gas in his own car. My brother argued, whined, complained, and even resorted to flattery, but it didn't work. My mom wouldn't budge.

As a last-ditch effort, my brother fired up his car, drove to the end of the driveway, and quickly pulled back up to the house. Running inside, he yelled for my mom, "I won't even make it out of the neighborhood! Please, Mom, just let me use Cammy's car."

She knew I would be upset, but in the moment, with his charming grin and pleading eyes, my brother won her over.

"Okay, but just this once," she relented.

Excited, Cavan grabbed the keys and raced across town to his meeting—in my car. My dream car. My baby blue '02 Audi A4. The one I received from my parents as an unexpected gift. My most prized possession, with automatic windows, a power sunroof, leather interior, an epic sound system, and a mighty engine that cranked out all the horsepower a girl could ever ask for.

On the way home from floating the river, I saw an Audi zipping toward me and my friends on the highway. As we passed at sixty miles per hour, I looked over and was surprised to see my brother behind the wheel.

"Hey! That's my car!" I shouted as I quickly dug my phone out of my bag and speed-dialed him.

"Why are you driving my car?" I asked as soon as he picked up.

"Cammy, it's fine," he tried to assure me. "My car didn't have enough gas to make it to town, and I was running late. Mom said I could borrow yours."

"Cavy, just be careful with it," was all I could think to say. He is my brother, after all, and it wasn't a huge deal that he was using my car for the night.

"Of course, Cam; don't worry. I'll drive safe."

Early the next morning my dad gently tapped on my door. It was part of our routine. He would come in and make sure I was awake for work; then he'd go make coffee for me on my drive in to the restaurant.

He whispered my name, and I rolled over in my bed. Slowly I

blinked my eyes open, and they adjusted to the light. He was standing next to my bed, and something looked a little off. His eyes were droopier than normal, and he looked haggard.

"Daddy, what's wrong?" I asked.

"I need you to drive your grandfather's truck to work this morning, okay?"

"Okay," I answered, a little worried. "Why?"

"Cavan was in a car accident last night," he said, sitting down on the edge of the bed.

"What? Is he okay?" I asked, sitting up and pushing the covers down to my lap.

"He got a little banged up but nothing bad. They checked him out at the hospital last night, and we brought him home. He's sleeping in his room. We tried to wake you up to go with us, but you were pretty tired."

"Yeah," I said, still a little hazy, "my back was acting up again, so I took a muscle relaxer. I was pretty out of it." I rubbed my eyes and asked again just to make sure. "So Cavan is okay?"

"Yeah, Cammy, he's okay, but it's a miracle."

"What do you mean?"

"Your car is completely totaled," he answered. "Your brother should be dead. He fell asleep and hit the back bumper of a parked semi. It sliced all the way through the cab to the passenger seat."

"What?" I asked, stunned.

"You won't believe it when you see it. The entire front end is smashed in and cut up. The air bags deployed. There was just enough room for Cavan to be safe in the driver seat. Everything else is destroyed."

My dad's eyes started tearing up, and I could feel my tears coming too. Still, I couldn't keep the thought from rising in the back of my mind: *My car is gone, and I'll never get it back.*

I didn't have a lot of time to waste before work; so I got up, showered, dressed, and got into the cab of my grandfather's pickup truck.

Midway through my shift as a server, I was walking up a long staircase with a tray of food. I was thinking about Cavan at home, asleep, recovering from the accident. I tried to imagine what my car looked like, crunched up behind the semi. I remembered what my dad said about the air bags and the Cavan-sized hole left in the driver seat. Then it hit me.

My car saved Cavan's life.

If he had been in his old, smaller, lighter Honda, without air bags, who knows what kind of damage would have been done? He could have been hurt, paralyzed, or even killed.

I thought through all the things that had to happen for him to drive my car. I had to be out of the house; otherwise, I never would have said yes. His car needed to be out of gas. My mom had to give him permission.

Suddenly a wave of remorse rushed through me, and I felt horrible for worrying about my car.

My brother is alive! I told myself. *Forget about the car!*

When I returned home that night, I found Cavan on the recliner in the living room, watching a movie. The shades were drawn, and it was dark. Light from the TV flickered off the walls, and I could see his face, resting on the chair, a few scratches on his forehead.

He rustled under the blanket and looked up to me.

"I'm sorry about your car, Cam," he said, his voice just louder than a whisper.

"Cavy," I said softly, "don't worry. You're my brother, and I love you. I'm so glad you're okay."

I leaned down, gave him a hug, and then left him to rest.

Today I drive a less-than-glamorous Ford Focus. It doesn't handle, sound, or feel quite as nice as the A4, and sometimes when I see an Audi pass me on the highway, I still wish I had my dream car. But I believe God sacrificed my car to preserve a far greater treasure: my brother's life.

CAMMY SCHOLZ was raised in central Oregon and attended college at Multnomah University in Portland, Oregon. Recently married to her husband, Corban, she is beginning a new chapter of life in British Columbia, Canada.

LEMON DROP

The morning after my son Cavan's accident, I walked outside and looked at his car—the one he'd *almost* driven the day before. As I looked at it, the realization hit me: no air bags. I began to weep. What if my wife, Brenda, had refused to let him take his sister's car? She would have lived with a lifetime of regret and pain. Thanks to God's grace, it was a close call, and sometimes that is exactly what we need to remember that we are not in control.

—Don

27

UNEXPECTED LAUGHTER

JODY MCCOMAS

D ear God, please help me to have a baby sister."

My two-year-old daughter was praying in her bed, her eyes clenched tight and hands folded up beneath her chin.

"No, a brother!" she continued. "No, both! Yes, both! Thank you, Jesus. Amen."

"Amen," my husband and I said in unison. Then he leaned forward and kissed her on the head.

"We'll keep praying, sweetie," he whispered in her ear. "Good night." We turned out the light and left her room in the glow of a night-light.

It wasn't for lack of prayer that we only had one child. We had been waiting in eager anticipation for years, long before our first daughter was born. The fact that we had a daughter to kiss at all was a miracle.

Before my husband and I were married, we agreed that we

wouldn't talk about having children for five years. But three and a half years into our marriage, I was surprised to discover a longing in my heart. When I passed a mother on the street, I made sure to look over the edge of the stroller. When I looked at images of families in advertisements, my heart welled with desire; I couldn't keep from thinking about the future with babies.

It was such a natural, inevitable transformation that I struggled to explain it to my husband, but one night I crawled into bed and did my best.

"I think God has changed my heart about children. I thought five years sounded right, but I think I'm ready now."

"How do you know?" he asked gently.

"I see babies everywhere I go. That is definitely a new thing. And I sense that God is calling me to do something other than college ministry. I think it's time to be a mom."

"You're sure you don't want to make it to five years?" He smiled.

"I'm sure."

Our newfound hope of having kids didn't come with immediate satisfaction. We tried our best, but our every effort came up fruitless. Frustrated and confused, I went to be examined by a fertility doctor. She performed several tests and discovered numerous difficulties.

"It will be hard for you to conceive," she informed us, "but not impossible. If you start on fertility drugs right now, there is a slim chance you will get pregnant."

Slim chance? I asked myself driving home. *That's it? Why would I develop a strong desire for children only to figure out I have a slim chance?* Enraged, I pointed my finger to God.

The only path forward was an expensive fertility treatment, and we agreed we would try it to a point. If it was unproductive, we thought the money would be better spent on adoption. Tentatively, I signed up for treatment, and the day before my first appointment, I received a call from the doctor.

"I have good news, Jody. We have the results from the blood test you took yesterday." She paused, and I anticipated her next words.

Could it really be?

"You're pregnant."

Joy instantly flooded my heart. *Thank you, Lord,* I prayed. *It really was meant to be!*

But it wasn't. Two weeks later I began experiencing tremendous pain, and the doctor discovered the baby was still in my fallopian tube. The pregnancy was terminated immediately, and the shades were drawn on my soul.

I wept in the darkness, alone and betrayed. I was so close to being a mom, and then my child was snatched away. To have the hope of a child and then lose it—I felt as if I was being punished.

Why is this so hard, Lord? Did I do something wrong? Is this desire from you? Will it ever be fulfilled?

The next few months were a dark stretch of time. I spent several days on my back, looking out the window, asking God to explain to me why he made me so poorly.

Why can't you fix me, God? I would beg him. *Please fix me!*

Four months after my miscarriage and several failed fertility treatments later, the doctor called and told us that once again we were pregnant. I couldn't help but guard my heart against the possibility of losing another child, but despite going into labor five weeks early, I gave birth to a beautiful baby girl, Jenna.

She is a miracle, I thought, looking at her in my arms, remembering back to all the long nights and bitter questions. *Thank you, Lord.*

Not long after our baby girl was born, the longing returned—I wanted another child. Again, we started the process, and again we were heartbroken. Years of fruitless effort passed, but I didn't want to complain. After all, we had a gorgeous daughter, among countless other blessings. But why was my heart filled with an almost constant longing for another child if I couldn't become a mother again?

My husband and I agreed to stop fertility treatment and began discussing international adoption. We even started to fill out the necessary paperwork, but something inside us told us to stop. Soon after we definitively closed the book on adoption from abroad, we got an unexpected phone call from family friends. They were thinking of us and wanted to set up a Skype call to discuss a possibility.

A bit anxiously, and not knowing exactly what they wanted, we logged on for the call.

"We've been thinking of you," my friend said, his face pixelated on the screen in front of me. "There is a young lady in our college ministry who is pregnant, and due to several circumstances, she can't raise the child. She asked if we knew anybody who could provide her baby a good home, and we thought of you."

Us? I wondered to myself. *Can this really be happening?*

After some questions and more explanation, we disconnected the call, and I struggled to identity my emotions.

Am I confused? Shocked? Hopeful?

I wondered if this could be the baby for us, and the more my husband and I prayed, the stronger we felt the baby was meant for us.

We agreed to meet the birth mother during her twelfth week of pregnancy, and we knew without a doubt her child was going to be a part of our family. We walked with the mother the next few months and were at the ultrasound appointment when the technician discovered the baby was a boy. Then we were present in the delivery room when a precious baby boy entered the world.

We named him Isaac, a Hebrew name that comes from the book

of Genesis. Abraham and his wife Sarah wanted to have a baby, but they believed they were too old—until God promised a son and delivered on the promise. His birth was so miraculous and unexpected they named him Isaac, which means laughter.

I never understood why a mother would name her son *laughter*, but after bearing the same burden as Sarah and lamenting a barren womb, I understand. Laughter is the only appropriate response to the impractical, unpredictable love of God.

Sometimes when we think things are impossible, God surprises us with the most incredible gift of all. We always knew our children would bring us joy, but we found out the hard way the unexpected child is the greatest joy of all.

JODY MCCOMAS has been married to her wonderful husband, Matt, for eleven years and is the blessed mom of two children. She and Matt have worked with college students for the past ten years and currently live in Portland, Oregon.

28

ONE SATURDAY MORNING

RICK WAGES

I open my eyes and immediately I know I am in trouble. It's Saturday morning, the best day of all, and I haven't even gotten out of bed, but I can feel it. My sheets are wet, and they stink. Even my pillow, which sometimes I hug when I sleep, is moist.

I hear Mama in the kitchen, humming along to the radio. The coffee is going *bloop bloop* in the pot, and the smell of bacon is filling the house. Outside in the backyard Dad is trying to start the lawn mower. Usually he is really good at getting it going, but today it isn't working. I hope he isn't mad at the mower, because then he'll be mad at me. Probably he'll be upset with me either way.

I roll over in my wet pajamas. Across the room I see my brother and sister sleeping in their bed. They get to share because they don't have my problem. Their bed is always dry in the morning.

If I could stop, I would, but I don't know how. Even when I don't drink anything after dinnertime, I still have accidents. Even when

I make sure to go to the bathroom six times before bed, I still can't help it.

My parents thought maybe I would stop when I turned four. But I didn't. Then they thought maybe when I turned five. But I haven't. I wish I could; I hate it.

I hate that Mama has to clean my sheets every day. I hate when I have to sleep on the towel. Most of all I hate when Dad gets upset and spanks me with Mr. Big, his leather belt. It hurts, and I don't think it helps me stop. I wish I didn't have to be spanked or wear the cloth diaper when people come over. It's not like I *try* to do this.

Most kids my age aren't like me. Both my brother and sister stopped a long time ago. On the television President Kennedy said they are going to send men to space. They will fly there in a rocket and walk on the moon and then come home. He said it will be real hard, but it can be done. They can walk on the moon, but I can't wake up with dry sheets. How come nobody can help me?

Everything in the kitchen smells so good that I roll out of bed and change into dry pants and a clean shirt.

"Good morning, Mama," I say as I shuffle into the kitchen.

"Hey, baby," she says, looking from the stove. "How'd you sleep?"

I know what she is asking. She is so pretty in her housecoat and blue slippers and hair rollers, and I wish I didn't have to tell her, but I do.

"I'm sorry, Mama. I did it again. Please don't tell Dad and ruin his day."

Mama doesn't answer me. Instead she tells me to sit down at the table. I obey.

"There's my boy!" says Dad, suddenly stomping in from the back porch. "How'd you sleep?"

I know I have to tell him, but I don't want to.

"I tried, Dad—really, I did. I promise I didn't do it on purpose."
I start to cry. "I'm so sorry."

Now Mama is crying, which isn't out of the ordinary. But when
I look at Dad, his eyes look wet too. That is definitely out of the
ordinary.

I know what is going to happen next, so I stand up. Dad is going
to teach me a lesson with Mr. Big, but instead of taking the belt down
off the wall, he sits down at the table. Maybe he is hungry and wants
to eat first.

Praise the Lord, I think. My granny taught me to say that when
good things happen, and this is a good thing. I quickly sit down
before Dad changes his mind.

Mama puts plates full of breakfast in front of us, and my dad digs
in. But then he takes one of his two pieces of bacon and puts it on my
plate. I quickly look at him, and he smiles. *Whoa!* Bacon is only for
Mom and Dad on the weekends, because it's expensive. My brother,
my sister, and I never get to have any, but we don't complain. Then
my mama reaches over and gives me a piece of her bacon too.

*Two pieces of bacon! And no whipping from Mr. Big! Saturdays
really are the best days of all!*

After breakfast Dad and I drive into town and park at Western
Auto because he needs a new spark plug for the mower. While he
looks around, I run over to the section with bikes and wagons.

After a few minutes Dad finds me. "Time to go, son," he says,
holding a really big sack to protect the spark plug.

When we walk back through the front door of the house, Mama
is waiting there. "Did you get the one I said to get?"

My dad nods. "Yep, it was right where you said it was, and on
sale too!"

I wonder what Mama needs a spark plug for. She doesn't know how to fix the mower, does she?

"Hustle up and bring your sheets and pillowcase to your mother," my dad says, reminding me of my accident. "Make sure you bring your pillow to me."

I sulk back to my room and start stripping my bed. Now Mr. Big is coming; there is no doubt. I walk into the kitchen with my shameful load, ready to take my licks.

I reach up and give my pillow to Dad. He takes it and looks down at me.

"Son, I'm sorry," he says, and then he pauses. I look to my mama, and she is in the kitchen, watching. I look back to my dad.

He's sorry? Sorry for what?

"I've been blaming you for something you can't control. Your accidents are not your fault."

I can't believe it. Does he really mean it?

"I know, son, because when I was your age, *I* did the same thing. My dad used to whip me, and I've never forgotten the shame. Now I see the shame in you, and I know it won't fix a thing."

My dad did it too? I think to myself as he keeps talking.

"This won't last forever. I don't know how much longer it will, but I'll tell you something: you've seen the last of Mr. Big. Don't worry about it anymore. It's not life or death—it's just money. I just hope"—he reaches into the big brown bag that I thought contained only the spark plug—"you can keep from wetting your new pillow."

He leans down and gives it to me. It still smells like the store; it's so brand-new.

Then all of a sudden Dad picks me up and squeezes me in his arms. He grips me really tight, and I don't even care that I can hardly breathe. It is the best hug ever. "We will get through this, son." I can feel his tears on my face.

It was a while before I stopped wetting the bed, but that was the last new pillow I would ever need as a kid. As always, Dad was true to his word, and Mr. Big stayed on the wall.

Dad is in heaven now, but I remember everything about him, especially how he surprised me with a hug and a pillow when I was an ashamed little boy. His example of grace and the power of his home-spun wisdom taught me a lot as a boy about our heavenly Father, and I passed the lessons on to my four children.

Like my dad said, *It's not life or death—it's just money.* Things in our house broke and went missing, but it didn't matter. What can never be replaced is the special relationship a child has with his father.

RICK WAGES has been married to his high school sweetheart, Kim, for thirty-seven years. They have four children, Kam, Keith, Karen, and Kevin; and five grandchildren, Kennedy, Sydney, Joel, Claire, and Gabe. Most live in Loganville, Georgia, a suburb of Atlanta, where Rick is best known as "Santa" for the city parade, churches, preschools, and children's hospitals in the area. He makes a living by building homes, selling roofs, and making friends.

29

TATTOOED ON MY HEART

ANGEL CHUNG CUTNO

I can't keep talking to you!" I shout. "I just need some time to think."
I put the phone down and slouch into the chair. Beyond the patio,
rising over the roofs of the houses across the street, I can see the
lights of San Francisco, glimmering against the black canvas of night.
What do they mean I can't go? I ask myself. *They can't tell me what to do.*

I jump up from the chair and start stomping down the street. I
turn and stomp back, then back down the street, then back again.
Ugghhh! I wail to myself. *This isn't fair! They don't understand! I have
to go!* I've been planning the trip my entire senior year of college. I'd
graduate, go home for a few weeks to see my family in Louisiana, fly
here to San Francisco, and then cross the Pacific to China. Then I'd
hook up with an organization, doing the one thing I believe I exist to
do: minister to North Koreans.

My parents do not understand the passion of my calling. Sure, my
mother is South Korean, and I have family in Seoul, but do they really
understand what is happening on the north side of the peninsula?

Maybe they do know, and they just don't care. "It's too dangerous," my mom says. "We aren't comfortable with you going. We will figure out how to get you home."

I'm not going home; that is for sure. My heart is in Asia, helping the most oppressed people on the planet. How can I turn my back on them and not go? My mom keeps calling, but I silence the ringer. She is going to tell me the same thing: "How can you do this to us? We are your parents! You want to travel all the way around the world to help people you don't know, but you're hurting your own parents!" I don't want to hear it. I keep pacing the street, fuming, mumbling to myself. *It's not about them. Why can't they see that?*

A few hours later my mom calls again, and I'm composed enough to answer. "Daddy and I decided you can return to South Korea because it is safer. You can stay with our family and work at the school where you volunteered." I instantly think back to my first summer in Seoul, teaching English to North Korean refugees. I was nineteen at the time and hardly aware of life behind the veiled curtain, but it didn't take long for my North Korean students to teach me about the hardships in their home country. They told me stories of their families being torn apart, their neighbors being sent to labor camps, unjust imprisonments, rampant censorship, and long, cold, hungry nights. When I flew back to school that fall, I knew I'd spend my life advocating for their freedom.

My mom is silent on the other end of the line, and I know it's the best compromise I'm going to get. If I can't be in China, I may as well be in South Korea. "Okay," I say. "Thanks, Mom."

"Good, then," she says, "but you have to promise one thing."

I sigh and think, *Now what? Why can't I just go?*

"As soon as you get to South Korea, you get the tattoo removed from your arm." I pass the phone to my left hand and look down at the inside of my right wrist. Last week I walked into a tattoo parlor and put eighty dollars down on the table. An hour later I walked out and looked at the fresh ink in the sunlight. It was perfect: the North Korean flag, with its red star set in red-and-blue stripes. Over the flag was the inscription I prayed every day: *Be the voice.*

My tattoo or my passion? I hesitate for a long time.

"Okay, Mom, I'll have it removed right away."

The next morning I board a plane for Seoul.

When my aunt picks me up, she doesn't waste any time sharing her—and my mother's—concerns about my tattoo. "These are not good here, no!" she says in Korean, wagging her finger, sitting behind the wheel of her car.

"I know," I say reluctantly. "I'll get it removed."

"It is a very long process," she replies. "But it must be done."

Later that week I find out it will take over a year to fully remove the colorful tattoo from my arm. Considering that is longer than I'll be in the country, I call home and strike another compromise with my mom. "Please, let me wait until I come home. I'll wear long sleeves every day."

She agrees, and I am content to make the small sacrifice. Finally free of the tattoo drama, I call the director of the school for North Korean refugees where I previously worked. He is happy and un-surprised to hear from me. My mom, it turns out, has called ahead to make sure the arrangements would work out. *Great,* I think. *Did she tell him about the tattoo?* After a quick conversation we arrange a meet-ing for the following morning, and right before we hang up he tells me, "I understand your heart and why you are here. I'll see you tomorrow."

Finally, someone who gets me. I wait for the next morning like a seven-year-old on Christmas Eve. I can't wait to get back to the work I love.

The next morning the director introduces me during morning assembly, and I recognize several of the smiling students. I'm happy to be back, but I can't help but be a little embarrassed. I have told several friends in South Korea, including old students here in this school, that I am going to China to work on the front lines. Yet here I am, back in Seoul, and there surely will be questions. I don't want to tell the story of my parents and the tattoo, and hope secretly the reasons for my return can go unsaid.

But suddenly the director grabs my right arm and thrusts it into the air. Startled, I resist, but the look in his eyes tells me to trust him. "This is why she is here," he says, as my sleeve falls away from my wrist, revealing the red-and-blue flag. Silence suddenly sweeps across the room. I look into the students' faces and see their confusion. They are probably asking, "Why does an American have our flag on her arm?" And I'm wondering the same thing. Overwhelmed, I collapse into a chair and start crying uncontrollably. Thankfully, the director recaptures the attention of the students and begins talking about something else.

By the end of his announcements, I have composed myself, but my shirt is wet with tears. A few students smile kindly as they exit the room; then a North Korean friend from my first time at the school approaches me. He stops just in front of me and reaches out for my right arm. He gently grabs me by the wrist and spins it around until my tattoo is in clear sight. Tears well up in his eyes, and he points to the flag of his homeland.

"Very thank you," he says.

Those three words are all I need to hear. I feel my anger about not being in China disappear and realize I may not be where I wanted to be, but I am where I need to be. My parents' concern, my family in Seoul, the tattoo on my arm—they are not random. God used them all to bring me here to the place I belong.

I smile at my friend. "Thank you," I say, tears streaming down my face. "There is no place I'd rather be."

ANGEL CHUNG CUTNO is known by close friends and family to have a spirit for adventure, new cultures, and serving people. This drive has allowed her to travel overseas for many years to serve in various capacities, most typically with children. She has combined her love for children, art, music, and cultures as she works to instill appreciation and understanding into the leaders of the next generation. As a self-declared "Jill of all trades," she is on a constant journey of learning new skills and fine-tuning what she already possesses in order to one day compile her own words into books for both children and adults.

30

KYLE'S LEGACY

PENNY WHIPPS

It was late summer in Atlanta, Georgia. Outside, the moonlit night sounded of distant traffic and droning cicadas. Inside, all was quiet except for the second hand ticking around the clock and the AC kicking on and off—the normal sounds of a normal night. What I wanted to hear—my three kids running around the house, playing music, and laughing until they cried—were just memories. They were all grown, living their adult lives in three different cities. It was just me now, falling asleep by myself, thinking of their smiles, thanking God for a family I love.

Thud, thud, thud.

I startled awake.

Thud, thud, thud.

I squinted and waited for the clock to come into focus: 12:46 a.m.

There is no way I'm going downstairs to get that, I told myself. *It's probably just some neighborhood kids playing ding-dong-ditch.* The knocking soon stopped, but in the silence that followed, my mind began to wander, and a strange seed of fear took root in my heart.

After several minutes, with my fear growing, I decided I was being silly and selfish. What if one of my friends was in trouble and needed my help? What if something happened to one of my kids? I climbed out of bed, dug my cell phone from my purse, and turned it on.

Three new messages.

Two were from my daughter, and one was from my cousin; all instructed me to call my daughter right away. Her cold, distant voice startled me.

"Mom, are you alone?"

It was a strange question: she knew I lived alone, and it was the middle of the night. What was she really asking?

"Mom, I'm really sorry you're alone—but Kyle is dead."

Kyle. My baby boy. Dead?

I could feel the waves of shock beginning to crash into me as I spoke.

"What do you mean he is dead? Was he in a car accident?"

"He died of a heroin overdose," my daughter answered. "He was with his friends, and this afternoon they found him dead. The police and coroner couldn't find your contact information, so they came to me."

Suddenly the silence of my empty house was overwhelming. I couldn't hear a thing or think a coherent thought. My heart pounded into my ribs, beating desperation through my chest. Was this really happening? Kyle? My Kyle? Of course not. Kyle couldn't be dead from a heroin overdose—he was always so scared of that stuff. There must have been a mix-up, a mistake.

But my daughter's voice was so thin, lifeless, sad.

"Mom. Mom, I'm so sorry."

Kyle was a delight from the day he was born, beautiful and kind-hearted, a talented teaser, and world-class hugger. He loved jam sessions with his brother and sister, sports, campouts, and picnics. His life was laughter and adventure. Whether it was a hike through woods by our house or planning trips to see the world, he was always eager to go farther, stay longer, and see more. Recently he'd moved in with family to save money for a trip to a school in rural Uganda. He didn't want just to go; he wanted to stay as long as possible to help the schoolchildren however he could.

By the next morning I was flying across the country, back to my hometown, with one question accompanying me mile after mile: *How on earth did this happen?*

When I landed, everything seemed to happen on autopilot—visiting the coroner's office, meeting with my family, planning the memorial service, viewing Kyle's body and saying good-bye to him, picking out the casket, preparing to speak at the funeral. At their request I met with the young men who were with Kyle the day he died and listened to their account of the story. As they spoke, I was filled with a horrible sense of disbelief.

They knew that Kyle was doing something dangerous, but no one felt they could say anything to him. Then suddenly the next thought rushed through my mind. *I need to tell Kyle's story and warn other kids!*

I called Kyle's former principal and asked him if I could speak to the students about Kyle's death. I had never been a public speaker, and he cautioned me that it was too soon, but my desire to do this was unwavering.

All in all I spoke about Kyle five times in the first three weeks following his death: at his memorial service, to my church's youth group, once at the high school, and twice at the middle school.

After each session I met with kids who knew Kyle and were personally struggling with his death. *If it could happen to Kyle, it could happen to me*, they seemed to be thinking. During the honest and heart-wrenching talks I had with kids and parents, one theme played constantly in the background: a lot of great kids are living dangerously, and their friends are keeping it secret. Any of Kyle's friends who were with him that fateful night could have saved his life, but a kind of unspoken pact silenced each of them. Kids tell themselves they are being good friends by keeping their mouths shut; no one wants to be a pest or a snitch. What they don't realize is their silence can be deadly.

As this passion—some might call it a calling—took hold of my heart, I began to understand that Kyle's story has the power to reach this generation with the urgent challenge to break the code of silence. That's how Just1x (Just One Time) came to be. Our intent isn't just to confront students who are living dangerously—involved with alcohol, drugs, sex, eating disorders, cutting, and so on. We also challenge the students who know their friends are living dangerously to speak up and get them help.

Today I speak to thousands of students a year, but it is still far from easy. In front of strangers across the country, I play the actual 9-1-1 call from my son's death. I'm reminded of the loss I have suffered every day, but I am also reminded that God did not allow this to happen in vain.

Do I miss him? Of course. Through his short life he was always *my* fierce protector. Now his story is helping to protect others. Just1x is Kyle's legacy, and for that I am forever grateful.

In 2009, PENNY WHIPPS founded Just1x (Just One Time) after her son Kyle died of an accidental heroin overdose. The message of Just1x is aimed not only at kids who live dangerously but also at students who keep their friends' dangerous living a secret. Penny travels to schools around the country, giving a forty-minute presentation that consists of two short videos, including the actual 9-1-1 call of Kyle's death, and a passionate call to action. For more details, visit just1x.com or e-mail Just1x at contact@just1x.com.

LEMON DROP

Death is not the end. I'll admit that wasn't my first thought when I found out my nephew was gone, but God has proven it over and over in our family. Though Kyle isn't with us to grace us with his wonderful smile at family gatherings, his legacy is living on through Just1x, and his story is saving lives. Kyle's death has reshaped our family, but it has not destroyed the plans of God; his love knows no bounds. As Paul said, there is no height, no depth, no pain, no grave that can keep his resurrecting love from us.

—Don

31

COVERED BY LOVE

YAMARIS ROSA

I knew the drill from my first pregnancy. First the ultrasound technician would smear the gel across my belly; then there would come a black-and-white blur; and finally we would hear the rat-a-tat heartbeat of my baby.

My husband and I weren't exactly intending to get pregnant four months after our first child was born, but we were excited. Despite the fact my husband was still out of work, we didn't have medical coverage, and we were living with my sister and her family in a small apartment, we couldn't wait to meet our newest child.

I looked over to the monitor and smiled. My husband was by my side, holding my hand, and waiting to see our baby for the first time.

The technician traced the cold ultrasound wand over my belly. She looped around my side and back over the top, then looped back down to the other side. She lifted the wand from my stomach and checked a setting on the machine. Her eyes narrowed with worry, and I broke the silence:

"Is everything okay?"

"I'm having trouble finding the heartbeat," she said cautiously, trying not to alarm us.

Again she traced the wand around my belly, and seconds slowed to minutes and hours and eternity. I closed my eyes and listened. The hum of the ultrasound machine was low and pulsing. My husband anxiously tapped his foot. How long did I wait before the technician pulled the wand from my stomach? Was it a year sitting there in the silence, waiting, before I heard her say, "I'm sorry; the baby does not have a heartbeat"?

She sounded a million miles away, speaking to me over a great expanse of water. Her words echoed through me.

"It can mean one of two things," she explained. "Either you are not as far along in your gestation period as we thought, or you are having a miscarriage. We will need to do some blood tests in order to be certain."

After they drew my blood, my husband drove me back to the apartment, and I sank into the sofa. Was our baby gone? Could it really end like this? I worried through the night. At eight o'clock the next morning, the doctor's office called and told us to come in as soon as possible.

"Mr. and Mrs. Rosa, we received the results from your blood test yesterday," the doctor said, sitting behind his desk. "I'm terribly sorry, but your pregnancy was unsuccessful. We will need to perform a dilation and curettage to remove the fetus."

His white coat became fuzzy around the edges and stretched out around the room. I couldn't see or hear him anymore. He faded away into the spinning white cloud. I became dizzy, and my stomach shrank. I cupped my hand over my mouth.

"I'm going to be sick."

The rest of the day was a nauseous frenzy. I couldn't eat or drink. I couldn't sleep. I couldn't stop the room from spinning. After I vomited the rest of the day, my husband drove me to the emergency room, and I was admitted for dehydration.

Quietly, I began begging God for an explanation. "Why is this happening?" I spent the night praying, listening, and waiting for an answer, but there was no clarity—only pain and confusion. I reminded myself of Jesus' words, "You do not realize now what I am doing, but later you will understand." I tried to hold on to the promise but wondered how long I would have to wait.

On the morning of my appointment, I was anxious. I had heard the dilation and curettage could be physically painful, but my real fear was the emotional loss. I was already heartbroken, and the procedure would only make it worse.

I reread the promise of Jesus and drove to the hospital. The procedure was successful, but the doctor discovered something that caused him concern. He told me it could be nothing, but he ordered a few extra tests just to be safe.

When the results came in, I once again listened to him explain my condition from behind his desk.

"You have a rare tumor called a teratoma on one of your ovaries. We are very lucky that we found it when we did; otherwise, it would have grown until it burst—and that would likely have been fatal."

"How do we treat it?" I asked, shocked by the news.

"Surgery. We need to remove it as soon as possible."

A month later I was recovering from a successful operation. The entire tumor had been removed, and I was quickly gaining my strength back. The day after my one-month post-op appointment, I received a letter from Medicaid. It looked, felt, and sounded like the letter I had received after my first pregnancy, when they had written to inform me that Medicaid covered me only during pregnancy. Though my son was covered for his first year, I was without insurance.

Reluctantly, I pulled the new letter from the envelope.

Dear Mrs. Rosa,

This letter is to inform you that we have updated your records, and due to your miscarriage, you are no longer eligible for medical coverage.

Understanding struck me like lightning. If I hadn't been pregnant with my second child, I wouldn't have been insured for the last several months. If I hadn't miscarried my second child at twelve weeks, the tumor in my ovary never would have been discovered. It was only because I miscarried my child that I am alive today.

Again I read the letter and remembered the painful question I'd prayed: "God, why is this happening?" At the time I didn't realize what God was doing, but now the answer was in my hands. By his grace I was alive, and now I could see.

No matter how many times I tell this story, it never brings me great happiness. I lost a child, and that wound will forever be tender. But it *is* a story that makes me grateful. I'm grateful to be alive, grateful to feel the love of my husband and my three children every day, and above all, grateful for a good God who has blessed me with a peace that surpasses my understanding.

Born and raised in Philadelphia, YAMARIS ROSA is married to a wonderful man and is the proud mother of three children. She enjoys leading the children's ministry program at her church and singing and dancing with her children, as well as sharing her lemonade story with anyone who will listen.

32

CAN I CALL YOU MOM?

CARLA WICKS

arla, your mom just called for you," the manager at the bowling alley said to me. "There is someone important at your house, waiting for you."

"Who is it?" I asked, sliding the bowling shoes off my feet. My friends looked on curiously.

"She didn't say; just needs you to get home. She said she'll meet you there."

The thirty-minute drive across town felt like a lifetime. My fingers tapped anxiously on the wheel, and every imaginable scenario raced through my mind. When I pulled into the driveway, the house was dark. It was 6:30 p.m., and two of my kids were away at work. My other daughter was at a school dance. My mother pulled in behind me and stepped out of the car.

"Is everything okay, Carla?"

"I don't know, Mom. No one is here. What is going on? Why did you call me?"

She told me we needed to go inside, and a few seconds later there was a knock at the front door. I rushed to the entryway and opened the door, but before the gentleman on my porch could say a word, I slammed it shut. I turned back toward my mom.

"I knew it," I cried. "He is from the navy. Something happened to Paul."

"Carla." My mom tried to calm me down. "You don't know that. You need to open the door and let him in."

"No, I can't; something happened." I continued to cry.

"No, we can," she said, and she helped me to the door. I slowly turned the knob, and he stepped into the room, the shiny brass on his uniform glimmering in the incandescent light.

"Ma'am," he said, sitting on the sofa across from me, "it is with deep regret that I am here to inform you that your son, Paul Stock, died this morning in Reno, Nevada."

I collapsed to the floor and wailed.

I'll never get him back. Oh Lord, he's gone forever. I cupped my hands to my mouth and closed my eyes. *Now he is gone for good.*

The officer sat, patiently waiting for me to regain my composure, and my mom softly rubbed my arm, but the grief was untouchable. I couldn't soothe it, calm it, prevent it, or end it; it tore into me like a predator, insatiably consuming my composure and peace of mind.

It stalked me as I traveled to Reno to visit Paul's body and say good-bye. It followed me to Virginia for the military service and gnawed at me as I hosted a funeral back home in Kansas.

"Here I am, Mom," I wanted him to say. "It has all been a mistake. I'm home, and I'm not leaving."

But he didn't come home. He couldn't.

He wasn't seventeen anymore, coming back from Florida with his little brother in tow. It had been six years since I put them on a plane to go live with their father. Despite my every effort to provide for him, his brother, and my two daughters, I couldn't keep the shoes under their feet from wearing through the soles. It was the hardest thing in my life, watching them board that plane, but that was before the officer knocked on the door and held his cap in his hand—before I knew the burning grief of outliving my son.

When he was in Florida, I visited when I could, but it was never enough. I couldn't be there with him. He grew up without me by his side, and when he finally came home after high school, I thought I had him back forever.

It wasn't long before he sat me down and looked at me seriously.

"I want to join the navy, Mom," he declared. "I can serve for a few years, then get my degree, and re-enter to fly jets."

A few more years, I told myself as he left home again. *Then he'll be back. We'll make up for the lost time.*

Years of grief unfolded before me. Over and over I replayed the memory of him walking down the Jetway as a kid, boarding the plane for Florida. I could see the backpack hanging loose on his shoulders, his hair bouncing with each step.

Turn around, Paul, I shouted within myself. *Just turn around! Come back. I'll work harder. I'll buy you new shoes. Just don't leave!*

The regret was unbearable. A strong, condemning voice narrated the memory:

You did the wrong thing. He never should have left. You are a bad mother. You could have done more.

I couldn't forgive myself. I should have stopped in the airport and turned around. I should have found a way to keep him home. I should have looked across the table and said, "No, Paul, I'm sorry. You just got home; you're not joining the navy."

But I didn't, and no matter how many times the memory played, I couldn't change it. He never turned around. The memories remained, but he was gone forever.

The grief was so isolating and lonely. My oldest daughter began pestering me to get out of the house. She suggested I try the Christian online dating service that helped her meet her husband, but I declined.

How could I begin a relationship with a broken heart? I asked myself, drawing the blinds on the house, staying home for yet another long, dark night.

My daughter didn't give up, and after weeks of constant begging, I finally relented and signed up for the service she suggested.

A few weeks later, to my great surprise, I was introduced to a man named Ken.

He was a single dad raising four kids one hundred miles away, but our conversations on the phone led to a date, then another date; and despite the distance, we began building a wonderful, unexpected relationship.

On New Year's Eve 1999, I was with Ken at his house, watching the ball drop on TV, and when midnight had come and gone, I started gathering my things.

"Maybe it's best you stay here tonight," Ken said. "It's late, and this whole Y2K thing might not be over." He sensed my hesitation. We had been dating awhile and believed in doing it the right way. We wanted to be a strong example for our children.

Ken smiled. "You can sleep in Donovan's room. I'll have him come in with me."

It made sense, and he was right; driving home seemed impractical and unnecessary.

"Okay." I smiled. "Show me the way."

At 4:30 a.m. I woke up and heard God asking me to look around the room.

I sat up and waited for my eyes to adjust to the dim light. I looked across the room to the baseball posters on the wall. There was a shelf with basketball trophies and framed, hand-drawn pictures. Toys were scattered around the floor.

I don't get it. What am I supposed to see? I wondered.

I looked around the room again, studying the details, and suddenly it hit me.

Everything belongs to an eleven-year-old boy.

I gasped. Eleven, Paul's exact age when I sent him to live with his father. The very year I began to miss the adolescence of my oldest son.

I began to weep as I welcomed the message from God:

You are going to marry Ken and be Donovan's mom.

Later that summer, just before Donovan began middle school, Ken and I were engaged. In September we were married, and I moved into a new house with my new husband and my new son.

Years later, after a tumultuous transition and a long list of altercations with Donovan, he mailed me a letter while at boot camp with the marines.

Surprised, I opened the envelope and read:

Carla, I was thinking a lot before I left and since I've been here. I meant to say something before but didn't get the chance. I've never really thanked you or told you how much I've appreciated you these past years.

You've been such a wonderful mother to me that I wish I could just call you Mom.

You do so much for me in a motherly manner that I've never had before; I didn't know how to respond. Basically you're amazing, and I love you more than you can know. I can't wait to see you in three months and give you a big hug and say this in person.

Love, Donovan

I could hardly read the words for the tears in my eyes. I had been a mother to Donovan ever since I married Ken, of course, but it had seemed through the taxing years that the affection was largely one-way. Now I knew otherwise. And in Donovan's asking to call me Mom, I saw the fulfillment of a promise made years before as I looked around his bedroom.

I have never expected Donovan to replace Paul's place in my life—he'll never be the son I lost. But he is the son I gained, and every time I pray for Donovan, I thank God for his loving faithfulness.

CARLA WICKS, a Kansas native, currently lives in Texas. She is married, is mother to eight grown children, has an adopted granddaughter who is seven years old, and is a grandmother to eight others. Her hobbies include freelance writing, reading, and scrapbooking.

33

TOUT BEGAY BIEN

SUSAN RICKEY

here is a three-year-old girl named Jenny waiting to be adopted," she said kindly, her voice crackling over the phone. "But don't look at the website until you and your husband are sure that you want a Haitian adoption. The minute you see Jenny, you'll fall in love."

The minute I hung up the phone, I turned on the computer. As the monitor flashed and the hard drive warmed up, I paced around the room.

A three-year-old named Jenny, I said to myself, over and over.

"Come on!" I shouted at the computer as it sluggishly turned on. "Hurry up!"

It couldn't start up fast enough—nothing could happen fast enough! Since learning about international adoption a few months back, I had been relentless in my investigation.

My husband and I desperately wanted a second child, but nothing seemed to work. We had suffered three miscarriages before our first son was born, and three more miscarriages after him.

Six times we watched the doctor walk into the room and break the news. Six times we drove home, silenced by pain and confusion. Six times we mourned a great loss and wondered if we were meant to have a second child at all.

We were tired of hurting and hoping, yet I never quit praying.

After my sixth miscarriage I met a woman who had adopted internationally. As she told the story of finding her daughter, I knew it would soon be my story, but I was quickly deterred by the expense. Thanks to a well-timed connection made by a dear friend, I ended up on the phone, learning about Jenny from a Haitian orphanage liaison named Ruth.

"It's much cheaper to adopt from Haiti," she explained to me. "Usually parents who want to adopt internationally have to work through a third-party adoption agency. In Haiti you deal directly with the orphanage."

Then she told me about Jenny.

I opened up my web browser and typed in the URL. The website appeared, and I scanned the names.

Jenny. I clicked on it without hesitating.

Slowly, pixel by pixel, line by line, my dial-up modem revealed her photo.

First her hair, strand by strand, gathered tightly in a topknot. Then her forehead, a calm expanse interrupted by two tense, wrinkled eyebrows over her wide, dark, yearning eyes. Her smooth cheeks. Her flat chin.

This is my daughter, Jenny, I told myself.

Eighteen months, a thousand forms, and several deposits later, my husband, our son, and I boarded a plane to Port-au-Prince, Haiti.

As we soared over the water toward the Caribbean island, I remembered Jenny's face first coloring my computer screen. I was hours away from picking her up and calling her by name, and it felt surreal. The long years of heartache stretched out before me, and I grabbed my husband's hand. We had been through so much pain. We had been waiting for so long.

"We get to meet our little girl," I said to him with tears pooling in my eyes. He smiled, nodded, and replied, "This is exactly how it was meant to happen."

Suddenly the Haitian woman sitting next to us jumped into our conversation.

"If you are going to Haiti, you need to know some Creole," she said with a thick, beautiful accent.

"When you see your little girl, you should tell her, *'Tout begay bien.'*"

I asked her to repeat it again. Then I began to practice saying it over and over, rolling the syllables off my tongue, every breath moving me one mile closer to my daughter.

When we landed, I knew she wasn't far. The orphanage director made plans to bring Jenny to the airport to greet us, and as we waited for our bags to come around on the carousel, I kept peeking through the doors to the crowded street.

When we emerged into the blinding afternoon sun, the chaos absorbed us. Pedestrians, vendors, taxis, and minibuses were in gridlock. Holding my son's hand, dragging him behind me, I looked into the eyes of everyone on the street. Kids were everywhere, running, standing, selling fruit.

I moved from face to face, and then there they were: the dark, yearning eyes. Her hair was tied up, and her weight was forward on her tiptoes. She was standing tall, looking into the crowd.

When she turned and saw us coming toward her, I dropped my

bags and fell to my knees. It took just one second of looking into each other's eyes to bond, and then I pulled her into my arms.

As I held her, I whispered the words I had learned just hours before. "*Tout begay bien*, Jenny. *Tout begay bien.*"

I said it for her years of orphan heartache and for my years of mourning lost motherhood. As I held her, I felt the pain of my unsatisfied longing disappear, and I knew all the suffering and waiting had been worth it.

One more time I whispered into Jenny's ear, "*Tout begay bien.*" *Everything is going to be all right.*

SUSAN RICKEY lives in far Northern California with her husband and two children, Eli and Jenny. They still like to take trips together, though none have been as monumental as this trip to Haiti.

34

THE LETTERS OF WAR

RAY AND BETTY WHIPPS

In each volume of *When God Makes Lemonade*, we hope to present a feature-length story that uniquely expresses the heart of lemonade theology. You'll quickly see that "The Letters of War" is significantly longer than other Lemonade stories. Our writer, Matthew Smith, would tell you that's because the story wouldn't quit writing itself! I hope you take the time to sit with this story and receive its powerful blessing. One tip before you get started—get a box of Kleenex. If you're like me, you're going to need it!

—Don

I n the early summer of 1945, an American army nurse stepped off the train at a harbor in France with her few possessions packed in a single bag. Her fatigues were neatly pressed, her brown shoes perfectly shined, and the name of her ship home was folded on the orders clutched tightly in her hand. She crossed the pier and joined the queue of army personnel waiting to climb the gangplank to the ship that would sail them home to a hero's welcome. Betty didn't feel like a hero, though; she didn't join the army to walk in parades or earn medals. She did it because it needed to be done, and now that the war was over, she didn't know what life would hold for her. *Go home and act like the years of blood and bandages never happened? Refashion a peaceful life after losing so much? Pick up where I left off?* As her mind wandered, she played with the gold ring on the dog tags fastened around her neck. The smooth metal was cold on her fingertips, and a chill jumped down her spine.

"Betty! Betty!" a familiar voice called to her from behind.

"Betty!" The voice came again, this time from her side, and her friend tugged at her sleeve. "Thank God I caught you before you left. This letter came for you, but it was sent to the wrong APO address." She passed the worn envelope into the space between them, and Betty froze, staring motionless at the three letters printed neatly across the envelope.

As World War II began raging across the globe in 1941, a young navy man named Ray Whipps was eager to climb into the cockpit and hunt down enemies in the European theater. But the competition for flight school was tough, and no matter how hard he tried, he couldn't secure a spot in a plane.

"Ray," his superior officer told him one day, "you're a good soldier and a good man. Don't worry yourself about not making it to flight school. A lot of men who want to fly don't make it in; that's just the way it is in the navy. Why don't you go back home and apply for the Army Air Corp? You'd make an excellent pilot, and they could use a good man like you."

"Yes sir. Thank you, sir," Ray responded, convinced his superior officer was right. He filled out the paperwork; received an honorable discharge; returned home to Columbus, Ohio; and immediately applied to the Army Air Corp. As he waited for his acceptance letter in the mail, he imagined himself as an army airman, flying daring missions, supporting ground troops, serving his country with all of his strength and courage. *I will finally get my chance to fly*, he thought to himself, remembering all the hours he had spent as a child, running through the yard with his arms spread wide, imagining lifting above the cornfields, soaring up, spinning through the clouds.

Ray pulled the letter from the mailbox, and his gut twisted into a knot of confusion. The envelope was the wrong color; the letterhead wasn't right; and the orders were a mistake. *Order to report for induction?* Ray asked himself, reading the orders over and over again. *This can't be right. I'm supposed to be a pilot.* It wasn't a mistake—the army sent the draft order before his application was processed—and there was nothing Ray could do about it. He packed his bag, kissed his mother, and boarded a train for Camp Banding, Florida.

On his way to basic training, coasting along the railway, Ray opened the New Testament and began searching Scripture for the answer to his question: *Why is God doing this?*

After seventeen weeks of learning to take orders; crawling beneath razor wire; and firing handguns, automatic rifles, and bazookas, Ray's unit was shipped to England. Upon their arrival they were ordered to join a massive Allied attack on the beaches of Normandy. But as Ray's classmates splashed down into the cold water of war, beneath heavy fire, he was on his way to England to join a different company.

Instead of shipping out with his training class after graduation, he had remained in Florida under orders as a cadre with a training outfit. He was responsible for teaching the incoming class of recruits all he had just learned, and then after six weeks he was ordered into active service.

When news reached him of the D-day invasion, his face grew pale. *All those men?* he pondered. *Gone forever. I should have been there, next to them, dying for freedom.* Once again he pulled the Bible from his pack and earnestly read the epistles of Paul. *Why am I still here, Lord? What are you doing?*

Ten days after D-day, Ray landed on the beach where many of his friends had lost their lives. He was one of the first replacement soldiers sent to the front, and the unit under his command pushed inland to the town of Saint-Lô. By the time they reached the once-quaint village that had stood for more than a thousand years, the entire town was a quagmire of mud and rubble. Scarcely one stone was standing atop another. Ray and his men took shelter in the smoking husks of family homes, taking cover from enemy fire, but they were unable to escape the reek of dead and decaying bodies.

During a lull in the fighting on their first night in Saint-Lô, Ray pulled his New Testament from his pack and opened the frayed cover. A wave of Allied fighters roared overhead, and for the hundredth time, he searched the Scriptures, praying, *Lord, I know you have a plan for me. There is a reason I'm down here and not up there, but what is it?*

The next morning, Ray received orders to lead his men on a street-by-street, house-by-house sweep for German defenders, but just before they embarked on their mission, the GI on lookout shouted back into the building, "Bomb!"

The platoon dispersed instantly, each man diving for cover, and the explosive detonated—sending a shock wave of destruction through the building, collapsing the walls, and burying men alive. Ray pulled himself from the rubble and organized his men to search for the soldiers missing in the chaos. Fortunately, every soldier under Ray's command was found alive and rescued. When they were all reunited, Ray finally took notice of his hands, bleeding from countless small shrapnel wounds. The damage rendered his hands unable to fire a rifle, so he quickly retreated to the medic tent for treatment.

"It could be worse," the field medic said as he bandaged Ray's hands. "This is nothing." Ray knew the medic was right. Even though he was still a young soldier, he had already seen the true cost of war: men limping through the smoky forest, looking for their arms, pools of blood steaming in the winter air, and more men dead than he could name. His first combat wound left him both scared and grateful. Scared that the war had the power to make any second his last, yet grateful he had been kept from harm so far.

Ray rejoined his men with orders to move 450 miles east into the Hürtgen Forest, a fifty-square-mile swath of steep hillsides, deep ravines, and dense vegetation. When they arrived a week later, the entire forest had already become a killing zone. More than one hundred thousand Allied troops had gone into the woods, and their lifeless bodies were being pulled out by the thousands. The enemy had anticipated the strong Allied assault and spent months preparing the forest for battle, laying mines, digging trenches, and camouflaging rockets in the undergrowth.

Mortars, men screaming, rifles firing, mines exploding—the war zone was full of the worst sounds Ray could imagine. Every time he looked up and saw a plane pass over the treetops, he swallowed a bit of bitterness, upset he was crouched behind a tree instead of firing from a cockpit in the air. German bombardment came once or twice a day and nearly every night. When the shrieking sound of bombs whistled to the ground, Ray ran up and down the trail, shouting at his men, "Foxholes! Everybody down! Take cover!" Then the massive shells struck, and craters erupted in the earth. Tree trunks snapped like flimsy matchsticks. Smoke hovered, stinging their eyes, and they coughed for a breath of fresh air.

Ray could still hear the props of German bombers overhead, and he raced through the maze of their encampment. "Stay down! Here they come!" Then he dove into a foxhole and covered his head. The earth shook beneath him, and then for the briefest of moments, everything went silent. He could hear himself breathing, but nothing else. The foxhole had opened around him, and the chaos was unfolding in slow motion. He fell back into the leaves, and a searing pain ripped into his leg. A mortar blast struck off to his left, and the earth rained down over him. He brushed the soil from his uniform and sat up.

"I'm hit!" he screamed, looking at the white-hot shrapnel burrowed in his thigh. It had sliced deep into his muscle, down to his bone, and the fire wouldn't cool. He held his leg between his hands and waited for help, but no one came. He gritted his teeth, forced himself to his feet, and limped past scores of dead bodies.

After a quick examination by a field medic, Ray knew the injury was worse than he had expected. "I can't help him here," the medic said. "He needs a hospital and bed rest. Send him to Brussels." Then the medic was gone, off to attend to the next in an endless line of wounded.

Ray was transported the next day along with other injured soldiers to a hospital in Belgium. He was checked in and given a bed in the main infirmary. Late that night, as Ray dozed in and out of sleep, the air-raid siren sounded, and bombs began falling from the sky.

Instantly, the hospital became a frantic scene of chaos—the walking wounded looking for a place to hide. After the dust settled and the casualties were counted, Ray was taken to Paris to board a plane for England. As Ray waited with his fellow wounded soldiers, they were told a thick fog had grounded their flight. Instead of waiting around all night, a train was prepared to take them to Cherbourg, France, to an army hospital far from the threat of bombardment.

On the train, Ray spotted a soldier from his platoon across the aisle. He was alive, but barely. The haunted look in his eye chilled Ray to the core.

"Lieutenant," Ray said to him, drawing him out of a long, deep gaze. "Are you okay?"

"There is nobody left, Serge," said the young man. "Nobody left but you and me." The entire platoon had been either killed or severely wounded in heavy shelling and subsequent combat. *God, please, God,* Ray pleaded as he slumped back down into his seat. *Why am I here? Why is this happening?* The ache in his leg and the wounds in his hands were nothing compared to the pain in his heart. The grief was unbearable. *Why was I saved?* he asked God, desperate for an answer. Again he cracked open the New Testament and read through the night, the print of God's Word barely lit by the moonshine pouring through the train window.

Twenty-two years old and fresh from nursing school, Betty Jean Carter enlisted in the United States Army as a first lieutenant in 1943. After being stationed in Spokane, Washington, for a short period of time, she was called into active duty and shipped to Cherbourg to serve at the 167th general tent hospital. The medical facility was a sprawling campus of temporary shelters containing fifteen hundred beds of wounded soldiers.

On December 4, 1944, Betty arrived for her shift and was told a new wave of soldiers had arrived in the night. She knotted her starched apron around her waist and entered the large, dormitory-style recovery tent. She busied herself with her normal duties: checking bandages, administering medications, refilling IV bags. She worked her way down the right side of the tent, one soldier after another. When she reached the third bed, she pulled the chart from the holster and read the patient's report:

TECH SERGEANT
WHIPPS, RAYMOND

- PUNCTURE WOUND, RIGHT LEG
- CLEAN, DRESS REGULARLY
- PENICILLIN: 3 DOSES PER DAY

Betty gazed over the chart to Ray, sleeping soundly atop the white sheets, his chest rising and falling with each breath. She placed the chart back at the end of his bed and stepped to his side. There was something about Ray that Betty couldn't quite place. Of all the soldiers she had treated, Ray seemed unique. He looked kind and inviting, like a gentleman. His brown hair, his jawline, the way his lips curled slightly, as if he were smiling. He was handsome.

As she removed the bandage from his leg, Ray slowly stirred awake and opened his eyes. He looked into Betty's hazel stare and felt as though he were dreaming. The last thing he remembered was boarding a train in the middle of the night, and now he was here, looking into the loveliest face he'd ever seen.

Betty nodded to a pen and pad of paper on the stand by Ray's bed. "You should write to your wife," she said, still working on his leg.

"I don't have one," Ray replied, never looking away from her hazel eyes.

"Well, then write to your girlfriend," Betty responded, not skipping a beat.

"I don't have one of those either." Betty looked up from her work, and Ray's eyes were waiting for her, looking, longing to know more about her. She quickly dressed his wound and moved on to the next bed.

Ray watched her tenderly going about her work, taking care to provide the best treatment possible. She was professional but personable, lovely, and strong. When she disappeared from the tent, he rustled his Bible from his pack and began reading.

"Are you a Christian?"

Ray looked up from the flimsy, gilded pages of the New Testament and saw Betty at the end of his bed. A tiny smile creased her face.

"I am," Ray answered. He lowered the book to his lap, and Betty's smile widened.

"Me too," she said. As they exchanged smiles, a deep resonance stirred in their souls. Something magical and unexpected was happening. Betty's chief nurse suddenly hustled down the main corridor of the tent, and Betty quickly busied herself. She was an army nurse under strict orders not to fraternize with the soldiers. Those were their rules, and it hadn't been an issue for Betty until now.

Over the next three weeks, Betty and Ray did what they could to spend time together. They sat next to each other at church, and once Ray was better, they went for walks around the base. Ray shared the story of how he'd left the navy for the army and was drafted as a solider instead of trained as a pilot. He told her about his life back home, his parents, and his dreams. Betty told Ray all about her childhood in Oregon and the aunt who had inspired her to become a nurse. Their conversations turned minutes into hours, and the reality of war seemed to slip ever on into the periphery of their lives. Everything seemed to fit: Ray's disappointment at not being a pilot, Betty's assignment in France, the miraculously timed injuries that saved Ray from capture and death. God had led them together. They believed it to be true just as they believed the sun in the sky to be true. They could see it, sense it, feel its warmth, and see everything else in its light.

Twenty-five days after Ray arrived in Betty's care, his new orders were delivered. He was being transferred to a recovery facility in England, where he would rehabilitate his leg and prepare to join a combat platoon. The night before he left, he called Betty to his bedside and produced a beautiful gold ring from his pocket.

"I want you to have this," he said, whispering. "It's a symbol of my love for you." Betty carefully took the cold ring from his fingers and gripped it in her fist.

"I'll wear it around my neck with my dog tags," she said, crying quietly. "And I'll write you every day."

"Betty," Ray said, "when this war is over and we go back home, will you marry me?"

"Of course, Raymond; of course I will."

The next morning, when Betty returned to the tent for her shift, a different soldier was lying in Ray's bed.

By the time Ray reached England, the Battle of the Bulge was still fuming on the Western front. The German offensive had pushed deep into the Allied lines, but the tide was turning. General Patton and the second armored division had been fighting their way through enemy lines, pushing the enemy back into German territory, and when Ray met his platoon, it already had orders to cross the Rhine River. Their mission was to invade a small, German-occupied village during a night raid. They set off in the morning, marching all day to reach their desired position by nightfall.

When the sun sank below the trees and darkness shrouded the forest, his unit started marching up a narrow ravine. Ray was ordered to hold the back of the line and keep his eyes on the group as they advanced. As he waited, the depthless darkness crouched in around him, and he became disoriented. In the shadows of the trees, he thought he could see soldiers sitting, waiting quietly to advance, but when he jogged up to their position, they vanished like a breath in the winter night. He turned around and traced his steps back to where he had been waiting, but nothing looked familiar. Growing dizzy in the dark, he was sure he'd be left behind if he didn't run up to his unit, so he dashed down the ravine.

When the terrain flattened out and he could see the outskirts of the village, he hunkered down behind a wall. There was no sign of his unit anywhere, and then suddenly, he heard a voice traveling faintly to his hiding spot. "Second company," it said, and Ray stood up. *Where did that come from?* he wondered. He was desperate to find his men, so he trotted into the village and knocked on a door, certain the house was where the voice had come from.

A German farmer opened the door, and Ray startled backward, gripping his gun in his hand. The German jumped back into the room, and raised his hands in front of his face. *What do I do? What do I do?* Ray thought to himself, trying to get his exhausted and terrified mind working. He stepped up into the house and backed the German farmer toward his family. The farmer reached out, trying to protect his wife and daughter from the American invader. Ray lifted his cheek from the sights on his gun.

"Go get everyone in the village," he said in his best German. The farmer stood, frozen. "Now!" Ray shouted, trying to intimidate the man. The farmer slowly crossed the room and then ran into the village center to wake his neighbors. When he returned, Ray asked the group if anyone could speak French. When a middle-aged man stepped forward, Ray switched to French, his stronger language, and asked if any German soldiers were in the village. The man shook his head back and forth.

"Okay," Ray said, relieved he was out of harm's way for the night. "I've been fighting all day and all night. I need to sleep. I want you to tell everyone here that they need to stay in their houses, or else!" The translator relayed the message in German, and Ray sent them back to their homes. When he was alone, he opened the door to a nearby barn and closed himself inside. He slid his heavy pack from his shoulders, lay down, and fell asleep with his rifle across his chest.

When a hail of bullets startled Ray awake, he dashed across the dusty floorboards for cover. Hunched in the corner of the barn beneath the spray of bullets, he knew he only had one way out. "Comrade!" he shouted. "I surrender!" The German soldiers advanced on the barn, and Ray leaned his rifle against an old wooden beam. *This is it*, he thought. *This is as far as I go.* The German soldiers flung open the door and stormed the barn. Ray was pulled out into the cold, starless night, stripped of his gear, and ordered to march.

When the sun rose over the frosty horizon, Ray could finally see the faces of his captors. They were marching in columns down an open road, bearing the bitter cold, eyes fixed ahead. Where they were going, he didn't know. He doubted he would make it back to Betty alive. He just marched.

Signs of spring were arriving in northern France, and Betty was excited for the coming warmth. It had been a long, hard winter, tending to the unending line of wounded soldiers. She'd met Ray in December, and it had already been three months since he left for England. The gold ring around her neck reminded her of him often. She could still see his smile and feel the gentle touch of his hand on her cheek. She had heard some talk about Allied victories in the European theater, but nothing was certain. She didn't know how long she'd have to wait to see her love again; she just knew she'd wait forever, if necessary.

It had been several weeks since she had heard from Ray. He was busy in England, preparing to deploy, and he promised to write soon. When her name was shouted at mail call, her heart leaped, and she rushed to grab the letter. Without looking at it, she pushed through the crowd, went back behind a tent, and found a quiet place to sit. She turned the envelope over in her hands, and her chest suddenly tightened. The army had stamped three letters on the envelope from Ray: KIA (killed in action).

Betty knew in an instant how much she loved Ray. The pain was fierce, numbing her entire body with shock and grief. A part of her very being was dying, and she could only watch it waste away. She clutched the ring around her neck and wept. The following day, still in shock, Betty heard her name again at mail call. Only half alive and weighted down by sorrow, she took the letter and looked at the name. It was another letter from Ray, this one also stamped by the army but differently.

MIA? Betty asked herself. *Is this a mistake? Wait! Was yesterday's letter a mistake?* Hope flooded her, and she rushed to find out the truth. Was Ray killed in action? Missing in action? Captured?

Missing? Fighting with another unit? The army couldn't give Betty a certain answer, so she chose to hope for the best. She began praying by the minute, *Please Lord, let Ray be alive, and keep him safe. Remind him of how much I love him.*

On Ray's fifth day as a prisoner of war, they were still marching. He had discovered that their destination was Munich, yet he feared the fate awaiting him. Was it better to march and suffer at the hands of German soldiers, or reach the city and find execution orders waiting for him? As they neared Munich, crossing a field, a low buzz coming from over the tree line caught his attention. Soon the Germans were hustling around, shouting with a look of urgency in their eyes. Then, almost out of nowhere, US planes flashed over the treetops and started spraying the road with bullets.

Ray jumped down into the ditch on the side of the road and covered his head with his hands. Next to him a German officer did the same. The planes circled, strafing the road, dropping bombs. *I'm going to die from friendly fire*, Ray thought, grimacing each time a bullet pierced the ground near his position. But the skies eventually cleared, and the Germans reorganized and finished their march to Munich.

Ray was handed over to an interrogating officer, who questioned him extensively about US movements, and then threw him into a cell with two other captured GIs. "It's good to see you guys," Ray said. "It's been too long since I've seen a friendly face." They traded tired, defeated smiles. "How long are we going to be in here?" Ray asked.

"Not long, friend," commented one of the prisoners. "We were told we are going to be shot in the morning."

Ray looked dead into his eyes. "Shot?" He nodded. Ray dropped to his knees and began praying. Later that night, while Ray was still on his knees, a commotion outside the prison distracted him.

"Do you hear that?" a prisoner said, sitting up. "Something is happening. They are scared." The air siren sounded, and the three prisoners huddled in the corner of their cell. Bombs started screaming through the air, and a German guard appeared at their door.

"Out, out, out!" he shouted in German. Ray followed the two men from the cell and joined a large group of prisoners waiting in the yard, hoping to God an American bomber didn't land a shell in their location. By the time the raid was over, the prison was severely damaged. With nowhere to put them, German guards sectioned them off into groups and started marching them north to Stalag VII-A.

Ray's swollen feet marched step-by-step toward his unknown future. His clothes hung loose on his body, as he was already losing weight. His cracked lips begged for water, but there was none to be found. He tried to remember life before the war, but it felt so surreal, like a brief dream he'd had last night before waking up in the dreary, gray reality of war. As they made the eighteen-kilometer march, Ray noticed a motorcycle with a sidecar coming down the road and knew instantly that it was an SS officer. He ducked his head down and looked at his feet, trying to remain inconspicuous. The officer passed, then suddenly came to a stop. He stepped out of the sidecar and started yelling at a German soldier, wildly waving his arms. When he finished, he sped off out of sight. The German soldier approached Ray.

"Do you know who that was?" he asked.

"Yes."

"He wants me to drop you off at the SS station in the next town." Ray froze, his heart sinking in his chest, knowing it meant instant execution.

"Don't worry." The soldier patted him on the back. "I won't do it. I don't like him any more than you do."

When they arrived at the infamous prison camp, Ray was alive, but barely. His finger had been wounded in the prison raid and was growing infected. With no access to medication or doctors, a fellow prisoner boiled a pot of water and forced Ray to submerge his wounded finger. The blistering hot pain dropped him to the floor, but his friend refused to take Ray's finger out of the water. They repeated this process three times a day for seven days until the infection was completely gone. The pain he stomached saving his finger was just the beginning of Ray's nightmare in Stalag VII-A.

All of the prisoners were suffering from malnutrition, and their bodies were wasting away. Ray was assigned to a crew responsible for clearing debris from the battlefields surrounding the camp. Prisoners died every day, and they couldn't bury them fast enough. If it wasn't starvation, it was exhaustion. If it wasn't illness, it was heartache. There were a thousand ways to die in Stalag VII-A, and Ray fought them all, clinging to the last shred of his life with all his hope.

On May 1, 1945, one month after he was captured, Allied forces liberated Ray's prison camp and set eight thousand Allied troops free. Ray was taken to a Red Cross facility, where he rested, ate, and then traveled back home to the United States of America. When his ship pulled into the New York harbor and the Statue of Liberty stood proudly welcoming home the soldiers who had fought so bravely in her name, Ray wept. The war was over. He was on his way home.

When Ray stepped up onto the porch of his parents' house in Columbus, Ohio, he drew in a long breath of clean, fresh air. It was the beginning of summer, in June, and his parents greeted him with emotional embraces and tearstained shirts. Their boy was back from the pit of hell, and they rejoiced. Ray's mother handed him a letter, and he recognized the handwriting instantly. It was from Betty, addressed to his mom, asking if she had heard any news about Ray's whereabouts. *I guess I know my whereabouts better than anyone*, Ray laughed to himself. He sat down, picked up a pen, and wrote the greatest love letter of his life.

"He's alive!" Betty shouted, grabbing the envelope from her friend. "I knew it; I just knew it!" She beamed, suddenly weeping with joy. "It's from him!" She wrapped her friend up in an emotional embrace, and they spun around the pier. Again she looked at the three most life-giving letters she'd ever seen: *R-A-Y.* Three months later, on September 29, 1945, Betty Jean Carter and Ray Whipps were married in a Baptist minister's home in New Orleans, Louisiana.

Sixty-seven years later, their enduring love remains, and the legacy of their fateful meeting lives on in their seven children, eighteen grandchildren, and twelve great-grandchildren.

To consider the events that brought about Ray and Betty's blessings is a lesson in heartache. Their paths crossed because of disrupted plans, injury, and war. The love they formed was forced to endure the dark night of death and to heal from the deep wounds of tragedy. Yet it is a story of faithful details: an injury at just the right time, a deployment to just the right place, and a German officer willing to save an American soldier's life. Each miracle is a wink from the divine, always present, behind-the-scenes, moving in mysterious ways.

Though this love story bears their names, Ray and Betty don't believe it is theirs to own. This story belongs to God, the Author, who used the letters of war to compose a story of life.

Ray and Betty Whipps live in Portland, Oregon, where they enjoy spending time with their children and grandchildren.

LEMON DROP

One of the things I love about this story is how Ray keeps going back to God with the "why" question: *Why are you doing this?* Even with his dreams crumbling around him and his life in danger, he continues to believe that God is in control, has his best in mind, and is aware of his pain. I love Psalm 56:8, where David says to God: "You have collected all my tears in your bottle. You have recorded each one in your book." Isn't that a beautiful image? God isn't on the other side of the universe somewhere; he is here, with us in our suffering, and one day he will reveal the full and good story of his book. Ray and Betty know firsthand that God can use suffering to bring about blessings, and I hope after reading their story, you do too.

—Don

35

ACCIDENTAL MINISTRY

JACLYN MILLER

W e will be home soon," I told Audrey, the little girl I was nannying, as she looked at me in the rearview mirror from the backseat.

Just a few more miles and we'd pull into the driveway of the three-story house where we lived with her older sister and parents. They had hired me about a year ago to be a live-in nanny for the girls, and I had just signed on for twelve more months. I loved the two girls dearly and expected another peaceful, well-paid year. I also didn't mind the added bonus of weekend-long trips to Boston's museums, restaurants, and theaters.

The song on the radio grabbed my attention. It was that tune again, played for the one-millionth time. I reached down to switch the station.

"Look out!"

Before I could look up, the world turned white, and a jarring impact brought us to an immediate stop. Steam hissed out of the engine, and I heard sobs from the backseat.

I coughed and slid away from the air bag. *No, no, no! Please, Lord. This isn't happening!*

I pulled myself out of the car and braced myself on the roof. Still wobbly, I shuffled to the back door on the driver's side and yanked it open. Little Audrey's face was pale, and she was still crying.

"Are you okay? Are you hurt?" Over her right eye I could see an angry lump growing on her forehead. I unbuckled her from the seat and lifted her out of the car. Quickly a crowd gathered, an ambulance arrived, and we sped across town to the hospital.

Eventually the doctor told me Audrey was okay. Besides the large bump on her head, she had no injuries, but that didn't erase the worry in her parents' eyes.

I was okay, too, except that I knew things would never be the same.

I wrecked their car. I injured their daughter. Will they forgive me? I wondered as we trundled home.

Fear, grief, worry, and anguish plagued me as reality settled over me like an autumn fog. In the few days since the accident, the parents had grown colder toward me. I expected the worst, and when a nanny friend in the area told me they were secretly inquiring about new nannies, I knew the ax would fall. Still, it didn't dull the bitter sting.

"We're sorry," the parents told me weeks later, "but we just can't trust you anymore. We have to let you go."

I packed my bags; said good-bye to the girls, my church family, and my friends in the area; and flew back to my hometown in Indiana.

Now what? I asked myself the entire way home. Miles and miles passed in silence.

I didn't know what to do with my life or my bitterness. Every time I thought of Boston, I grew angry. *What did I do wrong? It was an accident!* Not knowing whom to blame, I pointed the finger at God. Nothing seemed fair. He was unfair.

Back home with a free schedule, I began to reminisce about my high school and teen years. My self-guided trip down memory lane resurfaced a lot of old feelings, and I was surprised to rediscover one passion in particular—writing.

I remembered when I was two years old, I begged my mom to record stories I couldn't write on my own; and all through high school I filled up notebooks with stories and poetry. After graduating, I turned my focus to college midterms, finals, and then career pursuits. I had a new ministry degree and was ready to make a difference but didn't know where to land, so I took a job in a day care. Then the nannying job opened up, and the bump in income would help me start paying back my loans, so I signed up.

My hands were full with two kids as a nanny, but sometimes when they were at school, I'd jot down ideas and play with them on paper. My words felt sluggish and unoriginal, as if they were borrowed instead of revealed, and I rarely found the motivation to rework an old draft.

Back home the old passion was seizing me, and I welcomed its return. I started writing again, and before long I seriously wondered if I could make a living as a writer.

I looked for work in the creative field and found a couple openings, but they didn't pan out. Diligently, I searched more job listings, but what I found came up empty.

After five months of applying and interviewing, unemployment still haunted me. Depression set in, and I complained to my family, "How do I show them I can write? They only want people with experience, but they won't hire people to give them experience."

Out of money, I was forced to resume my previous job at the day care. I was right back where I'd started after college, doing the same job. I felt as if I'd backtracked, and my frustration fell on God.

"What do you want?" I seethed. "What am I supposed to do?"

The answer was so quiet, simple, and sudden; I almost missed it.

If you're unqualified, go get qualified. Don't waste my gifts.

Two days later I gathered my courage and walked into the adult student department at a local college. I stopped at the front desk and said, "I want to write. Sign me up."

When I walked in the graduation ceremony three years later, I accepted more than just a degree. I had a community of peers who shared my passion for words, including God's Word. I had a honed skill, sharpened by criticism and encouragement. Most of all, I had accepted my place in God's will.

Toward the end of my writing program, I discovered he had been preparing me for not just a career in writing but also a ministry to children. What I thought was a day care job to pay the bills was a valuable training ground to equip me for my future calling. Everything seemed to make sense: my passion for writing, my history of working with children, my time as a nanny, even the accident that cost me my job, moved me back home, and sank me into depression.

I didn't know it at the time, but God was deliberately moving me in the right direction. He used a crushing blow to turn me 180 degrees straight down the path of his purpose for my life. Now I don't just work with kids or pay the bills as a writer; I do both, sharing a ministry of words with children, and it is the ministry I was made for all along.

JACLYN MILLER is a freelance writer from Indiana. She is working toward a career in children's writing.

36

AYDEN THE TROUPER

CARYN RICH

Help me hold it, and I'll put the nail here," I said to my daughter, Aubrey. She was helping me build a set of stairs up the large tree in our backyard. It towered over our swimming pool, and we thought it would be fun to build steps up the trunk for her and her brothers to climb up into the branches and jump down into the water. "Okay, watch your fingers," I said, as I drove another nail into the board. Behind us, my two boys, Corbin and Ayden, were playing in the sandbox. It was the hottest part of an August day, and we couldn't wait to cool off in the pool.

"Hi, guys!" my husband, Chad, shouted from the back porch. I turned around and lowered the hammer.

"Hey! I thought you were at work!"

"Yeah, just came home for a quick bite." His eyes scanned the yard. "Where's Ayden?"

"He's in the sandbox," I replied, but when I turned around, Corbin was alone.

"Corbin, where is your brother?" Corbin shrugged and kept plowing his trucks through the sand. I stood up and looked around. My husband crossed the yard and joined me.

"Ayden?" he shouted. "Sometimes he is like Houdini; I swear. Ayden?" he called again, but there was no answer. We both shouted his name, walking around different parts of the backyard, looking around corners, behind trees. Then my daughter screamed, and my heart began pounding in my chest. Then Aubrey screamed again.

"Ayden's in the pool!" I ran around the yard and found Aubrey sitting in the tree, looking down into our aboveground pool, pointing down to her little brother, floating facedown in the water. I reached over the edge of the barrier, and everything became a blur. I pulled him close to me, lifted him from the water, pounding on his back to clear his lungs, and started doing CPR.

"No, no, no!" I screamed while compressing his chest. His lips were blue, and his skin was ice-cold. I repeated the breaths and compression, but the air just hissed out of his lifeless body. I faintly heard my husband yell to the kids, "Run! Get help! Go to the neighbors!" Then he called 9-1-1. "Please help us; my son has drowned!" he cried. I'd never heard him sound so helpless. As I continued compressions and breathing, I begged God to reverse the clock. Ten minutes was all I needed, just ten short minutes.

Behind me, I heard faint cries from my two other children. Then the sound of jingling keys approached. A man in a uniform hurried and knelt on Ayden's left side. I froze and watched as he took over, gently compressing Ayden's tiny chest with his fingertips. Another emergency worker took me aside and tried to calm me as he asked what happened. My mind was too scrambled. I didn't remember hearing him scream. I didn't remember hearing a splash. He told me they were doing everything they could and then asked me to wait in the ambulance. I stumbled into the house, past Corbin and Aubrey, and began sobbing on the sofa. My neighbors had come over to comfort them, but one of them was currently on hands and knees, calming our dog, who was so scared by the activity that she had thrown up.

"I'm sorry, thank you," I mumbled and walked out to the ambulance. I climbed into the cab and immediately smelled rubbing alcohol and bandages. I started to plead with God. *I'll do anything, Lord; just bring him back. Please!*

They hoisted Ayden into the ambulance on a stretcher, and we sped away. I followed them into the ER but couldn't bear to watch, so I joined my family in the waiting room. The look of anguish in their eyes was soul crushing. "It's going to be okay," I said as I sat down, praying to God it was true.

After an excruciating wait, we were finally led upstairs to the pediatric intensive care unit. Everything about the place felt wrong. I didn't belong there; my son certainly didn't belong there. He was so young and innocent. His tiny body was buried underneath layers of tubes and wires. Monitors beeped on every side of him. I didn't recognize him, and I hated it. I watched the anxious nurses scurry around him, and then Chad and I were called into a cold, dark conference room.

I didn't want to go. I wanted to believe he was going to get better, and I didn't want to hear about all the bad things that could still happen. I trembled as we sat down and listened to the doctors explain his condition. "It's very likely that due to the amount of time he went without oxygen, serious brain damage will have occurred," they said. "We also need to lower his body temperature to help his brain." Chad and I nodded, telling them to do whatever they needed to do to save our little boy.

Word of Ayden's accident spread quickly, and we were overwhelmed to hear about people fasting and praying on his behalf. A friend from Fiji called to tell us their church members were praying. A complete stranger approached me in the hallway at the hospital and told me her son had nearly drowned too. He was fighting for his life just a few doors down from Ayden. We prayed for each other often, and her visits were always encouraging.

Time passed slowly, and I watched closely for signs of improvement. I stood by Ayden's bed all day, wishing I could pick him up and cradle him in my arms. I wanted to comfort him and take him home, but I couldn't. I could only pray and hope. When Ayden fought through pneumonia and was weaned off of his medications, the doctors warned us that it would be tough to watch him fight through the cravings; but nothing could have prepared us to see him shake and sweat so much.

After the painful withdrawal process, we noticed the first sign of hope—his eyes fluttering. Then his fingers moved. Then he tried to smile. Each little response filled our hearts with joy, and within just a few days, Ayden had made more progress than he was expected to make in a month. They removed most of the tubes and cords from his body, and I was finally able to pick him up. It was such a good feeling to have him in my arms again, to feel his warm skin and his own voluntary movements.

We felt optimistic about his recovery, but the doctors continued to warn us. "There is a possibility his brain may never fully recover," they said, but he just kept getting better. His eyes opened wider and wider, and his grip got tighter and tighter. He was removed from intensive care and began therapy. Ayden latched on to a toy shopping cart and started crawling around, playing and giggling. One night we took him to see the fish in the hospital aquarium. We asked him to point out the yellow fish, and he did! It was incredible! We told his therapist the next day, and she was blown away. Ayden was recovering faster than expected, and after only twenty-five days in the hospital, he was released to come home.

There was still a chance that he wouldn't fully recover, but over the course of the next few weeks, and after a few surgeries on his vocal cords, Ayden made a 100 percent recovery. I believe with all my heart that he would not be here if not for the power of prayer. It saved his life, restored my faith in God, and taught me that he doesn't give us more than we can handle. When we trust him and his strength, miracles really can happen. Our little trouper Ayden is proof of that.

CARYN RICH and her husband, Chad, live with their three children in Boise, Idaho, and they are surrounded by loving family members and an incredible community of friends. Caryn was so inspired by the story of Ayden's miracle that she hopes to share it, and other encouraging stories, someday as a full-time author.

37 ═══

THE PARKING LOT PREDICAMENT

TODD GORTON

Whoa," my son shouted, running up to the RV. I had just parked on the street in front of our house. He circled the entire thing, with his eyes as big as the tires. "It's huge, like a whole house on wheels!" We weren't much of an RV-ing family, but some friends had just loaned us their late-'80s model Fleetwood Tioga Arrow for a camping trip we wanted to take up in the San Gabriel Mountains.

"Come on," I hollered at my son, who was crawling around somewhere inside the RV after having "tried out" the toilet. "We have to pack, or we won't be ready to leave tomorrow!"

After church the next day, my wife, our two kids, the dog, and I loaded into the not-so-shiny, thirty-foot-long house-on-wheels and lumbered toward the freeway.

"Maybe we can climb a mountain," my son dreamed aloud from the back.

"Or look for snakes." His sister joined the fun. "Are there rattle-snakes, Dad?" We mentioned every possible thing a family can do while camping, and we couldn't wait to step out into the fresh mountain air to get started.

I flipped on the blinker, and we soared up the on-ramp, only to come to a sudden halt. My wife looked at me with an "oh no" face, and I shouted at the kids, "Nobody worry; it's just a little traffic. We'll be up in the mountains in no time!" I turned back and looked through the windshield. The line of taillights stretched out and disappeared over the California horizon. I let up the brake pedal; the RV rolled forward five feet, then lurched to a stop. Just like that, five feet at a time, topping out at a max speed of three miles per hour, we wound our way through the freeways of Los Angeles. This was not exactly the vacation we had been dreaming of, but finally, after who knows how long, the freeway cleared, and we sped up to forty-five miles per hour.

"Now we're moving!" I encouraged the kids. But at our newfound high speed, I discovered a new problem: wind. It was whipping across the road, directly into the broad side of the RV, testing the limits of my driving skills and my sanity. I wrestled the rolling house down the road, hugging the lane lines, trying my hardest to keep it going straight. It was an epic struggle of Todd versus wind, traffic, and machine.

After fighting as long as I could with my hands gripped on the wheel, I exited the freeway and pulled us to a stop in a shopping center. I unbuckled the seat belt, walked back into the living area, and flopped down onto the couch.

"I'm done!" I declared, using my best two-year-old voice. After a short rest—and after a Frosty, a couple of cheeseburgers, and some sea-salt fries—we were back on the road. This time my wife was driving, and she made it one exit down the road before pulling over to manage her rising blood pressure and profuse sweating.

"Not that easy, is it?" I joked, trying to lighten the mood. She gave me the "shut up and drive this thing to the mountains" face, so we switched seats, and I fired up the engine. A few exits later I had to bring the beast to another stop. It wasn't accelerating very well up the hills, so I crawled under the engine and did what every self-respecting dad would do: use my phone to Google "poor RV performance." My search came back fruitless, and after poking a couple things and looking at the oil, I decided nothing was going to blow up. I hopped back into the driver's seat.

"Not sure what happened," I said to my wife as I cranked the key. "But we should be okay." Wrong again.

We merged onto the highway at thirty-five miles per hour and quickly slowed to fifteen. Then the engine died, and suddenly I was the guy everyone hates: blocking a lane of traffic with an RV he doesn't even really know how to drive on a holiday weekend.

"Lord, please help us out here," we prayed together on the side of the road. "Keep us safe and help the RV to start working." Over the next hour the engine would roar to life, we'd move a little down the road, and then it would die. We nursed the dying beast through the narrow streets of Glendale in search of a mechanic or an auto parts store, but nobody was open. After all, it was Memorial Day weekend.

We rolled to a stop in a Home Depot parking lot and listened as the RV coughed itself to death. We were stuck, looking at the bright glow of a home improvement store sign, far from the mountains and adventure we had imagined. Who knew if we'd ever make it? My wife and I sighed in unison. *What now?*

It is very difficult to explain what happened next. We ordered some pizza and began laughing when the delivery guy rolled up and stepped out of his car with a look of complete confusion on his face. After we ate, we played cards and laughed, then decided to go roller-skating right there in the parking lot. We laughed some more and spent the night away, goofing off and loving every minute of being together, and it all happened just past the floor models of the build-your-own sheds. Even though we were not nestled in the beautiful San Gabriel Mountains, we had tremendous fun together in a parking lot, and it was a gift.

Sleep eventually found us, and we brought in the morning with cold cereal. I dialed a few mechanics and received the same message: *Sorry, we are closed for Memorial Day.* One auto parts store picked up, listened to our ordeal, and told me he couldn't get the part we needed for two days. I wanted to throw myself on the floor and get it all out, tantrum-style. Thankfully, before I went into four-year-old meltdown mode, I found a guy named Byron. His shop wasn't open, but he was kind enough to personally inspect the RV.

"It's the catalytic converter," he said, crawling out from the belly of the beast. "It's completely melted. But not to worry; it's a quick fix." What wonderful words, *quick fix.*

"Come on," Byron said. "I'll take you guys to my favorite bakery while you wait." We filled up on baked goodies, played with iPads at a Best Buy next door, toured an Indian food market, and even walked past Chevy Chase Park. How's that for irony?

While we waited for the call from Byron, I wondered if I had made a mistake trusting a guy I never had met. For all I knew, he could have fixed the RV and been on his way with it down to Mexico. Or he could have stolen all of our stuff. Or done some weird mechanic math and left us with a bill for $4,000. But when we went back to the RV, everything was just as we had left it. Well, except for one thing: the engine was running. Byron charged us $180 for the fix, and we pulled out of the surprisingly undervisited Home Depot Resort Destination for our drive home.

Several years later our kids don't remember that as the worst vacation of all time. The truth is, neither do my wife and I. It was an unappealing slab of asphalt in front of a huge retail store, but God used it to bless us with time together as a family. We got to find our own fun, not in the mountains or on a peaceful hike but simply with each other. We used our imaginations and realized a broken RV can be as fun as Disneyland. Well, almost.

At times I wanted to stomp around like a child when things weren't going my way; there is a little kid in me still. What I learned from our vacation disaster/blessing is the difference between childish ways and childlike faith. I'm going to keep opting for the latter, and who knows? Someday you might find our family vacationing at a snowed-in airport. If you do, I hope you'll join us; it's a lot of fun to find joy in unexpected places.

TODD GORTON is a pastor and learner at Coast Hills Community Church in Southern California. He leads an amazing team of staff and volunteers who make disciples every day. He has served as a visual arts director, youth worker, TV producer, and high school teacher. In his spare time he treasures every moment with his wife, son, and daughter who enjoy burying him in the sand on the beach and making fun of his Spanish.

For more, visit toddgorton.com.

38

THE PERFECT FIT

KIMBERLY SUTTON

K imberly," said my manager, "you're just not a good fit for our company." I can still hear his voice and see his face as he sat behind his desk with a dark-blue tie knotted around his neck. "The decision has been made," he told me, and that was it. There was no further explanation or conversation. I sat, dumbfounded and confused, surprised to discover my job could vanish in an instant. I looked over to the representative from human resources sitting next to my manager. Her face was blank. She said nothing.

In the car on the way home, with my belongings in a box next to me, I cried. I couldn't help it. What had I done? Why was my effort unacceptable? Did I make a mistake? The questions piled up and weighed me down. Then panic arrested me. *It's all over. Our health insurance. The extra income from my paycheck. Paying down our family debt. Saving for retirement.*

I couldn't quiet the concerns. They grew louder and louder. *Our three teenagers are going to eat through my husband's paycheck in no time flat. We will go hungry. The bills will pile up. The debt will rise. Our ends won't meet. They will never meet again.*

When I arrived at home, I burst through the door and found my husband watching the evening news. "It's not fair; they can't fire me!" I cried. "He didn't even have a reason! I gave my all! Never once has anyone complained. My reviews were always positive. Everyone liked me. I can't believe this, and it doesn't make sense. What are we going to do?"

"It's okay," my husband tried to assure me. "This is no accident. God has provided and will provide for us." I couldn't help but doubt the confidence of his faith. *He is a pastor*, I thought to myself, staring out the window into the pale moonlit night. *He has to say stuff like that.*

The next morning I updated my résumé and started searching the classifieds for a new job. A week later I was still e-mailing and calling employers for interviews.

"Sorry," they all said. "We aren't hiring at this time."

Another week later, with still no leads on a job, I went to cash my final paycheck. The amount was so small, and our checking account was so low, I knew I'd have to stretch the check as far as possible. I quickly imagined myself walking up and down the aisles at the grocery store, checking the prices of every item, only to arrive at the checkout counter with milk, eggs, and bread. I knew I couldn't go to our usual grocery store, so I went to the local thrift store that doubled as a food pantry. I could also get financial assistance in paying my utility bill there.

As I waited in line, I watched the woman behind the counter help the customer in front of me. It made me think of my old job and how I missed making our clients smile. It was natural for me, and I enjoyed the challenge of working with their individual needs. Would I ever find something as rewarding—personally *and* financially?

When it was my turn, another woman invited me to her office to explain my situation. There was something tender in her smile. "Hi. How can I help you today?" she asked kindly. I tried to hide my distress.

"It's been a long few weeks. I lost my job, and I need help with an electric bill."

"Okay. I can help you with that. Would you mind if I prayed with you?" she asked, surprising me.

"Sure," I said, thankful for someone to come to my aid. She reached across the desk and took my hand. "Dear Lord, please help Kimberly find the right job, in the right place, where she can make a real difference." Instantly a sense of peace warmed my body. I opened my eyes.

"Thank you so much," I said softly. The woman returned my smile, finished helping me with my utility bill, and gave me some sacks of food to take home to the family.

Two days later I was at home when the phone rang.

"Hello?"

"Yes, hello, Kimberly?" The voice was kind and welcoming.

"This is she."

"Hi! I'm the director of a local nonprofit that runs a women's rehabilitation center. As part of our program we employ women at the resale shop downtown. One of our girls told us about you and said you were looking for a job." My heart skipped a beat. "We have two positions open, and I was wondering if you wanted to come out to our facility and meet with me?"

"Of course, oh my goodness, of course, I would love to!" I could hardly contain my excitement. As I drove through the countryside to the rehabilitation center, the sense of peace returned to me. It warmed my body and lifted my spirit. The director greeted me in her office and described the two open positions: one in the office and the other as a teacher.

"I have experience teaching," I told her.

"Excellent," she said, smiling. "You would be teaching women who are here instead of in jail or prison. Many of them have been abused, rejected by their families, or addicted to drugs and alcohol. Some have had their children taken away because of their addiction." As she told me story after story of the women in the shelter, my heart broke wide open.

I can work here, I told myself, *and make a real difference.* Quickly I remembered the prayer of the woman at the resale shop: *the right job, in the right place, where she can make a real difference.*

"This is amazing," I told the director. "This job is an answer to prayer."

I have been teaching at the rehabilitation center for a little over a year. Not only do I teach women, but also God uses this position to teach me many things. My salary is not nearly as much as my previous job, and I don't have any benefits, but God has provided our family with everything we could ever need.

At the time I was fired, I thought my family was losing everything we needed. Turns out, I was only losing the things I wanted. A paycheck. A good reputation. A place where I thought I was needed and important. God knew I needed to learn some life lessons about trust, faith, and purpose, and he provided the opportunity to become a rehab teacher so I might be willing to learn as well. I joke with the ladies about how they are "inpatients," but I'm an "outpatient." Every day I go to work with a brave group of women and practice what really matters in life: faith, forgiveness, trust, and love. I couldn't ask for a better fit.

KIMBERLY SUTTON lives near Houston, Texas, with her husband, Rick, and three children, Kayla, Rachael, and Josiah. She graduated from Evangel University with a degree in journalism and has worked for more than twenty-two years in ministry as a youth pastor, Bible teacher, church planter, missionary in Paraguay, and Teen Challenge rehabilitation teacher. She is fluent in Spanish, and she and her husband are the pastors of All Nations' Worship Center in Conroe, Texas, where all three of their children are musicians on the worship team.

For more information about New Life Women's Center, the organization featured in this story, visit creativeoutreach.com.

39

ROAD TO RECOVERY

APRIL LALAND

You have to come over," I said desperately, my mouth dry and my stomach nauseous. "I need your help. I'm about to do something stupid."

"I'm coming," my sponsor said. "Wait where you are." I'd been paired up with my sponsor at the recovery clinic, and she was helping me with my steps; but on that day, it didn't feel like any psycho-recovery therapy was going to help. I needed a fix, bad.

My addiction was my constant companion. After losing my mom when I was eight, being molested when I was ten, and being raped as a teenager, drugs were the only thing I could find to numb the pain. By the time I was fifteen, I was an addict.

When my sponsor arrived, I was beyond reasonable. I didn't want to listen to her talk about the steps or the higher power or the progress I'd made. I didn't want her to remind me of my kids and my responsibility as a mother. None of that mattered now.

"Come with me," I asked her. "Let's just get something small to take the edge off." For some reason, which I still do not understand today, my strong, reasonable, experienced sponsor agreed. We walked across town and found a dealer. Side by side, we forked over money for a handful of drugs, but unexpectedly I turned to her. "No," I said. "I shouldn't be here." Then I turned and ran back to the drug facility and asked for help.

Three days later a counselor at the clinic called me into her office. "Did you hear the news?" she asked.

"About what?"

"Your sponsor. April, it's terrible. She was found behind a Dumpster. Someone decapitated her."

I shook my head violently back and forth. "No, no, no . . . that can't be right. Please, no." I began crying, and my body started shaking.

The pain took over and carried me back to when I was an eight-year-old girl at my mother's funeral. Then the face of my molester flashed in my mind. I could hear the voice of my rapist. An entire lifetime of pain crippled me, and I thought I might die. Thoughts of suicide filled my mind and tormented me nonstop. Depression gripped me, and medication hardly numbed the pain at all. I wept for days, in and out of hysteria and uncontrollable grief. I felt as if it were going to consume me.

When I had a chance to get the one thing I knew would help, I did. My husband at the time, a user himself, slipped me something while visiting me at the clinic. I smoked it that night, inhaling the fumes that my body craved, hoping they'd set me free, but they didn't. I was caught, removed from the treatment facility, and sent before a judge who sentenced me to ten years in prison. I was thirty-one years old.

Prison was an unending nightmare. I was surrounded by violent felons and wracked to my core with guilt. I cried my eyes out every night and was hospitalized for dehydration several times. I couldn't shake the remorse. My addiction killed my sponsor, it was keeping me from my kids, and it had me locked up behind bars. One night, crying on my top bunk, I rolled over in desperation and reached up to God. *I don't know if I'm doing this right*, I prayed, *but I can't keep living with this pain. Save me from myself and from what I've done.* Immediately a calming presence filled the cell, and I knew I needed to get help.

The next day I began writing anyone I could think of. A few months later, the Georgia Justice Project wrote me back, and eventually went on to assist me in my release and help me start a court-appointed recovery process. Even with that help I struggled to stay clean. I battled my addiction every day, and sadly, it won most of the fights. When I wasn't high, I was in and out of court, fighting for my family, but in time I lost custody of two of my children.

Losing them was the true beginning of my recovery. It opened my eyes to the deep destruction of my behavior, and I finally began asking the right questions. *What do I need to do for my family? What is best for them?* I got clean, went back to school, and graduated with honors. Most important, I accepted an invitation to visit a church in Forest Park, Georgia, where I met Pastor Daniel Fagan. He taught me the truth of God's Word and led me to accept Christ into my life.

I wish the dictionary had more words to describe the freedom I found in Christ! In him I have remained drug-free, and now I am an author, poet, mentor to women in crisis, and inspirational speaker. My mission is to spread the power of God and help addicts and victims of abuse, especially women, find the truth in the story of God. Only the light of the Lord can wash away the kind of imprints addiction and abuse leave on a person's spirit. And it is only because I suffered those tragedies that I am able to help others heal.

APRIL LALAND is a talented author and dynamic inspirational speaker with empowering workshops on drug-free living and mentoring to addicts. These give her an incomparable foundation in making a positive impact in her community. Her twenty-five-year battle with addiction became the stepping-stone to a life of service to the kingdom of God. She now shares her inspirational and empowering story of hope, health, and healing through her book, *Memoir from a Glass Rose*, and her divine vision to turn pain into progress through her organization, In My Own Words, Inc.

40

THE FINAL DAYS

MARYBETH MCCULLUM

The rehab center was growing quiet as the day's last light waned. My brother had just left to make the three-hour drive back to his family, and my mom was on her way home too. It was the second night for my father in that particular facility—he was there on doctor's orders to rehab from a fall that bruised his hip, but he was growing weaker, and we feared leaving him alone through the night. My mom couldn't sleep on the fold-out chair in the room as my brother had the night before, so I reluctantly volunteered. It was just my father and me, together, for the night.

I didn't know if I should dread the next twelve hours or welcome them as a rare gift. I cared for my dad and was glad to be helping, but I'd never been "Daddy's little girl." He rarely said "I love you" and struggled with displaying his emotions. He showed his love by working hard and providing for our family. As I grew older, I resigned myself to the fact that my dad and I just didn't get each other. I was busy attending to my own life, and every now and then he'd invite me out for breakfast or a hike. I always halfheartedly agreed, convinced he was only reaching out to me to make himself feel better.

Seeing him bedridden was still a shock. He was always a strong, active man, and when we went on family hikes, the two of us always raced up ahead of the family. Those were my best memories of him, out on the trail together, silently connecting through our shared love for the outdoors. It was the one thing that brought us together over the years, but as he got older and grew sicker, the hikes had stopped.

I sat down in the chair next to his bed, listening to the hiss of his oxygen tank. Anxious about the night ahead, I breathed a prayer, asking for courage and wisdom. My dad was suffering from a rare disease called *progressive supranuclear palsy*, a brain disorder that incapacitates the victim both physically and mentally. He could still think clearly, but it took a long time for him to form thoughts and respond with words.

My husband and I helped my mom care for my dad when he was initially diagnosed. We set up a weekly dinner at their house so my husband could do odd jobs around the house, my mom could have time with our boys, and I could visit with my dad. At times I wanted to jump up and break the decades of silence and tell him I loved him and was sorry if I made it hard for him to connect with me, but I couldn't. He couldn't either, and I feared our time was running out.

"Dad," I asked quietly, "would you like me to read to you? I brought my Bible." He nodded in agreement. I pulled the leatherbound Bible from my bag and turned to some of my most cherished verses. I read to him for about an hour before he nearly dozed off to sleep. Watching him lying peacefully in bed, I knew I had to grasp this moment to share my heart. I leaned forward and asked, "Can I pray with you?"

It wasn't strange for me to pray out loud, nor was it unusual for my father to accept prayer. He was a man of deep faith, but we had never prayed alone, together, intimately. I moved to the side of his bed, lay my hands down on his chest, and began praying. "Lord, thank you for my father, for all he has done for me . . ." The words spilled out of me, coming from a surprising place of tenderness, and by the time I was done, the room was filled with God's peaceful, loving presence. It was the most intimate moment we'd ever experienced, and I was surprised by a deep joy.

I turned out the light and curled up on the fold-out chair, thankful I'd taken the risk. But as the night passed, I realized there were still things I wanted to say. I prayed all night for the courage to be honest, and when my dad finally awoke the next morning, I didn't let the moment pass.

"Dad," I said, speaking slowly for him to follow, "I know we haven't always communicated very well. You've tried over the years to connect with me in different ways, and I didn't make it very easy for you." He looked at me, his eyes lazy and blinking, but I knew he was listening. "I want you to know that I'm sorry and I know you were trying. I don't think we understood each other very well, but I hope you know that you've been a good dad to me, and I love you."

He whispered back, "I love you too." Then he patted my hand. "You're like an angel from heaven. You're an amazing woman." Never before had he spoken so tenderly to me. On the way home that morning, I reflected on our night together. My back was aching, my muscles were stiff, I desperately needed a shower, and I was beyond exhausted, both physically and emotionally. Still, I felt a deep satisfaction and a peace knowing my father and I had finally connected.

Over the next two weeks I went to visit my dad daily as he slowly slipped away. Courage begat courage, and I wrote a eulogy that I shared with him during one of his rare moments of lucidity. It was one of the few times I was able to express my gratitude and appreciation for who he was. In his weakened state he couldn't diffuse my words with his characteristic sarcasm. He just received them, squeezing my hand to let me know he was listening.

I thought my dad's disease was going to cut our time short, robbing us of the opportunity to truly connect with one another. But his illness was the very thing that brought us together, lowered our guard, and allowed us to share our love.

God gave us the gift we'd always longed to receive.

MARYBETH McCULLUM enjoys writing and blogging about her Christian faith and how it intersects with everyday life. She has a bachelor's degree in English and master's degree in education, both from UCLA. She taught high school English and leadership before choosing to stay home with her kids. Marybeth grew up as the youngest of five siblings. She lives with her husband and two boys in the San Francisco East Bay area.

41

GRANDMA'S LOVE

KATHLEEN KOHLER

We have something we need to tell you," I said. My boyfriend, Loren, and I were sitting across from my parents at the dinner table. It was early March, and while Loren had already graduated from high school, I still had my senior year ahead. I reached under the table and squeezed Loren's hand to gain courage. The knot in my stomach grew tighter, and I took a deep breath.

"I'm pregnant."

Daddy's smile vanished instantly, and his face began steaming bright red. His lips stretched into a thin, flat line of anger. My mother sat next to him, stunned, unblinking, holding an artichoke leaf between bites. "And," I choked out the rest, "we want to get married in April." It wasn't the best timing for my confession. My older brother had left home the previous summer, and now, without warning, my parents were going to be empty nesters and grandparents. The news didn't settle well.

Over the next few weeks, the house grew quiet, and I could feel my shame hanging in the air like a dark haze. Mom and Daddy tried to cope with the shock, and they decided it might be easier if they told Grandma the news. I was grateful for their decision. Grandma and I were close, and I knew the situation would cause her anguish. I wanted to delay the inevitable look of shame as long as possible.

A few weeks later, on Easter, Daddy drove across town to pick up Grandma for dinner at our house. I hadn't seen her since my parents talked to her, and I knew the moment was coming when I would have to look into her blue eyes and see the same look of disappointment I had seen in my parents. As I waited for Dad and Grandma to arrive, I retreated to my room. Anxious with energy, I nervously bounced around the room of my childhood, cleaning and packing. I dusted off some old kids books, organized my clothes that would soon no longer fit, and began wondering about the future. Loren and I had dated for more than a year; he was my first boyfriend and the only boy I'd ever even kissed. But was the love we felt enough to last a lifetime? I was both excited and scared to find out.

Just after one o'clock I heard Daddy's car roar up the driveway, and minutes later I could hear faint voices. The aroma of fresh-baked ham filled the house and flooded my room, carrying with it hints of the conversation coming from the kitchen. *What does Grandma think of me now?* I wondered. *Will I still be her special girl?*

I grew up going to Grandma's little white house on State Street as far back as I could remember. During the school year, I stayed overnight at her house on the weekends, but when June came and school let out, I got to stay for weeks straight. Together we picked flowers in the gardens blossoming around her house. Because Grandma didn't drive, we walked everywhere, to the post office and downtown to the Safeway. Sometimes she treated me to a root beer soda at the corner drugstore. Often we combed the old Woolworth's, looking for treasures to use in her endless craft projects. On warm, sunny days we strolled down to Lake Washington, each carrying a loaf of bread to feed the ducks. Grandma taught me to keep still and hold each slice out for their hungry eyes to see. "Don't be afraid," she said. "They won't hurt you." The brave ones nipped our fingers as they grabbed the bread from our hands, but it didn't hurt, just like Grandma said. At night we ate ice cream and watched movies. On the Fourth of July we squeezed together on the small back porch and watched the fireworks from her peekaboo view of the lake. When rain splattered the streets, we snuggled inside, and Grandma showed me how to make yarn dolls. I crafted the bodies and added their faces while she crocheted their clothes. Now, caught in a strange place between childhood and adulthood, I needed reassurance that I would be okay. I couldn't afford to lose my best friend.

A gentle knock on my door made me jump, and my heart raced with fear. "Come in," I said. Ashamed, I kept my head down and stared at the floor when Grandma entered my room. She walked right over to where I stood and wrapped me in her arms. I leaned back and searched her face. I saw no embarrassment, no disappointment, and no display of angry condemnation. Only love shined from her powder-blue eyes.

"Nothing you could ever do will change my love for you," she said. She pulled me close, and I laid my head against her shoulder, burying my face in her pink sweater. Silent tears spilled down my cheeks and dampened her simple cotton dress. We clung to each other for a long time. In that tender moment I knew that no matter where I went or what happened in my life, my grandma loved me. My anxious thoughts subsided, and I felt strong enough to confront whatever my future held. Her hug said, "You're not a loser." And most importantly, it revealed to me that I was loved based not on what I did but on who I was.

Two weeks later Grandma helped prepare the flowers for our wedding. Loren and I recited our marriage vows in a small ceremony, surrounded by family in the church he had grown up in. We found a huge second-floor apartment near Lake Washington, just three blocks from Grandma. On an early morning in late September, Benjamin arrived, bringing more love into our lives.

Oh, and that boy I married? Well, last April we celebrated thirty-three years of our lifelong commitment to each other. We weren't expected to "make it," but the love we share today is deeper than the day we said "I do." Love really does make all the difference.

KATHLEEN KOHLER writes for magazines and anthologies, drawing from her real-life experiences to offer hope. She and her husband live in the Pacific Northwest, and have three children and seven grandchildren. Visit kathleenkohler.com to read more of her published work.

LEMON DROP

Kathleen's grandma sounds a lot like God to me. She loved unconditionally, spoke words of life, and lifted the weight of her granddaughter's shame from her shoulders. God, who says "come unto me all you who are weary and heavy laden," takes us as we are. We only have to respond to his reaching embrace.

—Don

42

SANTO DOMINGO SUNRISE

TERRI ELDERS

I'm jealous, my friend's note said. *Every time I see a Club Med ad on television, I think of you . . . You must be having a marvelous time on your island paradise!* I lowered the note back into my lap and looked up into the clear Caribbean sky. The sun was hanging low over the horizon, coloring the streets of San Juan de la Maguana with warm, soft hints of orange. The humidity condensed on my bottle of Presidente, the local beer, and the beads of water rolled down the side of the cold, green bottle.

Island paradise? I questioned my friend's words, taking a bite of salty plantains. I was in the Dominican Republic, serving with the Peace Corps, working with families who lived in mud huts. Women carried water from the river on their heads and cooked on makeshift rock stoves in their yards. Once every seven days I got to sit in silence at my favorite patio café and read my mail, but other than that small weekly reprieve, nothing in the DR sounded, looked, or felt like paradise.

I placed her letter back down on the stack of mail and grabbed the blue envelope postmarked from Guatemala. It was the letter I'd been waiting all week to read. I thought of it every day as I roamed the high western desert near San Juan, visiting preschools, and as always, I saved it for last. I carefully opened the gauzy blue envelope and pulled out the letter from my boyfriend. He was living in Guatemala and had visited me in Santo Domingo the previous Christmas. We'd been together off and on for more than ten years, and when my assignment ended in a few months, I'd planned to join him in Guatemala.

The letter unfolded in my hands, and I began reading, smiling at the sight of his handwriting.

Dear Terri,

I'm sorry to have to say this in a letter, but I've met someone else.

My heart skipped a beat, and I started shaking my head. It must have been some kind of mistake.

We are going to be married soon. I hope you understand.

Married? Understand? Was he kidding? I read the letter again and began to weep. What was I supposed to understand? That the last ten years of our lives meant nothing? That our future plans were suddenly erased? That the person I cared about most in the world had basically just said, "Stop caring about me"? I stuffed the letter back into the envelope as tears poured down my face.

What do I do? I asked myself. The song on the radio changed from the usual merengue melody, and Air Supply suddenly, fittingly, started belting out "All Out of Love." I couldn't believe it, I didn't understand, and I didn't know what to do, so I stumbled down the street to the house where I rented a room and threw some clothes into a bag. I scribbled a note to the landlady on a scrap of paper, left it on the door, and rushed to the bus depot to catch the last ride of the day to Santo Domingo.

I had to see Father Luis.

When I first met Father Luis, I was browsing books at the Episcopal church library, and I noticed him eyeing the *Newsweek* sticking out of my bag. I knew English magazines sold out quickly in the few stores that carried them, so I gave him my copy, and we struck up a conversation. Soon, despite not being a regular church attendee back home, I started going to hear Father Luis preach in English every Sunday morning. I'd bring my weekly copy of *Newsweek* for him, and after the service we'd talk politics, faith, and world issues. One of our favorite topics of conversation was former president Jimmy Carter, a man Luis praised for his humanitarian efforts and a man who inspired my own participation in the Peace Corps.

I slumped down into the bus seat and glared out the window at the Dominican countryside passing in the distance. *Please be there*, I kept saying to myself, hoping Father Luis hadn't gone for the day. I didn't want to wait all night thinking about the Dear Jane letter. I knew I'd grow bitter. I just needed someone to sit and listen to me.

The moment the bus stopped in Santo Domingo, I hopped off and rushed across town to the church. As I came up the street, I saw Father Luis locking up the doors of the parish hall for the evening.

"Father, sorry to surprise you," I said, breathlessly, "but can I have a few minutes of your time?"

"Child," he replied, surprised at the desperation in my eyes, "you look as if you've lost your best friend. Come on inside." He opened up the doors and led me into the cool air of the old sanctuary. We sat on the old wooden benches, and before they stopped creaking beneath us, the story poured out of me.

"I thought he loved me too," I concluded, fishing another tissue from my tote.

After a few moments of silence, Father Luis said quietly, "Romantic love ebbs and flows. But maybe God has another plan for you—and you can count on his love forever."

"Another plan? What could it be?" I asked. I thought my original plan had been a pretty good one. What else could I come up with?

"It will unfold," Father Luis said. "Just open your mind and heart and wait. Direction will come." That sounded suspiciously vague, but I wasn't looking for the priest to instantly solve my problems.

"Thank you for listening," I said, pulling a crumpled copy of *Newsweek* from my bag. "It was squeezed between two chickens on the bus ride up."

He chuckled. "Sometimes life is like that. We can get squeezed, too, but God has a way of smoothing things out for us."

The next morning I woke at dawn, hoping the fresh sea air and the rising sun would be a good time for God to start smoothing things out for me. I strode along the coast, listening to the small waves crashing against the levee. The smell of the sea filled the air, and I wondered, *Where do I go from here?*

I thought of all the places I could go in the world: Asia, Europe, Polynesia. The list included every place on the globe except for one— the *only* place I wanted to go and couldn't—the arms of my boyfriend. *Where do you go when you can't go where you want?*

Suddenly I noticed a squadron of husky Dominicans jogging toward me. They looked like professional wrestlers, and their heads were on a constant swivel. As they neared, I could see they were surrounding a small gray-haired man in blue sweats jogging down the road. He looked like a kind old grandfather, and as they passed, he raised his wrinkled hand, smiled, and waved at me.

I waved back, trying to place his familiar face, and about a hundred yards later it hit me: I'd just walked past Jimmy Carter! And just like that, everything was clear. I realized if seventy-year-old Jimmy Carter could still serve his country and promote peace, instead of retreating from the world to enjoy a life of ease, then I could too. I finished my walk and marched straight into the office of the director at the Peace Corps office. "I'm staying in the Corps when my time here is up," I said. "Sign me up, and send me somewhere."

The road of my life didn't instantly become a smooth highway, but it did unfold in a way I could have never anticipated, just as Father Luis predicted. I went on to volunteer with the Peace Corps in the Republic of Seychelles in the Indian Ocean and later came back to the States to work at the Peace Corps headquarters in Washington DC. Life wasn't all work either. The ebb and flow of romantic love brought a wonderful man into my life, and I eventually married. My new husband and I were happy together for nine years before he succumbed to cancer a few years ago.

When I thank God for my blessings, I'm reminded of Father Luis and his wise words. I also remember the Santo Domingo sunrise and the smile of Jimmy Carter—the very thing I needed to keep my eyes on the right path. I often wonder: If God uses presidents themselves to answer prayers, what won't he use?

TERRI ELDERS, LCSW, lives near Colville, Washington. Her stories have appeared in dozens of periodicals and anthologies. She's a cocreator and editor for Publishing Syndicate's new anthology series Not Your Mother's Book. A public member of the Washington State Medical Quality Assurance Commission, Terri received UCLA's 2006 Alumni Award for Community Service. She blogs at atouchoftarragon.blogspot.com.

43

UNEXPECTED FAMILY

KIM MCKINNEY

N o, I'm fine. I don't need to go to the doctor," Marc said, brushing his long hair back over his forehead.

"Did you bump your head? Does it hurt?" I asked him again, worried about the growing lump over his left eye.

"I told you, it's okay." He smiled. "Now how about we talk about something else?" Something didn't seem right. Marc was a picture of health, and he was just twenty-two. What could this bump be from? I picked up some headache medication and packed it in his suitcase before he returned to California to start his spring semester. I thought the stress of school, ministry, and volunteering at the Dream Center in LA was getting to him.

"Just in case," I said, as I handed the pills to him. Two months later he called and said his vision was getting worse, his balance was off, and he was having a hard time concentrating. My husband and I packed up the car and drove from Seattle to LA to see for ourselves.

When we pulled into the parking lot of Marc's school, he was waiting for us, waving his lanky arms, smiling with his entire six-foot-five body. I opened the door to receive his warm embrace and asked to see his head. As he pulled his hair back, I felt like a fastball hit me in the stomach. His head protruded out on the left side, like a mutant alien trying to push its way out of his brain. Not wanting to alarm him, I calmly said that we would find a doctor in LA to take a look, immediately.

In the meantime Marc gave us a tour of the Dream Center, introduced us to his friends, and invited us to participate in a Saturday night "Adopt a Block" event, where he and others walk a specific block in LA to meet community members and learn about their needs. Keeping up with Marc was a lot of work, but in between events and meetings and conversations, we started looking for a doctor. Our three days came and went in LA, and my husband and I had to get back to Seattle.

The first doctor visit was scheduled, and I wished a hundred times over that I could stay in LA with Marc, but we closed the car door and left him standing on the pavement. It felt cruel. He was my baby, for heaven's sake; couldn't I just pick him up and find a giant-sized car seat to buckle him into? Couldn't I make him come home with us and be around his family? The trip home was like the colors gray and brown. I tried to see the vibrancy of life but felt a wash of droning, dull paint brushing over my world. Home became a place of constant waiting for tests results and conversations with insurance companies. I paced. I grabbed the phone every time it rang and hoped for some relief from the anxious, acidic emotions.

"Mom, the doctor is going to call you," Marc said one day when he reached me by phone.

"Why? What is it?" Silence threatened. "Marc?"

"He doesn't know; he's referring me on to a specialist." His voice was flat, worried. The doctor called later that day. "Mrs. McKinney, what I am seeing is not normal. He needs some blood tests and a CAT scan."

"Oh, this is just a precaution, right?" I was still thinking it was something simple. "You probably just want to cover your bases. Do you think it will be a quick outpatient operation? I'm sure he's going to be just fine," I rambled.

He stopped me. "Mrs. McKinney, I'm sorry, but this is not something simple. I know this is hard with you being in a different state . . ." I tuned him out and sat down, breathing heavily. "We'll take care of him," I heard him say.

No! I am the mom—I should be taking care of him! I thought to myself. I called Marc back and told him I would fly down for his tests. He insisted it was too soon to spend the extra money and convinced me to wait. One test led to another, and eventually he was sent to a team of specialists. A neurologist, an ophthalmologist, and an ENT all examined Marc's head and compared their findings.

"You have a tumor," they told him. "It is larger than most we see like this. It is next to your left eye, lodged behind your sinuses and next to your brain, but between bone plates. It is most likely benign, but is growing and needs to be removed." There was no time to find a doctor in Seattle and fly him home, so a date was set, and we arranged to come. My husband and I; our children, Amy and Justin; and my sister, Sherri, purchased tickets to California and made arrangements to move into a rented, furnished apartment. The expenses were adding up.

When we arrived, we met with the doctors, and they walked us through the procedure. "We will cut him from ear to ear," they said, "pull down his face, and drill into his bones to remove the tumor." I stood up, walked out of the room, and collapsed in the hallway. I could see the gray carpet through my fingers and smell the chemicals in the fibers. I inhaled and exhaled, trying to find my strength, but it had rushed from my body. The description of the surgery played in my mind.

No! I begged God. *Please don't take him!* I closed my eyes and suddenly envisioned myself before a mighty throne. I held my son in my arms, placed him in the lap of my heavenly Father, and heard him say, "He is safe, Kim." Slowly, a peace calmed me, and over the next few days I felt God's gentle hands holding me. I worked out travel arrangements with family members and started contacting our insurance companies. Both companies denied the claims, and estimates for the surgery were around $130,000. My husband and I began praying about selling our home.

As the surgery drew closer and closer, calls kept coming in. People were praying for Marc all over the country. Word spread about his condition, and two different insurance companies agreed to cover the operation. I had never heard of a health insurance company that took pity on a mother's tears and decided to provide coverage. The remaining challenges were little things, such as picking up family members from the airport, filling prescriptions, providing meals, learning to drive in LA traffic, and taking care of Marc. The Dream Center provided students and a van to pick up family members from the airport, bring food, go to the grocery store, and chauffeur us back and forth to church. Marc's friends visited us often, made us laugh, prayed with us, and assured us they would help in any way possible. Standing in the hospital the day of the surgery, we gathered around Marc like one big, supportive family and prayed.

Ten hours after the operation began, to remove the tumor and insert metal plates into Marc's head, the surgeon came out and told us we could finally see him. My husband, our son and daughter, and I hurried into his room and found him hooked up to wires and machines, with tubes coming out of his temples. Overcome with emotion, we held each other and cried. Then Marc opened his eyes, smiled, and said to the doctor, "Hey, someone could shoot me in the head now, and I would be all right with these metal plates." We burst out laughing and knew he was on the path to healing.

At a time I felt so lost in fear and helplessness, God surprised me with unexpected blessings and a newfound family. I resisted their help at first because I wanted to be the one helping, but God taught me about surrender, and he taught me how to say thank you. He let me be on the other end of life, receiving instead of giving, and I've been receiving his grace ever since.

KIM MCKINNEY is a freelance writer and life coach. Wesleyan Publishing House, Standard Publishing, *Echoes* magazine, and Review and Herald Publishing have published some of her inspiring stories and devotionals. Her work at a Christian camp provides her with resources to promote outdoor adventures for women and children. She loves hiking and traveling with family and friends. For more, visit coachkimmckinney.com.

44

SURVIVING SUICIDE

LISA LANE

The fifth bottle of liquor is half-empty, and I am half-numb, but I still feel the pain. I take another drink from the bottle.

Tonight there is only one way out of my room, my problems, my life, and I am looking for the courage to take it. The bottle of pills is next to me on the floor. The prescription is for my friend, but she was happy to sell them to me. She says they will help with my anxiety. That is what I want: to be free from this stress. Forever. To lay my head down and never rise into this anxious world of heartache and burden.

My divorce. Raising my son. Losing my job. Searching for work. My car breaking down. Being evicted. This is not my life. My life was supposed to be something else, not this. I don't want this life, and I can't change it. I've done everything I can do. No one will hire me. No one will help me. I've called every number, stood in every line, filled out every form, but nothing! A single, out-of-work mother, about to lose my house, and no one will help me! Is this the world I live in?

No. No more.

I take another drink. The alcohol burns my throat. I hear the TV in the other room. My five-year-old son is out there, sitting quietly, watching his show.

He'll be better off without me, won't he? Yes. I'm no good for him. I can't provide. I can't protect him. He'll be okay. He'll go live with his father and forget about me. It will be for the best.

I take a deep breath. The air is musty and cold.

I pick up the little orange bottle, and the pills cascade into my hand. I try to count them, but my eyes are blurry. There are enough, at least twenty.

This is the only way to escape. I raise my hand to my mouth and grip the liquor in the other. I'm shaking.

My eyes close, and everything goes dark.

This is it. It's time.

Suddenly I hear something at the door. It sounds like rustling paper, and I am distracted. I open my eyes and look to see a piece of crumbled paper slide under the door. I lower my hand and let go of the whiskey with the other so I can lean forward.

The paper is white, and his messy handwriting is scribbled in black.

I love you, Mom.

I read it again. And again. I read it until I can't see anymore because I'm weeping. Tears are burning down my cheeks, and I drop the pills back into the bottle.

I crawl to the door and pick up the paper.

My son loves me! Dear God, he is my son! What am I thinking? The debt doesn't matter. He doesn't care if I have the best job in town.

He'll eat anything—it doesn't matter what. He loves me, and I love him. Is that enough?

There is a pen resting on the nightstand, and I grab it. Beneath his note I write, *I love you, too, more than you will ever know!*

My love note trembles in my shaking hand as I kneel down to slide it back beneath the door. Just as I push it through the threshold, it's pulled from my fingers.

He is still there? Waiting to hear from me?

I jump up and fling open the door. My son is sitting on his knees, holding the note, and I scoop him up into my arms. He kisses my neck, and I kiss him back. I can't stop kissing him.

"Why are you crying, Mommy?"

"Oh, baby, because I love you so much!"

My son is thirteen now, and we are doing well. Life isn't without little problems here and there, but we get through them together, just as we did that dark night so many years ago. I still have his note hidden away somewhere safe. When things start to look hopeless, I pull it out and remember that once upon a time I almost gave up, but love never gave up on me. In fact, it saved my life.

LISA LANE is now a dispatch operator, raising her son and doing her best to provide him with a good life and a good example. She still struggles with depression and bouts with bipolar disorder, but she has never again given thought to taking her own life. She aspires to be a writer and hopes her story will help others struggling with depression and feelings of helplessness.

LEMON DROP

In Psalm 77:19, Asaph wrote about God saving Israel while they were trapped between a hostile army and the Red Sea. He said, "Your road led through the sea, your pathway through the mighty waters—a pathway no one knew was there!" When I read Lisa's story, I marvel at the incredible timing of God's unlikely provision that provided a different way out of her pain and problems—the way of love.

—Don

45

BALM FOR BURNOUT

LOIS HUDSON

t was an ideal California Sunday, postcard perfect, sunny, and warm; but I was in a gray fog. My spirit was languishing—hanging desperately to the end of the rope, with no knot to stop my slide. I was on the verge of tears all morning. I couldn't sing, pray, or concentrate at church. I knew as soon as the service was over, I'd get back into the car with my husband and two sons, drive home, and find my mother-in-law waiting for me.

She had been living with us for almost seven years, and caring for her was wearing me out. I had done my best to welcome her into our home. We shifted our two sons into new rooms down the hall so Grandma could have the one closest to the bathroom. I unboxed her belongings and decorated the room with her own furnishings. We hung family pictures, connected her television, brought in her easy chair, created her own personal space in the bathroom, and discussed with our sons the reasons for this arrangement.

As an optimist—maybe cockeyed, as the song says—I expected her to settle in, adapt to her beautiful new room, and enjoy being with family. Instead, she ignored closed doors and private moments. She challenged our sons' conversations and activities. She hid household items in her room. She napped on the living room sofa in the middle of the day. She left her shoes and false teeth on the coffee table. Rather frequently she stormed down the hall, saying with a snarky tone, "Well, don't worry about *my* dinner. I'm going to my room."

At other times she seemed so normal; and when visitors stopped by, they couldn't believe she'd ever be a problem. She was fun. She was witty. She was her old self, bringing the party to life. But as soon as the guests left, she would ask who they were and why in the world we were friends with them.

I kept waiting and waiting for her to adapt to our family life, but as the months went by, she deteriorated. It wasn't uncommon for my son to come home from school and ask me, "Mom, did you know Grandma is up on the street corner with her pillow under her arm?" I finally hung a large jingle bell on the doorknob to alert me to any movement through the door. Sadly, I learned to hate the sound of jingle bells.

I didn't know at the time, but she was in the early stages of dementia. She was forgetting things. She didn't recognize my husband or me. Things weren't getting any easier, only harder.

When I heard a favorite radio program was featuring a panel of family caregivers, I tuned in, eager for whatever advice I could glean. But the discussion was so lovey-dovey, everything-is-wonderful-since-Grandmother-came-to-live-with-us, sickeningly sweet that I had to turn it off. It just wasn't realistic. Not in my world anyway.

Was I the only one who felt this way? Was I out of line? Were my experiences the unrealistic ones? When another stroke left Grandma unable to walk, I was mentally relieved that I wouldn't have to worry about her running away anymore. But the physical load increased with grooming, bathing, dressing, feeding, laundering, medicating, and chauffeuring. She seemed to fight me at every turn, and when things didn't go her way, she let me know. One day she even stretched out of her wheelchair and stomped on my bare foot, breaking three toes.

On that Sunday afternoon my spirit was dangling from the frayed rope, so I declared a personal retreat. I took my Bible, a notebook, and a glass of lemonade and sank into a deep chair on the patio. I put my feet up and closed my eyes, and before long, negative thoughts began scolding me. *You shouldn't feel like this. You know better. You call yourself a Christian. You claim to trust God.* Alone, sitting in the shade of an avocado tree, leaf-dappled sunlight warmed my skin, and my very breath became a prayer. "Lord, I am so needy right now. I really need to hear something personal from you, something just for me . . ."

Instantly Isaiah 40:30–31 came to mind. "Lord, I know that one. That's not what I need. I need more." Again the verse stole my thoughts.

Look it up. Read it from the page. The words were inaudible but no less real, so I curiously reached for my Bible and turned to the familiar passage: "Even youths grow tired and weary, and young men stumble and fall; but those who hope in the LORD will renew their strength. They will soar on wings like eagles; they will run and not grow weary, they will walk and not be faint" (NIV).

"Yes, Lord, it's beautiful, but I know that one. I want—no—*need* more."

Read on.

"That's the end of the chapter," I grumbled.

I know. Read on. Sputtering in spirit but desperate, I read on into the next chapter. It spoke of nations and kings, islands and judgment, and fear. Nothing seemed to fit at all, but then I arrived at a verse I had underlined and forgotten: "So do not fear, for I am with you; do not be dismayed, for I am your God. I will strengthen you and help you; I will uphold you with my righteous right hand" (Isaiah 41:10). Suddenly the burns on my spirit seemed to cool. It was such an obvious answer to my needy plea, and the result was instantaneous—I felt the blessing of renewed strength, revitalized energy, restored spirit.

Sipping my lemonade, I continued to reflect on the verse and noticed that God referred to himself four times and the reader five times. "I am with you . . . I am your God . . . I will strengthen you . . . and help you . . . I will uphold you." I read the promises over and over, claiming each one as my own. I was the "you" God was speaking to, and he graciously nurtured my soul.

Caring for Grandma went on for a total of fourteen years, the last seven of which she was bedbound. Thankfully, I had learned that Sunday on the patio that I wasn't alone, and I felt God sustaining me. The answered prayer carried me through many more difficult times. It even helped me to laugh and take things more in stride. Once, when I rolled her over and accidently hurt her arm, she shot me a death stare. But I just smiled, laughed, soothed her arm, and gave her a kiss. It was good to see her old spunk.

Then one morning when I went to tend to her, she was gone—no health crisis, no warning of the end—she had simply gone to sleep. I sat next to her body, waiting for the coroner, clutching the note from the doctor that said she had experienced a planned, natural, at-home death. It was written to free us from an investigation by the authorities, but as I held it, I was reminded of the answered prayer that freed me from anger and impatience. I held her hand with tears in my eyes, sad to see her go, but relieved her long stretch of suffering had come to an end.

To this day I keep on my desk a piece of twine with a knot at the end. It reminds me that even though I cannot tie the knot when I am at the end of my rope, the great I AM will.

LOIS HUDSON is the coauthor of *Ending Elder Abuse: A Family Guide*, and she has been published in a number of devotional collections. She is currently living in Sparks, Nevada, and is working on her first writing love—a series of novels.

46 ═══

ROOM 234

GINA GRAHAM

He hunched down low to the leaves scattered over the cold earth and looked through the thick underbrush. The woods were quiet, and his eyes scanned the trees, moving from one mossy green trunk to another. Any sign of movement and he was ready, the gun firm in his hand, the shell loaded and waiting.

Hurchial knew the best deer blinds in this part of Maine's woods; he'd been hunting and working the same stretch of land since he was a kid. He started out by helping his father when he was a boy, but now, as a strong seventeen-year-old, he made a good living felling trees and hauling them out to the mill. He knew his way around the terrain like the rooms in his own house, and he was certain there were deer feeding near the creek he had just traversed.

Still hunched low, he crept around a tree and ducked beneath some branches. A small twig snapped beneath his weight, and he paused, patiently waiting for the noise to fade.

239

Suddenly a burst behind him broke the silence, and he fell to the ground, grasping at a sharp pain in his neck. When he hit the leaves, he rolled to his side, wailing in pain. He stuck his index finger into the hole beneath his chin, just over his Adam's apple, and followed it through to the exit wound. The metal jacket bullet had traveled clean through his throat.

As he grasped at the wound, trying to stop the blood, he heard steps enter the clearing where he lay.

Lorestin, a World War II veteran just released from the army, ran up to Hurchial and knelt down beside him.

"You shot me," Hurchial said, looking into his eyes.

"I thought I was alone," Lorestin said, panicking. "Oh no, Hurchial! I thought you were a deer!"

Hurchial reached around into his back pocket, pulled out his white handkerchief, and stuffed it into one side of the wound. Instantly blood colored it dark red. He fished out another bandanna to help stop the bleeding, then whispered to Lorestin, "Get me out of here."

Lorestin helped him to his feet and started leading him from the scene of the accident.

"No, no," Hurchial whispered, pulling at his arm. "You're going the wrong way. We have to go this way to the road." Hurchial turned around, and Lorestin followed, too traumatized to lead the way.

"I'm so sorry," Lorestin kept saying as they wore through the woods and toward the road. A mile later, when they finally reached the clearing for the road, the blood had trickled all the way down Hurchial's chest and legs into his boots. His socks were soaked, and he could feel the liquid between his toes.

He collapsed on the road, and Lorestin flagged down a trucker. They loaded Hurchial into the cab and raced toward the small, rural town, where they figured they could find help. As they approached the town center, Lorestin pointed down the street.

"There!" he shouted, excitedly. "Your father's car! He can help!"

The driver screeched to a halt, and Lorestin began unloading Hurchial's wounded body. Carrol, Hurchial's father, watched in horror as his bloodied son was pulled from the truck. He rushed up to the cab as Lorestin tried to apologize.

"I'm so sorry, Carrol; it was an accident!"

Carrol didn't waste a minute. He grabbed Hurchial and led him to his car, turning and shouting over his shoulder to Lorestin, "Go inside and call the doctor. Tell him we are coming and need help!"

Hurchial slumped down into the front seat of his father's car and closed his eyes. He was growing light-headed, dizzy, and nauseous.

"It's okay, son," his father encouraged him. "You'll be okay." But five miles down the road, a loud thump jolted Hurchial awake. Something misfired under the hood, and the car slowly rolled to a stop. His father quickly jumped out of the car and opened the hood but was swallowed in a cloud of steam rising from the engine block.

Fortunately, just a minute later, Hurchial's uncle drove up and stopped.

"I heard Hurchial was hurt," he said, jumping out of the truck. "I was coming to the doctor to see if I could help."

"We can't get there!" Carrol replied. "We need your truck!"

Again Hurchial was unloaded from one vehicle and loaded into another. By the time they reached the doctor's office, the doctor was outside on the road. He took one look in the cab at the bloody rags and waved them on to the hospital down the road.

"I can't help him," he said, "but I'll call ahead and make sure they are ready for you."

All in all, it took an hour to get Hurchial from the woods to the hospital. When they burst through the lobby doors, they didn't wait but were rushed straight into an operating room.

The next evening at work a young nurse's aide named Florence was given the unusual assignment of working on the men's floor.

I don't believe it, she thought to herself. *I'd rather work with thirty women than one man!*

But true to her nature, she resolved to do the best job she could even if she didn't like it. She'd been at the hospital for a few years, working after school to help her parents provide for her and ten siblings. She was the responsible oldest child, and after her shift she'd make the two-and-a-half-mile walk home to do her homework and help her brothers and sisters get ready for bed.

She entered the room assigned to her and looked first at the chart.

Gunshot wound, infection around wound, treat with two rounds of penicillin shots.

Florence glanced over the chart to the bed, where Hurchial was lying quietly and reading a comic book.

When she wasn't looking, busy with her work on the other side of the room, Hurchial was peeking over the page, watching her, noticing her dark hair and beautiful eyes.

Every time she entered the room, his heart leapt a little, and his eyes always wandered from his book.

"Here is your dinner," Florence said one night, placing a tray in front of him. He looked over the comic book and smiled. "This isn't mine."

"It is too!" she volleyed back. "Now, eat it all!"

A few minutes later, the dietitian grabbed Florence by the arm and told her, "Here is the food for Mr. Noyes in room 234."

"But I already gave him his tray," Florence replied, suddenly aware of her mistake. Florence rushed back into Hurchial's room and placed the new tray down in front of him.

"Now, that's more like it!" he said, smiling mischievously, with a twinkle in his eye. Florence smiled back, guilty as charged, captivated by his charm.

Over the next few days, sparks of conversation lit room 234 in Rumford Community Hospital. Then Hurchial was discharged.

Three months later Florence opened a letter simply addressed, *Florence, Back Kingdom Road, Mexico, Maine.*

She pulled a fragile valentine from the envelope and turned it over in her hand. *I'm falling for you*, it said, and it was signed, *Hurchial.*

That was the beginning of the beginning, and more than sixty years later Florence still has that valentine carefully wrapped in a dresser drawer. Hurchial and Florence were married one year to the day from his accident and have three wonderful children, five grandchildren, and five great-grandchildren. They have always enjoyed a simple, natural life, focused on family and faith in God. If you ever have the chance to meet them and ask about their story, do. You won't regret it. They will point up the river a mile from their house and smile.

"That's where it all began," they'll say, "with the accident that was no accident at all."

GINA GRAHAM and her husband live in the sunny South. Her most important job is keeping her three teenage boys happy, fed, and productive. Visit Gina at ginagraham.com. She hides a heart symbol in all of her art and often draws a Scottie dog in her illustrations.

47

TWIN CHANCES

ALISA WAGNER

It was three in the morning when nausea forced me awake. I sat bolt upright in bed, panting with my entire body, and then my stomach clenched, and I lurched forward.

"I don't understand," I gasped to myself, my face scrunched with confusion. The sensation wasn't coming from inside me. It was external, as if I were in the grip of a phantom giant slowly squeezing me in his fist.

I got out of bed and padded into the baby's nursery, where my nine-month-old slept soundly in his crib. I looked at his sweet face, and for a moment I felt relief.

He is okay, I thought, stroking his thin hair. The nausea began to fade, but then instantly it wrenched around my waist. I picked up my little boy and cuddled his warm, pliant body to my chest.

What is this feeling? I asked, as the phantom menace gripped me tighter. *Why do I feel like I'm scared? What is happening?*

Just as I reentered my bedroom, the phone rang. I closed my eyes, and my head fell to my chest. *Please, Lord, let everyone be okay,* I prayed as I turned around.

Still carrying my baby, I walked into the living room and picked up the phone. My brother-in-law Eric's voice sounded as if it were inside the earth, bouncing lifelessly off the stones of a deep, dark well. "Your sister's been in a car accident—they're airlifting her to San Antonio."

I dropped to my knees and placed my baby softly on the carpet. "How is she?"

My hands were trembling, and my voice sounded like a stranger's. Why was it suddenly so cold, and why was I kneeling on the floor? The giant was squeezing my chest even tighter. His voice came from the well again. "Not good. They don't know if she'll make it."

I arrived in the ER in San Antonio just after my sister. A doctor put his hand on my arm to stop my headlong rush. He held my eyes in his for a long moment.

"We're doing everything we can," he said. "There's nothing you can do right now."

As we sat anxiously in the waiting room, details from the accident began to emerge. A truck ran a red light and pinned my sister in her car for hours as the emergency responders performed the excruciating task of extracting her body without killing her. She nearly died waiting for them to pull her from the mangled mess of steel, and despite the agony of a crushed chest, she stayed conscious every minute of the long rescue.

The doctor said she was in tremendous pain, and I believed him. I could feel it. The invisible menace that had gripped my stomach had crushed my sister, and I could sense the depth of her suffering as her body lay shattered and dying in a white room down the hall.

She lived through the night, but because of her failing lungs, they couldn't perform essential operations. We waited and waited, and two weeks passed before she was cleared for surgery. During that time, I sat beside her bed, holding her hand. She was in too much pain to talk much, but she did ask me if she was going to die. She even asked me if it was okay to die.

I told her she was going to make it and before she knew it, she would be dancing with Eric and goofing around with her kids.

She would take long, labored breaths, and then ask me again, "Am I going to die?"

I answered her question a thousand times.

After her surgeries my sister continually fought for her life. She endured breathing machines, permanent nerve damage, addictive painkillers, and unrelenting pain, but every time death offered to end her suffering, she declined the invitation. She never gave up, and we never stopped praying, *Lord, we believe in your power to heal, and we ask for a miracle!*

Six years later we see the miracle, and it isn't that she was healed instantly, because she wasn't. The miracle is this—we sit at the park while our children race up steps and launch themselves down a twisty tube slide. It could be a Tuesday morning in March or a Saturday afternoon in June. It could be balmy or threatening rain. What never changes is the presence of my sister, my ever-fixed mark, sitting beside me, alive.

When I think back to the phone call from Eric and the grip of fear that nearly crushed me, I remember something else that I felt: regret. I thought my sister was gone forever and we'd never fulfill our dream of sharing our adult lives together. We had always longed to be side by side, raising our children, sharing holidays, but marriage and jobs had kept us in different cities.

I feared I'd never get the chance to relive our relationship, but thanks to God's mercy, we do. Now we recognize the uncertainty of tomorrow and welcome each day as a miracle. We live in the same town. We compare gray hairs. We sit in companionable silence. We trade tips on how to get our kids to finish their homework and eat their vegetables. We laugh about stories from our childhood and wonder how we got so old. Then we stop and let the truth sink in—we are growing old together.

My sister's accident gave us the gift of a second chance, and every time we see each other, we unwrap the gift as if it's the first time, more grateful for God's grace than ever before.

ALISA WAGNER proudly wears the righteousness of Christ because of her faith in Jesus' sacrifice for her sins. By grace she received the gift of the Holy Spirit, and he and the power of God's Word guide her life and writing. Alisa and her husband, Daniel, enjoy raising their three amazing children: Isaac, Levi, and Kiki. Alisa's identical twin sister, Crissy, is her ministry helpmate, doing all aspects of ministry that writers usually dislike. Alisa writes on her blog, *FaithImagined.com*, and her true hope for her writing is that it communicates the attainable God.

LEMON DROP

Could it be that suffering can actually be a gift, what Sheldon Vanauken called a "severe mercy"? I think so. When we lose the ones we love, or nearly lose them, the world changes—we see things differently. I believe those seasons in life are a severe mercy from God, allowing us the perspective to see what truly matters in life. They help us to stop taking things for granted, they cultivate a grateful spirit, and they remind us that God truly is a good giver.

—Don

48

THE NIGHT YOU WERE BORN

CAROLYN HILL

Y ou can't go!" I glared at him. How dare my husband even suggest going out of town—much less out of the country—the
exact week our daughter, Amy, was expected to give birth to her
first child? Mical pulled the car into the park and stopped under an
ancient oak tree. He rolled down the window and turned to face me.
"Carolyn, I really think I need to go." He spoke in his *patient* voice,
which infuriated me even more.

"You aren't the only man that can lead the mission trip," I stated
flatly, despising the whiny twang in my voice.

"Pastor Bob asked me to lead the team. I am the only builder
going."

"Mical, you've been on more mission trips than I can count. You
know I've never complained, but I need you here this time. What if
something goes wrong? What if Amy has problems or . . . the baby? I
don't know what I'd do if something happened and you weren't here.

I need you." I looked at him, willing him to hear my heart, but he shook his head.

"There's nothing I can do to help here. If I go, it can change people's lives in Jamaica. We're building a church. They've been meeting in a shack." He moved closer and put his arm around my shoulder. As I stared up at him, my heart sank. We'd been married twenty-five years, and I'd seen that look plenty of times—his mind was made up.

Three days later, with Mical and his team on their way to Jamaica, my daughter's contractions began, and we checked her into the maternity ward. Eddie, Amy's husband, joined me and my son, Jonathan, at Amy's bedside, and we began waiting. We tried to take Amy's mind off the pain, but as the contractions intensified, my heart began to compress with each one.

Her eyes registered fear, and tears rolled down her face into her long auburn hair. I tried to comfort and encourage her, but in the dark hours before dawn, we realized something was wrong. "It's her cervix," the doctor explained. "It isn't moving into the right position."

"What does that mean?" Eddie asked.

"It means it can cause harm to the baby. We just have to keep waiting and hope it slides into place." So we waited, all night, and as the first rays of dawn stole through the windows, I traipsed down to the lobby for a cup of coffee. Jonathan's six-foot-three-inch body was sprawled out over a sofa. Across the room Amy's friends Lisa and Randy were asleep on a couch. Another couple, Shannon and Todd, had joined them at some point, and they got up to greet me. I hugged Shannon.

"When did y'all get here?" I asked.

"Last night. We couldn't stay away any longer." I explained that we were still waiting and walked back to Amy's room, feeling comforted that we weren't alone.

Another ten hours wore on, and I again watched the sun slip behind the horizon through the window beside Amy's bed. She had been in labor for twenty-four hours now, and nurses continued to move in and out of the room, saying very little. I watched my daughter, always so full of energy and life, grow tired and pale as contractions continued to exhaust her. Finally, she was given an epidural and mercifully fell into a fitful sleep.

I dozed in the chair beside her, and the night seemed like a disjointed dream. Amy moaning, nurses moving in and out, monitors blinking and bleeping. As the sun came up on Tuesday morning, I brushed the hair back from Amy's face and prayed. "Father, bring this baby here. It's time. Don't let Amy suffer anymore." I had never wanted to talk to Mical more than I did that moment, to lean against him and let him take all the weight and fear away. He'd always been my strength. I needed him so much.

A few hours later while I was still sitting in the darkened room by Amy's bed, my sister called. "Hi," I whispered into the receiver, trying not to wake Amy.

"Sis, an ambulance just picked up Mama Julius. She's had a heart attack. They are taking her to the same hospital you are in." I couldn't breathe. *My precious grandmother—a heart attack? Not now. Oh, please, God. Not now.* Tears washed my face. I had been so excited to introduce her to my first grandchild, and now it might not happen.

I walked down to the waiting room, trying to hold my emotions in check; but as I told the still-growing crowd about Mama Julius, my composure melted, and I cried out the details. I begged them, "Please pray that she lives at least long enough to see the baby."

They gathered around me and prayed for God's mercy. Two hours later I was pulled from Amy's room and told that my grandmother had passed away. My knees buckled, and I sank to the floor, but our crowd of saints once again gathered around me and prayed. After the tears subsided, my friend took my arm and said, "Come on. Wash your face. You've got to get back to Amy's room. She needs you."

In a haze I walked to her room and opened the door. Amy was as white as the sheet she was lying on, and I chose not to tell her about Mama Julius. She needed all her strength, and so did I. Hour after hour passed with Amy still in labor. Every time I walked down the hall, there were more friends and family in the halls and waiting room. I couldn't believe they were still there, waiting, some of them up to forty hours to support us. In spite of the desperate sorrow of losing my grandmother, the weight of worry over my daughter and my unborn grandchild, and the distance of my husband, I knew I wasn't alone.

After forty-five hours in labor, the baby finally moved into the birth position. My son-in-law and I donned the paper scrubs and went into the delivery room. Bright-pink spots flecked Amy's cheeks as she worked to deliver the baby. Eddie coached her like a pro, telling her when to breathe, push, breathe, push. I was giddy with excitement, when suddenly the doctor's voice became urgent. Two nurses quickly jumped onto the bed, one on either side of Amy, and began tugging and pulling on her belly. I dropped to my knees. *Oh, God, what now? I prayed. Save my daughter and granddaughter.*

Tense moments passed in silence, the only sounds coming from the beeping monitors and the nurses' heavy breathing as they pushed my daughter's belly as if they were kneading dough. I held my breath, watching, waiting, and then, almost as quickly as the drama began, the doctor shouted, "That's it!" and a beautiful, perfect baby girl slid into his waiting hands. A lusty wail filled the room as the doctor laid the baby on Amy's stomach. I breathed a prayer of thanksgiving and watched as Amy and Eddie examined their new daughter, total wonder lighting their eyes. I swung open the door to the waiting room and grinned. "She's perfect!" A cheer erupted, and everyone began hugging and crying along with me.

Looking back on that day, I'm reminded of a song recorded by Andraé Crouch years ago called "Through It All." In it he says that without problems, "I wouldn't know that God could solve them." When God allowed my husband to be away during a traumatic time, he brought scores of other people to support and pray for us. I've never felt so much grief and joy at the same time. And I've never felt so loved.

CAROLYN HILL is a retired interior designer living in New Orleans with Mical, her husband of forty-one years. She has written many short stories and is currently working on her first novel.

49 ===

THE EDUCATION OF A
JOBLESS TEACHER

DEREK SMITH

hy did I become a teacher? That was the question—but what was the answer? Certainly it wasn't doing what I had been doing at my last school: using a school-approved curriculum, watching kids flip mindlessly through their workbooks, and anxiously seeing their potential waste away in front of me.

I wanted to teach and scheme and find new ways to reach kids. I wanted to trick students into learning and celebrate with them when their eyes lit up with exciting "aha" moments. Sadly, my school—my home for five years—was going in a direction I didn't want to go, and it was time for a change. I sent out my first round of applications, expecting my résumé, experience, and test scores to make me a shoo-in at any school in the city. I imagined my phone would ring any day, and I'd answer with a clear, professional voice, "Hello. This is Mr. Smith."

"Yes. Mr. Smith, I'm the principal at a very important, influential high school," the voice would say. "Tell me: you worked at a school where 80–90 percent of your students passed the reading and writing exams?"

"That is correct," I'd reply, already awaiting the next question.

"Will you bring your talent to our school?"

"That depends; how much are you offering?"

Not surprisingly, that conversation never happened. What was surprising was the lack of calls I received. Of the thirteen schools I mailed résumés to, only two called me back: Nathan Hale and Renton High. Performing some online research, I discovered Nathan Hale was a school a lot like mine, with high test scores and a middle-to upper-class student body. Renton, on the other hand, was in a low-income community and had the lowest scores in the district. The percentage of students on free-and-reduced lunch was more than double my current school's. I was used to teaching in a 94 percent white school, but Renton was 31 percent Asian, 32 percent Pacific Islander, 37 percent black, 16 percent Hispanic, 14 percent white, and 1 percent Native American. I looked at the numbers on the computer screen and added them up over and over. *That's over 100 percent*, I told myself. *How is that even possible?* I took interviews with both schools, and though my interview at Nathan Hale went exceptionally well, I didn't get the job.

The Renton High interview started with a question about classroom management. "If a student yawns," I said, "I ask him to get out of his chair and show me the pencil sharpener."

"You don't know where it is?" The principal looked at me, confused.

"No," I assured him, "I do, but I'm pretending I don't. It's a management trick."

Somehow, most likely through God's grace, I salvaged the remainder of the interview, and two days later the principal called to offer me the job. When I hung up, I looked around my old classroom, at the collapsed cardboard boxes, half-full Tupperware bins, and swollen manila folders, proof of my pending departure. I needed a minute to think, but more than that, I needed time to stall. Other schools were still reviewing my application. Ballard High School might want me. The people at Holy Names Academy were reaching for the phone at that moment. Weren't they? And then I realized: I was skeptical of Renton because Renton was different. I worried about demographics. I worried about my qualifications. In five years I'd taught 750 students, but only two of those didn't speak fluent English. Much of the student body at Renton was bilingual, and for many, English was a second language.

I called my good friend, a fellow teacher, and asked his advice. He listened to me complain about my fear of the unknown and then cut me off. "You're lucky to get any offer in this economy. Teachers are out of work everywhere. Take the job." He was right. Any offer was a good offer. I called the principal back and took the job.

Four years later, writing these thoughts from the third floor of Renton High School next to a window with a view of downtown Renton, I realize my friend was right. I am lucky. But he's also wrong because I wasn't lucky to get any offer. I was lucky to get *this* offer. Renton High is a special place. I know that now. Five days a week, twelve hundred students gather beneath this roof to spend seven hours learning. It is a diverse student body, coming from all over the world, speaking languages I still struggle to understand, but they are one student body.

Many of our kids show up at parent-teacher conferences alone; some bring single moms; others bring dads, aunts, grandmas, grandpas, and siblings. Many translate for their relatives. During the day a number of Muslim students retreat to the prayer room in the library. In the spring the Vietnamese fan dance brings down the house. Boys sport bright belts and hats that match the neon laces in their shoes. Girls compare Nicki Minaj ringtones. Together they stand in the stairwell, eating Little Caesar's pizza, using their adolescent minds to dream up new ways to get in trouble.

I have learned the school and the students don't need me to figure out their demographics or do the math on the ethnicity survey. The students will tell me who they are, so I need to listen. Sometimes I don't listen, and I rush into speeches about graduation, navigating a tough job climate, or applying to competitive universities. My students look at me and wait for me to come down to earth, where they live day to day, and I apologize for the lofty rhetoric. Every time they give me grace, which is what I give them when their lives get complicated and they ask for understanding. Every day we take a few small steps.

Renton is a lot like church: full of diversity, grace, music, dancing, and unity. Three times a year the students and faculty all crowd the gymnasium floor after the pep assembly and link arms. Together as one voice, a thousand or more people sing the Renton High alma mater.

> *Midst the leafy trees surrounding,*
> *'Neath the spacious skies*
> *Stands alone our hall of wisdom*
> *Knowledge, great and wise*

I thought I joined the staff at Renton so I could teach, but it turns out I go to school every day to learn. My students teach me patience, hope, gratitude, and joy, and I thank God for the knowledge—great and wise.

DEREK SMITH teaches reading and writing and advises the *Arrow* newsmagazine at Renton High School in Renton, Washington. He is currently working on a book about his first year of teaching.

50 ===

UP, UP, UP

KEVIN KALMAN

The early-morning sun stretched over the runway in golden columns of light. Beads of dew glimmered on the grass that lined the long stretch of asphalt, and the sky was a perfect robin's egg blue. I climbed into the cockpit of my best friend's 1954 Luscombe single-engine hand-crank plane and latched the door.

"Good day for flying," I said, buckling the harness around my waist.

"Always a good day for flying," Bob said, smiling. He went through the start-up procedure—checking the gauges, the oil pressure, the tanks—and then hand spun the prop. It slowly turned and sputtered to life, whipping around faster than I could see, cutting into the quiet morning. Bob taxied down the tarmac and steered the nose around until it aimed directly down the runway.

"Let her rip, Bob," I said, and he pulled back on the throttle. We skipped down the black tar asphalt, pulled up into the air, and banked left. The air caught beneath the smooth, rigid wings, and we soared weightlessly into the morning light. The altimeter kept climbing, three hundred feet, four hundred feet, and the world fell away beneath us. The green patches of sectioned Nantucket moors gave way to tan stretches of wave-battered sand, and the shadow of our little plane crept across the surface of the deep Atlantic blue.

"Beautiful," I said, looking down at the Nantucket Sound. We climbed past nine hundred feet, nearly to a thousand feet, and the fishing boats looked like specks of white paint dropped carelessly on a canvas of ocean. Bob reached forward, tapped a gauge, and then sat back with a puzzled look in his eye.

"I'm not sure why—" he began to say, but then the engine cut out. Everything was eerily quiet, and all I could hear was the pounding of my heart and the wind whipping past the plane.

"What?" I shouted, looking at Bob.

"It's not good," he said, quickly reaching for the radio.

"Mayday, mayday!" he said, his voice panicked. "This is SP47Y, and our engine is out. We're going down!" The plane quickly nosed down, and we started losing elevation, fast. Bob steered us back toward the beach and locked in on a dirt parking lot. The wind whistled past, shaking the plane, pulling us back down to earth. The parking lot grew bigger and bigger in the narrow windshield, and my body tensed. I braced myself on the dashboard.

"Up! Up! Up!" I shouted.

"We're all out of up!" Bob screamed. The plane smashed into the dirt lot, jamming the fixed landing gear through the floorboards and up to the roof. The passenger cabin instantly compressed around us, and we skidded down the abandoned lot, flipping over. When we finally came to a stop, I was still conscious, but my back was on fire. I unbuckled myself and crawled out of the wreckage, smelling fuel as it leaked from the shredded tank. I limped around the pile of mangled steel and pulled Bob from the cabin. We lay motionlessly on the dirt, looking up into the serene sky that had nearly hurled us to our deaths.

When the emergency responders arrived, Bob was quickly strapped to a stretcher and flown to Boston for facial reconstruction surgery. I was transported via ambulance to the Nantucket Cottage Hospital, where they stabilized my broken back.

The doctors didn't know how long I'd be in the hospital. A lot depended on how well my back started healing, and I tried to get them to send me home. Surely I could sit around my house, doing nothing, instead of lying around in a tiny, sterile-smelling hospital room, but they refused to release me. During my second week, just before I was about to lose my mind, in walked Betsy, a girl I had known in high school. She was a year older and way too cool for me back in our high school years, but there she was, standing at the foot of my bed.

"Betsy, hi. What are you doing here?"

"I heard about the plane crash," she said, looking just as beautiful as I remembered her. "The entire island is talking about it. The guys in your office said you were going nuts with nothing to do, so I brought you plans for my new house. I figured you could work me up a price while you're sitting around doing nothing!" A quiet moment passed, and we looked into each other's eyes. "Well," she said, "want to take a look?"

I was more than happy to do so.

I did her estimate from my hospital bed, and later that fall, when I was back to work, we broke ground on her house. As the job was progressing, I had a front-row seat to see the way she loved her two sons. She was a wonderful mom, full of joy and patience and energy. I couldn't stop thinking about her, and when her house was about halfway complete, I dug up the courage to ask her out on a date. Everyone told her it was a bad idea to start dating her builder, but she gave me a chance. We went out to dinner for her birthday, and in a magical moment it started to snow. As we walked up Main Street in Nantucket under the streetlights and falling snow, we fell head over heels in love.

My plan for that plane ride day didn't include breaking my back, falling in love, or getting married. But that was twenty-five years ago and too many kids, dogs, stories, and laughs to recall. I tell people I'm the luckiest guy in the world, and they think it is because I survived a plane crash.

I know differently.

KEVIN KALMAN is a native Nantucketer who now resides in Charleston, South Carolina. He is married to Betsy, the love of his life, and has four children, as well as soon to be four grandchildren. He has won several custom home construction and remodeling awards over the last twenty-five years and was featured in a thirteen-part TV series with Bob Vila.

LEMON DROP

Do you think Kevin would choose to go through the plane crash again if he knew so much joy was on the other side? I kind of think so—I know I feel that way about my hunting accident. Usually the things that come with a cost are the ones worth holding on to. I hope Kevin's story encourages you to hang on and not give up; the hardships in your life may be the very thing God needs to bring his greatest blessing.

—Don

51

FATHERLESS

ROBYN DAVIS

The dirt roads around my house were long, windy, and quiet—the perfect place to take a walk and think about life. It was another tough day, and I'd just hung up the phone after another fight with my boyfriend. I needed somewhere to be alone and catch my breath. The gravel crunched beneath the soles of my sneakers, and I kicked the larger rocks off the road into the ditch. I looked up into the endless blue and felt the world spinning beneath my feet.

I could hear a truck coming along, so I stepped over to the side of the road and kept walking. The engine roared up behind me and stopped. The door opened, then closed.

"You doing okay out here all by yourself?" a man's voice said.

I turned around and smiled politely. "Not really; just need to clear my head a little."

"I see," he said, looking into the cab of his truck. "Want a ride?"

Can't I just have some peace and quiet without being interrupted? I thought to myself. He was still waiting for an answer, with his arm outstretched, pointing to the empty seat and inviting me in.

"No thanks. I'll keep walking." I turned around and started back down the road. Then I heard his footsteps behind me, starting slowly, then faster. By the time I turned back, he was right behind me. He put his hand over my mouth, forced me to the ground, and pinned me to the road.

"You just keep quiet," he said as he tore my clothes from my body. His hands grabbed at me and held me down, and all I could do was look up into the endless blue and wait for him to finish. When he was done, he threatened me: "You tell anyone, and I'll come hurt you." Then he drove off.

Who would I tell? I wondered, walking home, ashamed and confused. *I don't know his name. I didn't get his license plate number.* I walked straight into my bathroom and turned on the shower. The hot water scalded my body, and I tried to wash away the feel of his hands. I scrubbed my skin and washed my hair over and over until the water ran cold and I started shivering.

Four weeks later I missed my period. Then I started waking up feeling nauseated. I bought a home pregnancy test and discovered I was pregnant. I held the test results in my hand, shaking, hardly believing this was my life in front of me. *Is this nightmare ever going to end?* I wept to myself.

My first thought was to get an abortion. I couldn't imagine having a child, let alone this child from this man who had used me, hurt me, and violated me. *Would the baby look like him? Would he find out and hurt the baby? What will my parents think? What will my church think?* I had kept the rape to myself because I was so ashamed. *Will anyone believe me now?*

I sat down with my parents in the living room and started crying.

Mom tried to console me, but I told her she didn't understand. I could feel the secret creeping up inside of me, begging to get out.

"I'm pregnant," I cried, "but it's not what you think. I was raped . . . on the road . . . and I was afraid to tell you." The three of us cried for the rest of the night. My mother was the first to suggest an abortion; she knew how time-consuming children were, and she felt it was unfair that I'd had pregnancy forced on me.

"I can't do it, Mom," I told her a few days later. "I have to keep the baby."

My mother was incredible. She embraced me, supported me, and encouraged me through the pregnancy. My father, the pastor of a small Texas church, felt the congregation had a right to know, but I didn't want them to know I was raped. My parents respected my wishes for the details of what happened to remain private.

I endured the usual morning sickness, sensitivity to smell, weight gain, and body-image issues, but the hardest part of pregnancy was coming to terms with the life inside of me. I didn't love my baby. I resented the baby for ruining my life. I was terrified of being a parent. When I found out the baby was a girl, I was overwhelmed with relief. I was positive I couldn't love a boy. I'd never be able to look him in the eyes without seeing the face of the man from the road.

The first time I felt my baby move was the first time I thought I could love her, and as she grew, so did my affection. At church, where everyone assumed I had gotten pregnant by choice, people stopped hugging me. Others stopped shaking my hand. Some stopped talking to me altogether. I decided to stop going to service and instead help my mother with the children's church, but it wasn't long before complaints were spreading. "She shouldn't be teaching the children," they said. "She is a bad example." When my friend called the church to reserve a room for my baby shower, she was told to keep looking because the church didn't support teen pregnancy. Then a deacon ordered me to confess my sin in front of the congregation. I refused and never went back.

I felt as if the church had abandoned me. I was young and pregnant. I was scared and uncertain, and I needed help and support from other mothers. I wanted to know that my child would be welcome at church, but her birth wasn't even allowed to be celebrated. She was unwanted, cast aside, not because of who she was but how she had come into being. Why was my child a problem and another child a blessing? Isn't every life precious? Didn't God also form her in the womb?

I started college that fall, prepared a room for the baby, and on January 29, 2010, welcomed her into my life. The first time I held her in my arms, I knew I had made the right choice. She opened her eyes and looked into mine, and my heart broke wide open, pouring out a love so strong and unconditional I knew it would last forever. I thought of Jeremiah 1:5: "I knew you before I formed you in your mother's womb." Then Psalm 139:13, "You . . . knit me together in my mother's womb," and John 10:10, "My purpose is to give them a rich and satisfying life." Feeling her soft skin on mine, I knew with certainty that God had come to give me and my little girl life.

A few days after she was born, I was watching her sleep in her bassinet. Slowly, letter by letter, I filled out the birth certificate. I penned in the date and my name, then paused at the line that read "Father's Name." I looked over to my little girl, smiled, and recited Psalm 68:5: God is a "Father to the fatherless."

I never would have expected the most traumatic event of my life to become a blessing, but being a single parent of a child born from rape has transformed me. My daughter has opened my eyes, captivated my heart, and led me to do some serious soul-searching. Just after her second birthday, we joined a new church. She loves to sing along and tell me everything she learns in Sunday school. I light up when I see her surrounded by loving friends and family. I watch her smile and dance, and I thank God for a living story that reminds me of his blessings and his love.

ROBYN DAVIS is a young mother to the most adorable little girl in the world and is currently studying as a junior in college. She hopes to someday start a shelter for teen mothers.

52

SINK OR SWIM

WYNDEE PHILLIPS

D o you see that slide that starts way up there?" my dad asked me, kneeling down, pointing up to the top of a white, shiny, plastic waterslide. I turned and looked at him, my eyes open wide with excitement.

"Do we get to go on that one?" I asked him in my cute three-year-old voice.

"Of course!" he said, scooping me up, heading for the stairs. We climbed all the way up, and he held my hand the entire way. Then we sat down, and he counted, "Three . . . two . . ." His body rocked back and forth on each count. ". . . one!" He thrust us forward down the slide, and I closed my eyes with his big hands holding me close.

When we hit the water, I wasn't holding my breath, and he couldn't hold on to me, so I started sinking to the bottom. I don't know how long I was underwater or if I almost died or not, but when my dad finally pulled me from the pool, I was deathly afraid of ever getting back in.

A few years later my fourth-grade class went on a field trip to hunt crawdads in the river, but I wouldn't get near the water. I was terrified, and despite my parents' best efforts to help me overcome my fear, I simply couldn't. I failed swim lesson after swim lesson.

As I started middle school, we made an ordinary trip to the beach near my relatives' house in Southern California, and as usual I made sure to stay a safe distance from the water. But somehow I got distracted, and a large wave snuck up behind me and pulled me into the frothy ocean. I kicked and screamed and panicked; with my arms weighed down with seaweed, I dragged myself back to dry land.

I stopped going to the beach after that, and aside from taking a shower, I don't think I went near water for several years. But during my sophomore year, a cute boy I liked and who was a friend stopped talking to me. Actually, he didn't just stop talking to me; he started saying really mean things about me and spread nasty rumors around the school. His sudden change of heart confused me, and I thought if I could spend some more time with him, he would see none of the things he was saying were true. I didn't know how or where I'd get close enough to change his mind about me, but then a mutual friend informed me he was joining the swim team. *The swim team*, I thought to myself. *I can join the swim team too.*

Somehow the years of terror and trauma had been mysteriously blocked from my memory, and sure enough, I signed up to join the swim team. Without saying a word about my lifelong fear, my mom signed the form and sent me off to school the first day of practice.

It wasn't pretty, my first month on the team. Every time I put my face in the water I started hyperventilating. I had to get out of the pool and sit on the side, breathing heavily into a brown paper bag. *Great*, I thought to myself. *Sitting on the pool deck, making a fool of myself—who wants to be friends with the hyperventilating nonswimmer on the swim team?*

I kept at it, though, and by the end of the season, I was actually competing in races. By the end of my sophomore year, I was a varsity swimmer, slicing through the water, breathing confidently between strokes, placing in several of my races.

It's funny, looking back. I don't remember what happened with the boy I liked. I don't think I ever discovered the reasons for his sudden change of heart, but it didn't matter. I had overcome my greatest fear, and that was the greatest blessing I'd ever known. It inspired me to help others overcome their fears too. So, oddly enough, the summer after my sophomore year, I went back to the same pool where I'd failed my lessons as a kid and received my certification. I've been instructing swimmers of all ages for eleven years.

My specialty is helping children and adults who are scared of the water, just as I was. I don't have to imagine or wonder what it's like to be afraid to swim. I know, and that knowledge gives me the patience needed to help others conquer their fears. Every now and then a thankful parent or student tells me about a successful family trip to the lake or the river or the beach. I smile when I hear those stories, but not as much as when parents tell me their children now have the confidence to try other things that previously seemed impossible.

I look back today and am thankful for my experiences. Even though they were painful on many levels—physically, mentally, and socially—they ultimately led me back into the pool, where I have the honor of working with wonderful, brave, courageous little swimmers. They remind me daily that we get to choose how to handle our pain. It can define us, or it can transform us. Many of my students are mocked by their classmates for their inability to swim, and many of them are truly terrified of the water. But here is the thing: they are at the pool. Their inadequacies do not define them. Sure, they start by splashing around the edge of the pool, but eventually they let go and float to the middle of the water. They look down and see the bottom of the deep end, blurry beneath their feet, and smile. I smile, and I think God smiles too, because it takes faith to overcome a fear.

WYNDEE PHILLIPS was born in Southern California and moved to central Oregon when she was five years old. After overcoming her fear of swimming, she had the confidence to pursue other dreams, which included moving to New York City at eighteen years of age. Wyndee is now married, has three beautiful daughters, and lives in Bend, Oregon.

53

A TOUGH BREAK

MATT MCGOLDRICK

The late-summer sun rose high over the Rocky Mountains to the sound of our ATVs tearing up the trail. My dad was in front of me, leaning into the turns, accelerating up the straights, climbing to the top of Vail Pass, and I was right on his tail. When we reached the top, we couldn't wipe the smiles from our faces. The view was stunning, and our hands still buzzed from the vibrations of the engines' power.

"Not a bad way to spend a morning," my dad said, looking out over the valley.

I turned around, enjoying the panorama of the mountains. "Not bad at all."

"Okay, let's take a picture for your mother and get back," my dad said, balancing his camera on the seat of the ATV. "We have three hours before your appointment." My appointment. The very reason we had traveled all the way from Atlanta, Georgia, to Vail, Colorado, was to visit the doctor about my knee. I had torn the ACL in my left knee three times in high school: once as a freshman, later as a sophomore, and, lastly, in the spring of my junior year. Needless to say, I spent most of my soccer career watching from the sidelines with crutches.

After the third injury I underwent two surgeries in Vail and was told I'd never play soccer again. I moped around for months feeling confused and angry, wondering why God would rob me of my childhood dream to play college soccer. *You took away my favorite thing*, I kept thinking, blaming God. I was so depressed I thought about not attending college at all. Fortunately I found out from the doctor that my limitations were mostly lateral, so sports like soccer, basketball, and football were forbidden. But I could still run. I researched schools with cross-country programs and was accepted to Lee University, where I could join their cross-country team. The first semester of my freshman year was set to begin in three days, and we were in Vail to get the final okay from the doctor.

"Okay, smile." We both grinned from ear to ear, and the timer on the camera counted down. "All right," Dad said, "be safe going down. Mom is going to be so upset if you have another accident."

I had heard it a thousand times before but played along. "Sure thing. I'll follow you." We hopped back on the ATVs and cranked the engines. My dad pushed the throttle, shifted into first gear, and peeled out down the trail. I followed him through a series of switchbacks and then accelerated up behind him. Pine trees blurred past me, and I managed to look down at the speedometer: forty-five miles per hour.

Dad turned again to the right, and it didn't look very sharp, so I held my speed. But before I could see the dramatic bend in the trail, the tires hit the sandy bank, and I lost control. The handlebars hit square against a tree, and the momentum threw me forward into the air and spun me around until I was stopped by a tree. My back cracked against the bark, and I tumbled to the ground.

The impact was so violent my shoes flew off, and my shirt ripped in half. I lay there for several minutes, curled up in pain, coughing, trying to catch my wind, when I realized I was at least forty feet from the trail. *You have to crawl back up to where they can see you*, I told myself, *or they will never find you*. I dragged myself up the incline and collapsed onto the trail. My dad was long gone, ripping down the mountain, unaware that I had crashed behind him. The forest was quiet for a long time, and my back was on fire. I lay there, looking up into the blue sky over the Rocky Mountains, wondering how badly I was hurt. *Mom is going to be so upset*, I thought, waiting for someone to find me and take me down the mountain.

Finally I heard the high-pitched whine of an ATV. A group of tourists rounded the corner, heading up the mountain, and quickly cut their engines when they saw me. One guy jumped off and asked me if I could walk, which I couldn't. They sent word to the bottom of the mountain for a rescue vehicle.

Fifteen minutes later my dad came back around the corner and found me lying on the ground, covered with jackets and surrounded by a large group of morning thrill-seekers.

"What happened?" he asked, leaning down next to me.

"I was going too fast; I couldn't turn." Then the truly terrifying thought struck me again. "Mom is going to die; she is going to be so upset."

Dad shook his head. "She definitely won't be happy." When the rescue truck arrived, they loaded me into the cab and drove slowly down the dirt road to our car. Mom met us at the bottom of the moun-tain and burst into tears when she saw me dazed and hurt.

"I'm sorry, Mom," I said, as Dad helped me into the back of the car. Despite the searing pain and stiffness in my back, I managed to hobble into the emergency room. They took me back to a room for X-rays, scans, and tests, and when the doctor came back into the room, he stuck the X-ray films into the light box. He flipped it on, illuminating the image of my back.

"You can see here," he said, pointing at a small crack, "and here, and here, and here." My eyes followed his finger down the picture of my spine. "You broke four transverse processes in your lower back." He turned and looked at me. "It's going to hurt for a while, but you will be okay."

The doctor was right—it did hurt. I struggled to focus in class and couldn't shake the pain while studying. As my grades dropped lower and lower, I took more and more painkillers, but nothing helped. I began to wonder how long I'd live in pain. *I don't understand, God,* I continued my accusations. *First my knee and now cross-country and school? Why do you keep taking everything from me?*

Halfway through my first term, my mom called and told me she was coming to take me out to lunch. She made the drive, picked me up, and took me to P.F. Chang's for a nice meal. We chatted about school and things back home, and right after the bill came, a look of fear flashed across her face, and her voice cracked.

"Honey, I have something I need to talk with you about." I could hardly hear her in the loud restaurant. "The doctors called us and said they found a tumor at the base of your spinal column. They want to see you again right away, so we have scheduled you an appointment for tomorrow." *A tumor?* I wondered to myself, driving to the hospital the next day. *How did they find a tumor?*

I sat down in the doctor's office with my parents and listened. "Matt, we noticed something in your MRI," the doctor explained, "and after looking at the results from the other tests, we are confident it is a tumor growing inside your spinal column. It is the size of my thumb, and without treatment it will eventually paralyze you."

I was frozen, suddenly face-to-face with the reality God had orchestrated. *If I hadn't torn my ACL three times, I never would have gone to Vail, wrecked the ATV, broken my back, had the X-rays, and discovered the tumor.* Suddenly all the questions and frustrations disappeared, and something new took hold of me: gratitude.

The surgery to remove the benign tumor was a success, and I'm still moving, walking, running, and enjoying every chance I get to participate in sports. I can't compete at the same level I did before my surgery, but I've been given a much greater blessing: an unwavering assurance of God's goodness.

Always outdoors and on the move, MATT McGOLDRICK continues to compete in a men's soccer league. He recently graduated with a degree in business administration and currently enjoys sharing his passion for athletics as a staff member of a local gym.

LEMON DROP

Matt's story reminds me to always look for the blessings going on behind the scenes. Usually my first response to something that hurts is to ask, "Really, God?" Thanks to Matt and other Lemonade stories, I'm continually encouraged to embrace Psalm 126:5: "Those who plant in tears will harvest with shouts of joy." Planting in tears certainly isn't easy, but it is an act of faith that trusts God to transform our pain into something beautiful.

—Don

54

THE SURPRISE CHILD

CONNIE COOK

Neil, we have to talk." He turned away from the TV—toward his wife, Mae—and looked blankly into her eyes. "I have to tell you what the doctor told me."

"You're pregnant again!" he cut in. "I was afraid of it."

"Yes, I am, but that's not—"

"We're too old for this," he interrupted again. "You're forty; you'll be forty-one by the time the baby's born. It'll be like starting a family again. The baby will be like an only child."

"Neil, do you want this baby?" Mae asked point-blank. He turned back to the TV. The colored pixels flickered off his face.

"What difference does it make what I want?" His voice was monotone. "It's happening."

"There are . . . options. That's what the doctor talked to me about."

Neil turned to face her again. She had his full attention now. "What d'you mean?"

"Things have changed. A woman no longer has to carry a . . ." She paused and took a deep breath. "Pregnancy. Not if there are risks to her health. The doctor thinks it may be better. I'll be over forty soon. And the baby . . . it might not be normal, you know. There's a greater chance, with me being older, that the baby will have issues. The doctor wanted me to know my options. I need to know what you think."

He looked back at his program to avoid meeting her eyes and mumbled, "What does it matter what I think? What do you want? It can't be up to me. Do you want this baby?"

"You know I don't." There was no sense denying it. "After five kids, there'll be ten years between this one and Tim. Do you think I want to do this all over again? I thought I was done. I'd hoped I was done."

"Well then," Neil said slowly, "it's got to be up to you, doesn't it?"

"I need your help."

"With what? It's got to be your decision. How can I help you with it?"

"I need to know what you think, what you want. I can't make this decision alone."

Neil refused to look at her. "I can't help you decide. It's got to be up to you," he repeated. Mae knew he didn't want the child, but it didn't help. She was no closer to knowing what to do. An abortion would be so easy, right? She tried to remember what she'd heard from friends and radio shows and her pastor, but it never mattered to her then. She hadn't had any reason to think about it until now.

It occurred to her that maybe she should ask God what he thought about her pregnancy and about the possibility of . . . what words had the doctor used? Terminating the pregnancy? She sat quietly with her Bible folded on her lap and closed her eyes. *Lord, I'm scared and so alone.* She thought back to her childhood and her grandmother Vida, teaching her about God's love in Sunday school. She could still hear her voice talking about the faithfulness of God and his constant provision. Then Mae felt a gentle nudge to answer one simple question: *God created the little life inside of you, right?* Her eyes welled up with tears, and she knew exactly what she needed to do. She blew her nose, swabbed her wet cheeks, and stood up. *Okay,* she said to herself, feeling her stomach, *it's decided.*

By the time I was born, Mom had adjusted to the idea of having another baby. Once the discomfort of pregnancy and the pain of childbirth were past, she was excited. I always knew I was loved by both of my parents, but Dad grew increasingly distant toward Mom. When I was thirteen, after all my brothers and sisters had left home, my dad left too.

Those were dark days for my mom. When Dad remarried, it just made things harder. It was during that time that she told me the story of her pregnancy and my birth—of the doctor who had recommended abortion, of her own uncertainty, of my dad's noncommittal response. She told me the story not to upset me but to help me understand what she had come to understand: that God doesn't make mistakes. In the midst of her pain and heartbreak, she often told me, "I can't imagine what I'd do right now if God hadn't given you to me. He knew I needed you." That was years ago, and now I'm a long way from thirteen.

Mom is eighty, and she has Parkinson's. She is no longer able to live alone or take care of herself, so a few years ago I moved back to my hometown to look after her. It was something I'd always known I wanted to do when the time came, and I'm grateful I was in a position to do so. Whenever I help my mom around the house or spend the night sharing stories with her, I'm reminded of what she taught me as a girl: that God doesn't make mistakes. God gave us to each other for a reason, and neither of us can imagine life without the other.

CONNIE COOK lives in Creston, British Columbia, where she was born and raised. She is a full-time, live-in caregiver. She has completed her training with New Tribes Mission and hopes someday to use her training on a cross-cultural mission field.

55 ═══

A GRANDMA'S HEART

ANNE FORLINE

M y husband and I are orphans. By the time we were in our early forties, both sets of our parents had passed on. I lost both my mom and dad to cancer. Steve's parents died from heart trouble and cancer. Both of our fathers died before we even met each other, and while both moms were alive to see us get married, only mine was alive to help us celebrate the birth of our daughter, Cara.

Steve hates it when I tell people, "We're orphans." But it's true. Steve and I don't have our parents around anymore, and we miss them terribly, but the true tragedy is that Cara has no grandparents to dote on her. She can't pull rank and call a grandparent to help get her out of trouble, and she doesn't have anyone to invite to "Bring Your Grandparent" events. She does have lots of aunts, uncles, and cousins to cheer her on at her softball and soccer games, but she has a grandparent void.

From the time we moved into our house several years ago, we

maintained friendly relationships with most of our neighbors. One neighbor, Rose, lives two houses down and is well into her seventies. We were cordial but not close. We'd smile and wave to each other as we put our trash cans away and exchange pleasantries if we saw each other at the supermarket. Other than that, we hardly interacted.

Then one day Cara came barreling through the house, yelling, "Mom, look! Miss Rose got a puppy. Can we go see it?" We went outside and saw Rose holding a leash that had a tiny, white puffball at the end. Cara made it to Rose's house before I got to the end of our walkway. Rose motioned to Cara and said to her, "Do you want to see the puppy? I just got her." Cara immediately sat down cross-legged on the ground, and the puppy hopped into her lap. By then, I had caught up.

"She's so cute. What's her name?" I asked, stooping down to rub the pup's head.

"Meesha," Rose replied. "My mother used to call people that name all the time. We think it means 'little girl' in another language." She continued, "I don't know if you heard, but my husband is very sick. He's been in and out of the hospital, and the doctors say he doesn't have long."

"I didn't know. I'm so sorry," I apologized.

"It's okay," Rose answered. "That's why I got a puppy to keep me company. Now, if I only knew someone who could help me walk her . . ."

"I can!" Cara interjected. "Can I, Mom, please?"

"Sure," I answered. And so began Cara and Meesha's daily routine. Each day we'd go to Rose's house and wait for her to hook on Meesha's leash. Then we would take Meesha to the park. Sometimes when we brought Meesha home, Rose would give Cara a candy bar. Once, she reached into her pocket and produced a few dollars, which

I unwisely tried to intercept: "No, Rose. You don't have to pay us. We enjoy walking Meesha."

Rose smiled sweetly and looked at me point-blank. "This isn't for you. It's for her," she said as she stuffed the money into Cara's hand. "You're my special friend," she told Cara.

"Thank you!" Cara exclaimed. "I'm saving my money for doll clothes. There's a cart in the mall that sells doll dresses, and I almost have enough to buy one."

Later that evening there was a knock at the door. It was Rose. "Is Cara here?" she asked.

"She's at youth group with Steve. Do you need me to walk Meesha?" I replied.

"No, I went to the mall, and I found the cart with the doll clothes. I wanted to surprise Cara with one of the fancy doll dresses," she explained. She carefully opened a package wrapped in white tissue paper. It revealed a cherry-red velvet dress with white fur trim.

I said, "Rose, you didn't have to."

"You're right," she responded. "I wanted to." Then she held up a pair of tiny white patent leather boots that went with the dress. She asked, "Do you think she'll like them?"

"Yes, Rose," I assured her. "She'll love them."

A few weeks later when we made our daily trek to Rose's house, several cars were parked out front. When we knocked on the door, her daughter Cheryl answered.

"Is Rose here?" I asked. "We usually take Meesha for her walk."

"She's at the funeral home, making arrangements," she answered. "My father passed away this morning."

"We're so sorry. We'll come back another time," I answered.

"No," Cheryl responded, dabbing her eyes with a tissue. "Mom said you'd be coming by for Meesha. Let me get her leash on."

It wasn't long after her husband died when Rose invited Cara and me into her house. After Rose unhooked Meesha, she announced, "I'm bored, and I'm going back to work."

"Good for you!" I answered.

"I have a favor to ask," she continued. "If I give you a house key, would you still be able to walk Meesha while I'm at work?"

"Absolutely," I assured her. So we continued our daily walks with Meesha. Each day we'd leave a note for Rose, telling her about Meesha's adventures. We would write, "Meesha chased a squirrel today," or "Meesha got a treat from the mailman," and then leave the note for her. Rose always left us a note in reply. "Thank you for walking Meesha. Help yourself to some of the bananas," or "Take some tomatoes."

Once we were bringing Meesha home as Rose was pulling up from work. It was dinnertime, and she was holding a box of doughnuts. She explained she was expecting company. As I put Meesha's leash away, I heard Rose offer Cara a doughnut. "Take a chocolate one; they're the best," she encouraged.

"I didn't eat my dinner yet," Cara answered.

"So what?" Rose told her. "Sometimes it's fun to have dessert first." I bit my tongue as Cara took a huge bite of a chocolate sprinkled doughnut.

I started to notice that Rose would often tell me to put Meesha's leash away so she could spend a little extra time with Cara.

"What's new?" she asked Cara.

"I'm taking a cooking class. I learned how to peel potatoes, and I made an apple turnover," Cara responded. Rose was fast on her feet.

"Do you have a potato peeler? An apple slicer?" She started rummaging through her kitchen drawers and produced one of each and handed them to Cara.

"These are great!" Cara answered. "These are just like the ones we use in class. Thanks so much."

"You're welcome, sweetheart," Rose said as she hugged her. "See you tomorrow." As Rose closed the door and we started to walk home, Cara said, "Mom, Miss Rose really loves me, doesn't she?"

"Yes, Cara," I responded. "She sure does."

ANNE FORLINE lives in Bellmawr, New Jersey, with her husband, Steven; daughter, Cara; and two bunnies, Patches and JoJo. Anne is a homeschool mom, a freelance writer, and a second-grade teacher at an after-school program. She and Steve teach in their church's junior department, coach Cara's sports teams, and volunteer with "For Bunny Sake," a rabbit rescue whose mission is to find homes for abandoned domestic bunnies. Visit her blog, *Write Stuff*, at anneforline. blogspot.com.

56

FALLING INTO GRACE

DAVID WATERMAN

What's your name?" I asked the stranger, looking at his pleated slacks and clean shirt.

"My name is Luis," he replied. "It's very nice to meet you." We shook hands, and I wondered if he'd hold up on the job site. It was midsummer, and I was working construction for a general contractor, gutting and rebuilding a fire-damaged building. I'd been on the site for a few weeks, working with a colleague, ripping the carpet from the floor, tearing out the drywall, sweeping up endless piles of ash. We had stabilized the structure the previous week, and we were finally ready to start work on the exterior brick.

But my colleague had called in sick, so my boss hired temporary help to fill in for the day. Luis, with the slick-looking slacks and soft hands, was my only help for the next ten hours. We climbed up the stairs to the second floor, and I explained the process.

"You'll mix the mortar here, then pass it through the window, and I'll lay the brick. We'll work from here"—I pointed to the corner

286

of the building—"down to that end there." His gaze followed my finger, and he nodded. "Good then. Let's get started."

It was just after eight thirty, and I knew it was going to be a long day. The scaffolding was already hot, and there was no way we'd get as much done as I wanted.

"So, Luis," I spoke up, tired of wondering why a guy would wear slacks to a job site, "how long have you been in construction?"

He looked up from the mortar and laughed. "No, amigo, I am not a construction worker. I am a doctor."

"Really? How did you end up out here today?"

"I had a little trouble this morning on the highway," Luis said. "I blew some tires and need money to buy more. Crazy, no?" The smile on his face was gone, and his gaze was unflinching. It was easy to see he was telling the truth.

"Really! A doctor mixing cement!" I said it out loud so I could hear it myself and maybe begin to believe it. Then I peppered him with questions, one after another. "What kind of doctor are you? Do you still practice? Why are you in here? Shouldn't you be in a hospital somewhere?"

He answered every question gracefully, and his story was so enthralling we talked straight up to and through our lunch break. It turns out Luis was a doctor in the military, and after he retired, he was on vacation when an American tourist led him to Christ. He went on to study in the seminary, and when he finished, he started a medical ministry in the most poverty-stricken part of Mexico. He was on his way to Denver to meet several donors when his car had a flat tire. Having already used his spare, and with no money for a fix, he looked for the first job he could find.

"My car came to a stop in the parking lot of your boss," Luis said. "I went into his office and told him I needed to earn money so I can buy new tires, so he sent me here." Inspired by his testimony, I began sharing stories from my work as an evangelist. But as I was sharing, still sweating beneath the sweltering sun, I suddenly became dizzy. I tried to brace myself on the wall in front of me, but as I reached forward, it began to fall away. I tried to shout a warning to Luis that the wall was collapsing, but it wasn't the wall; it was me. I fell three stories and landed flat on my back atop the sand heap used for mortar mix. Across the street from the job site, an emergency room nurse who was at home, sick for the first time in thirteen years, shuffled into her kitchen for a cold drink. With the water running into her glass, she looked up through her window and saw a man falling.

Waiting at a red light on his drive home from work, a paramedic crept out into the intersection. As the traffic cleared, he looked up at the burned-out building wrapped in scaffolding and saw a man fall three stories.

When the nurse reached the scene, she found a Mexican construction worker performing chest compressions on my lifeless body.

"I saw him fall," she said, rushing up to his side. "I'm a nurse, I can help."

"Yes, my name is Luis. I am a doctor." The nurse looked at him quizzically.

"We were working," Luis continued, "and he became dizzy. He is dehydrated from the heat." The nurse knelt down and took over the compression, and Luis began artificial respiration.

"Do you need help?" the paramedic shouted, rushing up to the scene. "I have a radio. I can call it in." He pulled his two-way radio from his emergency bag and dialed in the frequency. Suddenly my eyes snapped open, and I sat up.

"It's okay, David; just keep still," Luis said, gently laying me back down. "You fell a long way. You need to go to the hospital." As I lay back down and closed my eyes, I could hear a stranger in the background calling for help.

"You're a lucky man," the ER doctor told me later that night. "You broke a few ribs. There are also a few hairline fractures, and your back will be bruised for a while. It will be uncomfortable, but you'll be okay." He put the clipboard back into the wire basket at the end of my bed and folded his arms. "I mean it when I say you're a lucky man," he said. "Your heart stopped when you landed on that sandpile. If it weren't for your coworker doing CPR, you wouldn't be here right now."

A few days later my boss came to visit me at home. He was a tough man with a worn face, weathered by a lifetime of hard work; a difficult relationship with his missionary father had led him to a strong dislike for all things Christian.

"We got the doctor off to Denver," he told me. "I gave him a set of new tires and paid him too." He talked as if my fall and survival were business as usual.

Still in pain and a little out of things, I chuckled. "First time I've had a doctor mixing cement for me—of all the days for you to hire him!" He nodded. "And the fact that I fell onto the sandpile," I added. "A few inches to the left or right, and I'd have split my head open on brick! God is good!"

"Not so good," he shook his head. "You fell. If he were good, he would have stopped the fall!"

"Well," I said, "I'm sure there is a reason why I'm still here. God didn't keep me alive on accident."

A year later my boss was working on a transmission when the tractor slipped off the jacks and crushed him. While he was in the hospital with severe injuries, our company secretary went to visit him often, and one day she led him to Christ. She told me that she used my story as an example of grace and provision, and it encouraged my boss to trust in the goodness of God.

I remembered the doctor telling me I was lucky to have survived, but *luck* is a funny word. It doesn't feel as though chance or coincidence put all the right people in the right place at the right time. And I don't even believe they were there for me that day. Sure, they saved my life, and that is a miracle all its own. But God was up to something bigger. I may have been the one who tripped from the scaffolding, but ultimately my boss is the one who fell into the grace of God.

DAVID WATERMAN is a bi-vocational missionary working in construction to raise money for missionary work. He has planted churches on reservations, pastored churches, and traveled as an evangelist. He also advises missionaries around the world on water supply development and construction projects.

LEMON DROP

I think David's story is a powerful reminder that our stories are never truly our own. No matter how small we think we are, each of us is part of a bigger narrative, the story of God, which he uses to reach countless others. David understands that his fall and recovery were not just for him. It changed his boss's life, and the thing is, his story has probably changed many others too.

—Don

57

THE LITTLE BIKER THAT COULD

KAREN HESSEN

"Mommy, Tom is on the phone," Tina called from down the hallway.

"Okay," I replied, shuffling over to the receiver.

"Hi, Tom. Is everything okay?"

"Everything's good!" he said, excited. "You'd better get up here and bring your camera. We'll be out back."

"We'll be right there," I said.

"Tina, put your coat on!" I yelled, running down the hallway. "We have to go see Tom." It was a cold, blustery day in mid-December. Our small, rural community had been recently blanketed with snow. The apple orchards were bare—only snow clung to the naked branches. It was about four miles from our house to Winnie Wakely School, at the top of the hill where my son Kurtis received his physical therapy three times a week. Lots of physical therapists had worked with Kurtis over the years, but Tom was special. He knew what was important to a six-year-old boy: things like wearing normal shoes without braces, riding a bicycle, and having little plastic caps on the ends of your shoelaces so frayed ends don't make lacing impossible. Tom also knew that boys who wore belts with hard-to-work buckles might end up peeing down their legs.

As Tina and I drove slowly through the barren orchards up the winding country road, I thought about how excited Kurtis must be and how thankful I was for Tom to be in his life. Every six months we met to set goals for Kurtis's development. Our goal this time around was for Kurtis to be riding a bicycle by Christmas. He had sent a letter to Santa requesting a new two-wheeler, and it was just nine days until Christmas. This was his last session with Tom until after the holiday.

Kurtis was an abused child whom I had adopted when he was twenty-three months old. He was a beautiful boy with hair like spun gold, eyes the color of warm caramel, and ivory skin as smooth as cream. The traumatic brain injury that occurred when he was fifteen months old had left him delayed in almost every area of his development. His left leg was two inches shorter than the right. The muscles of his left thigh and calf had atrophied. He wore a heavy lift and leg brace on his left shoe to allow his foot to reach the floor. His left leg was essentially just a stabilizer for standing; it could not function to pedal a bicycle. God would need to work a miracle for Kurtis to learn to ride a bike.

I parked my Jeep in the snow-covered parking lot under the ponderosa pines. Tina and I went through the special education building to the covered play area behind the school. We could see Tom running alongside the bicycle with Kurtis balanced on the seat. Tina and I began to clap and cheer, but Kurtis just gave us the "What's the big deal?" look. He thought Tom was still holding the bike upright behind him. So as Kurtis turned the bike to head back in our direction, Tom changed his pace and ran up ahead where Kurtis could see him.

Kurtis looked at Tom, then looked at me. The happiest smile I'd ever seen flashed across his beautiful face. "I don't beleeb it! I don't beleeb it!" he shouted with joy as he rode past, his right leg doing the work for his left. Tina, always his biggest fan, clapped and cheered him on. I wiped the tears from my cheeks and shouted, "Look at you, Kurtis! You're riding a bike!" He just kept pedaling, watching, and grinning. Proud of his accomplishment, he rode out of the covered play area, onto the basketball court, and straight into the basketball goal. Undaunted, he picked himself up, threw his left leg—brace and all—over the bar, then rode back to receive his congratulations.

When he dismounted the bike, I wrapped him up in a huge hug and lifted him up off the ground. *Thank you, God, for this miracle*, I prayed silently, still crying. It was a very merry Christmas, indeed!

KAREN HESSEN is an author and speaker. She and her husband, Douglas, live in Forest Grove and Seaside, Oregon. She has two adult adopted children. She considers her genre inspirational nonfiction but has found her niche writing humor. Visit Karen's website at karenrhessen.com.

58

BEHIND BARS

DANIELLE BARRETT

Laura walked tentatively into the room and sat down in the back. The chairs were lined up, facing the front of the room, and a microphone was plugged into a speaker system. She glanced around at the other women, some sitting silently, others chatting quietly. She readjusted herself in the chair and looked toward the door. *This is a bad idea*, she told herself. *I shouldn't be here. This isn't going to help anything.*

As she stood up to leave, a woman approached her through the aisle of chairs. Her hand was out, and she was smiling. "Hi. Welcome to Kairos Outside," she said.

Laura reached up and shook her hand. "Hi," she said, struggling to look her in the eye.

"Is this your first time here?" the woman asked. Laura nodded. "Well, we are so glad you came. My name is Julie, and I help organize. What is your name?"

"Laura," she replied, and they both sat down.

"Nice to meet you, Laura. Tell me, why are you here tonight?" Laura paused. It wasn't an easy thing to talk about. It had been several years since her two sons were sentenced to time in prison, and she'd spent every day since feeling embarrassed, ashamed, and depressed. *What kind of mother raises criminals?* she often asked herself, heaping guilt atop her broken heart. Convinced her life was destroyed beyond repair, she had kept her pain to herself. But now Julie was sitting quietly beside her, waiting for an answer.

"Um," she stuttered, "both of my boys are locked up in San Quentin." Julie reached out, took her hands, and began nodding slowly.

"You're in the right place. Everyone here knows what you are going through." Laura looked into her eyes and saw her genuine concern. Her body relaxed, and she took a deep breath. It felt good to tell someone and not be turned away. "You picked a good night to come too," Julie continued. "We have a great guest speaker. His name is Mike."

Mike, a man who watched his son go through the prison system, spoke openly about his pain and fear of rejection. Laura listened intently, amazed at how accurately he described her emotions. "I didn't want to go anywhere or talk to anyone," he said, his voice carrying loudly through the sound system. "I was embarrassed. I thought people would reject me because my son was a criminal. I thought they would label me a bad person. I didn't want people to know, so I hid."

When Mike finished speaking, Laura sat down with him and spoke openly about what she was experiencing. He listened with an attentive ear and understood her pain. Over the next few months they shared several conversations, which led to a few dates. A year after meeting at Kairos, Laura and Mike were married. Who would have thought that the most painful experience she had been forced to endure would lead to the most amazing love of her life?

Their love is as uncommon as the place they met. They understand each other's pain, encourage each other in hard times, and support each other at court appointments and visitations. They share it all, and it unites them in a powerful way. Because of their unique experience, they routinely visit juvenile hall to speak with young boys locked up for the first time. It still feels like pouring salt on a wound when Laura speaks publicly about her boys, but she does it, believing her experience will help others change their story. Together, she and Mike ask those boys to imagine their entire life behind bars, and they help them understand how hard it is on parents to lose their children to prison. More important, Laura and Mike show them love and forgiveness. They accept them. They give them compassion and mercy. They listen to their stories. They talk to all of the kids as though they are their own, telling them that no matter what they have done or where they go, God's love will never leave them.*

DANIELLE BARRETT has been part of the Rock Church Prison Ministry in San Diego for five years and has spent the last three years on the juvenile hall team.

---

*Names and locations in this story have been changed to protect the privacy of the family.

59 =====

SWEPT AWAY

ERIKA HOFFMAN

I squeezed the dirty water from the sponge and wiped the sweat from my brow. The stove was only half clean, and the annual scrubbing for the upcoming rental season was wearing me out.

"Let's go for a short swim," I called to my husband in the other room. It was late afternoon, and I could see from our beach house window that the shore was nearly abandoned. I pulled off my sticky work clothes and slid into my black swimsuit and skirt accessory. Call me old-fashioned or just old, but I am of the age where I prefer buying bathing suits with skirts. I never go swimming without one.

Reluctantly my husband traipsed after me toward the water. He and I had been short with each other earlier, and I could tell he wasn't particularly excited to be getting wet. When I sauntered into the water, he stood only calf-deep.

"Come on! It's not cold if you immerse yourself!" I urged, rolling my eyes at his hesitancy. "Cold water won't kill you!" I paddled about in the gentle waves, and my husband finally swam out to meet me.

We were floating ten feet from the shore when a large wave came over us and pulled us both out. I realized I was over my head and asked my husband if he could touch bottom.

"No." He shook his head, spitting seawater from his mouth. I started the breaststroke toward shore but made no headway. I tried an Australian crawl, fighting against the current, but the undertow pulled me farther out. I exerted. I strained. I went nowhere.

"Hold on to me!" I yelled. My husband reached for my fingers, but the waves pushed us apart.

"Swim in with the next wave," he answered. We both tried. Like being in a vortex, we were pinned down in a current of water that tugged us backward. The beach was thirty feet from us, but it might as well have been miles. We were losing the battle. I was weak. I couldn't stay up. I couldn't even float.

"I can't make it," I said.

"Help!" yelled my husband, with anxiousness in his eyes. He began waving his arms, crossing them. "Help!" he cried out, scanning the shore. No one was in sight. We bobbed helplessly with our heads barely above water. In the pit of my stomach, I knew it was over. I thought of our kids. I thought of the headlines. I thought how we'd die here, a stone's throw from shore.

"I can't go on. I can't," I murmured. He looked worried and was still an arm's length from me. He grabbed for my fingertips but couldn't hold them. With the last touch of our hands, hands that had touched for forty years, I knew we were goners.

A swell pushed him in a little. His toe hit sand. He turned sideways, reached back, and grabbed my skirt. The wave relentlessly tugged me out, but he clutched that scrap of fabric and struggled forward.

"I'm too tired," he said.

"Don't let go," I begged him. He thrust on, fighting the waves as they tried to pull us apart forever. The skirt's stretchy material tightened. The waistband surged away from me. He yanked me forward, and my toes scraped land. Too weak to stand, I crawled uphill, clawing the sand, and collapsed. My husband lay next to me, waves smacking over his exhausted body. *Where's help?* I thought. I couldn't lift my head. I couldn't turn. My head was pounding. I lay inert, limp as a dead fish.

"Byron?" I called for my husband, but there was no answer. I dozed off. I woke to a noisy machine and lifted my chin to spy a dune buggy with a lifeguard bolting up the coast. He was high up on the beach, near the houses, and he passed without ever looking over at the ocean.

"You okay?" I yelled into the wind. My husband wasn't as high on the incline as I. He was still partially submerged.

"My heart is racing," he said. "Someone will come." I have no concept of the time that passed. We were like castaways portrayed in movies, enervated from fighting the relentless sea. Stillness enveloped me. I heard a dog bark.

"Can you move?" I asked.

"Let me stay here awhile." We lay still. My mind still couldn't grasp we hadn't died.

Nothing was different about the sea that day. Nothing gave us pause. There were no red flags to warn that our little dip would turn into an epic struggle for survival. But we had survived somehow.

After a while we headed to the wooden bench on the public stairway overlooking the sea, where we had deposited our towels and flip-flops a lifetime ago. A couple there studied us and asked how we were.

"We almost drowned," I said. The guy smiled and then realized we were sincere.

"I saw you lying at the water's edge. I wondered. I didn't know . . ." he said.

"The wind kept people from hearing us," I said. "But my husband saved my life."

Tranquillity has settled over me since our brush with death. I learned that I am on borrowed time. I learned how uncertain the future is. I rediscovered how deeply I love my husband. When a cross word forms on my lips, directed at my spouse, I take out that black swimming skirt, stretched out and frayed, and remember how I was doomed and reborn. I thank my husband again and again for not letting go.

Accidents happen, and by God's grace we survived. We have found a new hope for the future, resilience we didn't know we had, and most important, love. We emerged kinder, gentler, and better. We smile more, enjoy life more, and accept every day for what it really is: a gift.

ERIKA HOFFMAN pens nonfiction narratives that appear frequently in nationally known anthologies, religious magazines, and e-zines. She also writes mysteries.

LEMON DROP

Sometimes we have to nearly lose someone to know how much we really love that person—why is that? Maybe our love grows cold and distant with time and distractions, but as Erika's story shows, it's never too late for a second chance. Her story has inspired me to imagine my life without my loved ones, and when I do, it sweeps me back into their arms with gratitude and joy.

—Don

60

PENNILESS BUT NOT BROKE

DIANE WILLIAMS

When I was thirty-seven, I woke up at 2:00 a.m. to sweat-soaked sheets and a fire in my body. My joints were swollen, tender to the touch, and my aching limbs lay life-less in the bed, burning and sweating from every pore. Unbeknownst to me, I was suffering from rheumatoid arthritis, and by the time I was diagnosed, it was too late for precautionary measures. I would remain immobilized the rest of my life.

My husband didn't like the sound of caring for a wife with special needs, so he packed a bag and disappeared, leaving me broke, unemployed, immobile, and solely responsible for raising our two pre-teen daughters. It also meant Tiffany and Jasmine were the only ones left to care for me, which they did—twenty-four hours a day, seven days a week—while going to school and preserving remnants of their own identities. It was hard, exhausting work, and it didn't take long for the stress to begin tearing us apart.

I told them as often as I could, "There are many valleys that need to be crossed while climbing toward the mountain." But they just stared at me blankly, as if to say, "Yeah, Mom, we get it; big deal." I wanted them to know everything would be okay, but truth be told, I didn't know that for certain. I myself felt scared and insecure; after all, everything I had trusted in had disappeared and left me hurting. To make it through, I made a promise with God that I would only allow myself five minutes of pity at a time. I'd let it hurt, I'd cry, but then I'd move on and get back to thinking about my girls.

We needed something to bring us together, something big, and I had been praying for a miracle the day Tiffany came home from school and told me about a summer program called Young Scholars. It was sponsored by the Junior Statesmen of America Foundation and convened every summer at Yale University. She immediately applied, and five weeks later, the mail carrier delivered a letter congratulating Tiffany on her acceptance. There was only one problem—she needed to raise three thousand dollars.

"How am I going to raise that much money?" Tiffany huffed, before leaving me alone in the room with her acceptance package on the table. I flipped through the program flyer that came with her acceptance letter and quickly became flooded with emotions. I was angry at the disease that had burned through our savings and kept me from working. I also felt guilty about not being able to help. Pity consumed me, and for five minutes I felt helpless and entirely hopeless.

Then suddenly I remembered the principle I had embedded in my daughters' minds: *there are many valleys that need to be crossed while climbing toward the mountain.* I bowed my head and prayed, *Please, God, show me the way. Show me how I can help Tiffany raise the money.* I began to visualize my daughter at Yale, doing everything the flyer described: walking through the museums, taking classes, asking professors questions, soaking up knowledge. *Help me, Lord, to make this a reality. Please.*

Randomly, a short phrase flashed across my mind—*penniless, but not broke*—and I remembered my old job as a community youth director. There I worked as a fund-raiser, helping to run many successful campaigns. *We can do this*, I thought to myself. *I know what to do!* "Tiffany!" I shouted for her to come back into the room. When she rounded the corner, I didn't waste a second. "Are you committed to work for this money?" Slowly she nodded, a little confused about my newfound enthusiasm. "Good. Now let's ask your sister for her help." Jazzy joined us at the table, and I outlined what needed to happen if we were going to implement an effective fund-raising campaign. By the end of the week we had prepared a media kit to be mailed out, and thanks to Jazzy's computer skills, it was a beautiful piece of work. During the second week, we began mailing, and at the beginning of week three, Tiffany awoke to my frantic yelling.

"The *Los Angeles Times* wants to interview you, your teachers, your sister, and me!" I shouted, elated, as Tiffany danced around with excitement. By the time Tiffany left home that morning, she had scheduled interviews with reporters for most of the week. Once the *Los Angeles Times* printed its article, *U-T San Diego* and several other nationwide newspapers picked up Tiffany's story.

The following week I woke Tiffany again with excitement in my voice. Two donors had just called, complimented Jazzy's work, and said Tiffany should start packing because they wanted to finance her entire trip.

"What?" Tiffany shouted when I told her the news.

"Yes! You're going to Yale!" I said it as loudly as I could, celebrating with every word.

"I'm going to Yale! I'm going to Yale!" she chanted, smiling from ear to ear.

"And that's not all," I cut in. "A third donor said your story touched her heart, and she wants to come meet you, at home, tomorrow." When the doorbell rang the following day, Tiffany rushed to swing the door open. On the porch was a well-dressed middle-aged woman who introduced herself and stepped inside.

"I am so proud of your daughter," she said, looking at me. Then she looked back to Tiffany. "The reporter didn't mention anything about clothing, accessories, or spending money in the article. Tiffany, you worked hard. Congratulations!" The woman handed her two money orders totaling fifteen hundred dollars. "Go shopping, and have some fun in New York. If that's not enough, please let me know. Money will not be the factor that keeps you from attending Yale and having a good time this summer." I tried to hold back the tears as Tiffany embraced the generous woman and promised to contact her with some pictures when she returned.

By the time the summer was over, Tiffany had received donations from her school's administration, teachers, friends, and anonymous supporters. Even the mayor of La Verne, California, mailed a check. Tiffany's time at Yale was richly rewarding, and she aced both of her courses. When she came home in the early fall, she had a long list of stories, lessons, and experiences. "Mom," she said one day after she was back, "when Dad left and Jazzy and I had to take care of you, I was angry. I thought my life was over."

So did I, Tiff, I thought to myself.

"But I'm not worried anymore," Tiffany continued. "I feel like I'm just getting started." It was true: it did feel as though God had renewed our spirits and given us a second chance. He brought us together when we needed it most, and reminded us all that the valleys of our lives may leave us penniless, but they will never leave us broke.

DIANE WILLIAMS is the author of *Angels in Action* and is currently working on her soon-to-be-released book *The Invisible Child—A Memoir*. Her work has been published in *Guideposts, Angels on Earth, Plus, Pray!* magazine, and the San Dimas Writer's Workshop's *Tales from the Authors: Stories, Essays, and Poetry*, volume 1. Visit her blog at mindofagoddess.wordpress.com.

61

A LONG, ROUGH RIDE

JIM COON

Kendra knew a lot about pain for a fifth grader. She couldn't do a handstand or a cartwheel. She couldn't clap for her friends when they jumped off the swings. She couldn't play the clarinet like most of the other girls in her school. She couldn't even raise both of her hands in gym class when the teacher said, "Reach for the stars!"

It wasn't her fault. She wanted to be like the other kids, but she was born with a severe birth defect that caused her right arm to stop growing at the elbow. As hard as she tried to forget about the one thing that made her different, the other kids wouldn't let her forget. They teased her constantly. The truly nasty ones even pulled their arms up into their shirtsleeves and ran around armless, pretending they were Kendra.

When I met her in 1997 through a mentorship program, Kendra was a very bold young lady. I would hear her tell other students to "get a life" when they taunted her about her deformity. But in private Kendra would tell me how tired it made her to be defensive all the time. "I just want to be normal for once," she said, sulking, with heavy shoulders.

"It's okay, Kendra," I told her. "You're beautiful just the way you are. Don't worry about them."

When Christmas came around, she surprised me with a thoughtful card. It was handmade, and when I opened it later that night at home, I couldn't keep from crying.

Dear Mr. Coon, she wrote, *all I want for Christmas is a new arm.* I could sense the desperation in her handwriting, and I agreed there would be no better gift for a young, beautiful little girl. I did a little research on prosthetic limbs and quickly discovered the prohibitive costs. It would cost at least five thousand dollars for a new arm, money my wife and I didn't have and couldn't save for at the time.

After the holidays passed, I returned to my normal routine of working, exercising, and mentoring kids at Kendra's school. One morning while I was suffering through an hour of aerobic exercise at spin class, I was thinking of Kendra's Christmas card. I was reminded of how much she had suffered in her short life and how it made my hard-breathing, muscle-burning workout seem insignificant.

Then it hit me. *If I can suffer a little bit, doing something extreme, maybe I can find sponsors and raise money for Kendra.* Sure enough, soon thereafter I spotted an ad for the two-hundred-mile Seattle-to-Portland bike ride and signed up on the spot. Not wanting to camp overnight and finish the ride in two days, I opted for the one-day option.

My wife was a little confused about my idea. "But you don't have a bike," she kept saying, which was true. So I bought an entry-level ten-speed, brought it home, and started riding around the neighborhood. I knew the Seattle-to-Portland ride was going to be a lot different from a spin class, but I knew I could do it.

When the morning of the ride arrived, I had lined up several sponsors willing to donate to Kendra's arm fund. All I had to do was ride two hundred miles and cross a state line, and it would be done. Kendra would have a new arm! I had no idea when I began pedaling at 5:00 a.m. that most riders had trained for several months for the event. Most of them, I found out later, rode two hundred miles per week with at least one ride more than fifty miles. I had ridden my ten-speed seventy miles a week at the most, so eight hours into the ride, when both of my knees looked like cantaloupes, I was surprised.

It is just bike riding, I told myself, trying to ignore the relentless pain. Each time I lifted my leg to crank the pedal, my knees pulsed and burned. I fought through, one excruciating stroke at a time, but twenty-five miles from the finish line, I simply fell over. I had been riding for thirteen hours straight, and my knees were refusing to move another mile. I tried to pick my bike up and straddle the seat, but my body disobeyed, and I tumbled back to the curb.

I can't finish, I told myself, upset that I couldn't pull through for Kendra. I called my wife, Gloria, and she and our daughter drove to St. Helens, Oregon, where they found me sitting on the curb outside a 7-Eleven with a bag of ice on each knee. Gloria looked at my knees, my heavy steel bike, the sad look on my face, and didn't say a word. She just drove me home and put me to bed. I was so sick I couldn't even eat.

The next morning I asked my wife to take me back to the spot where I had stopped riding. I didn't care how much it hurt or if I was alone: I was going to finish and earn the money people had pledged toward Kendra's new arm. But just like the day before, my body refused, unable to take even a small, unsupported step. As I stumbled back to bed, I wondered how I would tell Kendra and her parents that

I came up short, that there would be no arm because the money was pledged with the knowledge that I would finish the entire course.

But over the next few days, as my donors found out about my pain-filled failure, they sent their donations anyway. I guess my effort was enough to inspire their generosity, and by the end of the week, I had the five thousand dollars to purchase Kendra's new arm.

Three months later I stood in the parking lot of Kendra's school and smiled as she rode a bike for the first time in her life. She zipped past, back and forth, with two arms balancing the handlebars. Her joy spread wide through the asphalt lot, as the sound of her laughter came from the depths of her healed heart. Then she stopped in front of me, dismounted the bike, and ran up to me, saying, "C'mere, Mr. Coon. I'm gonna give you a big hug with both my arms!"

I have experienced lots of trials since that ride from Seattle to Portland many years ago. When I do, I remember two things. First, Kendra was a pillar of strength and fought to gain respect from those who teased her. If she could do it, I can do it. Second, all things are possible with God. Even when things hurt too much to carry on and the finish line feels a million miles away, we can always dig a little deeper and go a little farther than we think.

JIM COON is owner with his wife, Gloria, of a real-estate firm in Bend, Oregon. He has been married for thirty years and has two wonderful daughters and a great son. The following year after raising the money for Kendra, he trained hard and rode the entire Seattle-to-Portland two-hundred-mile cycling event in one day. His entire family met him at the finish line.

62 ⹀⹀

EMPTY COKE BOTTLES

LUKE BELING

The ache was deep and pulsing, burning from his foot up to his knee. It had been five years since the accident at the plant, and he still couldn't work. He could hardly walk, and after two years of fighting insurance companies for a claim, he gave up and gave in to life on the streets.

He'd been begging for three years, waking up every morning with cracked lips, a dry mouth, an empty stomach, and the aching leg. He'd hobble to the intersections with the most pedestrians and wait for someone to look him in the eye. He wanted their money, but not as much as he wanted a conversation. Would anybody see him? Could they see him? He waited every day, hungry and hoping for a friend to share his story.

One Saturday morning he was warmed awake by the slow rising sun. He sat up beneath a scraggly oak tree and rubbed the sleep from his eyes. The residential neighborhood was a good, quiet place to sleep but a tough place to beg. He wondered where the day would take him. Maybe to the curb by the market? Possibly the block of restaurants downtown?

Inside, just behind the wall where the beggar sat, Luke heard the kettle hissing with hot water in the kitchen. He extinguished the gas flame and poured a cup of coffee. He leaned on the counter and looked out into the morning light. He had the entire day before him, open and free. No school, studying, or homework. He imagined the possibilities. Football in the park. A bike ride. Relaxing on the beach with friends. Finally, a day without responsibilities—except for one. Fetching the newspaper for his dad from the driveway was a Saturday tradition in their family. Dad woke up, drank coffee, smoked cigarettes, and read the paper. Luke couldn't remember it being any other way.

Luke put down his cup of coffee and unlocked the gate to their driveway. He stepped out onto the street and grabbed the paper from the sidewalk, then opened the mailbox and retrieved a handful of letters. He turned to go back inside, but a voice caught his attention.

"Please, boss, please." The voice was quiet and desperate, and Luke could hardly hear him over the traffic. He turned and looked to the beggar now sitting in the shade of the oak tree. His eyes were wide with hope and his hand was up.

Luke knew he wasn't supposed to talk to the beggars outside the house. He could hear his dad's voice: "Don't talk to those guys; they will only make trouble!" He thought about stepping back through the gate, delivering the paper, and getting on with his Saturday, but he was stuck, staring at the tattered man.

Another voice was speaking within him, strong yet gentle. *He lifts the poor from the dust and the needy from the garbage dump. He sets them among princes, placing them in seats of honor.*

This man should be seated like a prince, Luke thought as he knelt down next to him. "I don't have any money, but I can get you water and food." The beggar smiled wide, and he nodded with enthusiasm. "Thank you, boss, thank you!"

Luke jogged back up to the house and pulled some apples, bananas, pears, and oranges from the fruit bowl. He tossed them into a grocery sack, added a loaf of bread and some bottles of water, and started back to the street. As he made his way down the driveway, the light refracting from a glass bottle on the porch shone in his eye. He squinted and turned his head, then suddenly stopped.

Empty Coke bottles! He can turn those in for money! he thought. Quickly he ran back up to the house, swiped his sister's backpack, and stuffed it with six empty Coke bottles.

Luke opened the front gate and knelt down next to the man.

"What is your name?" he asked.

The beggar licked his lips and nodded his head. "Henry, boss. My name is Henry."

"Henry, it's nice to meet you. I'm Luke. I found some things for you that should get you through the day. I also have these Coke bottles. You can take them to the deli and redeem them for money."

Henry nodded, and Luke put his hand on his shoulder. "Before you go, can I pray with you?"

"Yes, boss, please. Thank you."

Luke began to pray. "God, you own the cattle on a thousand hills. Provide a job for Henry, restore his life, and give him money. Lots of it!" Luke opened his eyes and saw Henry smiling, looking up to heaven.

"Thank you, boss, thank you," he said over and over, as he collected his belongings and shuffled painfully away down the street.

The next morning Luke's mom burst into his room shouting, "Luke! Wake up, Luke! There is someone at the gate, yelling your name!" He raced down to the gate, half-dressed, wondering what could be so urgent on Sunday morning. When he reached the gate, he swung it open and found Henry, jumping up and down, smiling from ear to ear.

"Boss! Boss, Luke! I have wonderful news! You won't believe it!" Luke stepped through the gate as Henry launched into his story. "After you prayed for me yesterday, I went right to the deli to swap those heavy bottles for money. Just as I was leaving, an *umlungu**** tapped me on my back. He was smiling and happy to see me, and I knew it was my old boss because of his nose. I can never forget his nose!"

"Your old boss?" Luke asked, trying to piece together the details.

"Yes! My boss from the power plant, from way back. He said they had been looking for me for a long time because the insurance company finally came through with the money, and they had three thousand dollars for me!"

Henry's voice softened, and his eyes became moist. "Boss, Luke, I didn't know what to tell him. I fell to my knees and wept out loud, thanking Jesus right there in the market! Everyone just looked at me funny, but I couldn't stop!"

"Henry, that is incredible!" Luke exclaimed, completely stunned.

"But," Henry continued, "the best news is that he told me they have a new job opening for me at the plant. I am going to train people to do my old job. He said I can work in the office and not hurt my leg. I get to work again!"

Henry's eyes were shining like diamonds as he finished his story. "Jesus saved me, boss, thanks to those empty Coke bottles and your prayer!"

Luke and Henry embraced and stained their shirts with tears.

Umlungu is a Zulu word for "white person."

Henry broke into song, his voice carrying the melody of an African folk tune, praising God for his goodness. Luke joined him, and soon the neighbors were staring through their curtains. An old black beggar and a young white kid, dancing and singing at six in the morning in apartheid-era South Africa, worshiping the God who owns the cattle on a thousand hills, seats the poor with princes, and answers the prayers of his children.

LUKE BELING is a native of the rainbow nation, South Africa. He has a heart for the poor, lonely, and forgotten of this world. His dream is to minister among the poor with the compassion and love of Jesus, and then tell of it through written stories. Currently he resides with his wife in Rochester, Minnesota, where he coaches tennis, teaches English, and writes.

LEMON DROP

Luke's story teaches me that if we want to be a part of the divine story, we have to value what God values, even if it means going against accepted social conventions. In Luke's case, he was a young white boy befriending a poor black man in a particularly race-divided culture. Luke knew his actions wouldn't please others or his father, but he couldn't quiet the voice of God urging him to reach out with a helping hand. He acted, and as a result, he became part of a miracle. Makes me wonder how many miracles you and I will be a part of if we listen to the voice of God, even when it means challenging accepted cultural norms.

—Don

63

TEN DAYS IN DALLAS

DONNA MATTHEWS

I didn't want to call him. I knew I had to, and eventually I would, but I called everyone else first. It wasn't easy news to hear, but they took it okay. I told them everything I had heard so far and said, "I don't know yet," to the questions they were bound to ask.

When? Where? Why? Should we come now? How long should we stay?

It was too soon to know the details. "I'll call back when I have more information. I'm so sorry," I said mournfully.

"I'm sorry too. Love you, Mom," they all said before hanging up.

Then it was his turn. I hated to call with such heartbreaking news; things were already hard enough as they were. The loss of his father, the military lifestyle, the three young boys at home, the tenuous relationship with his wife, and now this.

"Lord, please be with him," I said as I picked up the receiver.

"Hello?"

"Nik, it's Mom." My voice was shaky and tired.

"Mom? Are you okay?"

"No, honey. I'm so sorry. I received a call this morning. Someone found your brother Jody. He hanged himself."

When my husband and I were married, I brought three children to the marriage, and he brought five. Then we had two kids of our own; Nik was the youngest. Our house was always full of energy and mischief, and Nik was usually at the middle of the mayhem. When his brothers and sisters reached the age to leave home, he dreaded saying good-bye. They were his best friends, and he loved them dearly.

When he graduated high school, he married his sweetheart, Krystal, and joined the air force. Their first son came along quickly, followed by twins. The pressure of serving in Anchorage, Alaska, memories of two tours of Iraq, and the stress of raising three boys was taking a toll on his marriage with Krystal. He was drinking a lot, she was emotionally disconnected, and they had recently decided a divorce would be best.

Nik didn't say much after I shared the news. He was silent for a long time, and then he hung up. A few hours later he called back and told me the air force would let him come home to Dallas. He would make the trip by himself.

"What about Krystal and the boys?" I asked, trying not to be too intrusive.

"She doesn't want to come."

"Are you sure?"

"Yeah. I have to go, Mom. I'll see you soon."

I lowered the phone from my ear, and the dial tone hung in the air.

Alone? I thought to myself. *I don't like this. They all need to be here.*

I wrote Nik and Krystal quick e-mails, checking in, saying hi, and hoping a conversation would start about the trip. I called as often as I could. And I prayed, a lot.

Lord, please allow them to come together. They need this time. We all do.

Then Nik called again. "Mom," he said, "I found out the air force will fly all five of us home. We can stay for two weeks."

In the days leading up to the memorial, we didn't have a spare minute to sit and be a family. It was the first time we had all been together in two years, but we were buried beneath an avalanche of details. Finally, with the whole family exhausted and overwhelmed, the service arrived, and we were able to celebrate Jody's life and begin grieving his loss.

After the service Nik and Krystal came back to our house with the boys. Everything was behind us now—the shock, the planning, the reunion, the service—and the house was so quiet. My husband picked up the boys and took them to the backyard to play while Nik, Krystal, and I sat silently on the back porch.

"I already miss Jody," Nik said, staring blankly at the horizon. "I haven't seen him in two years, but now just knowing I can't see him makes me miss him."

Nik erupted with tears, and Krystal and I joined him. As the afternoon faded into night, we sat circled on the porch, crying, hugging, talking, and sharing the grief together. We had begun to mourn, and the emotional outpouring freed Nik and Krystal to begin talking about their relationship. It wasn't easy listening to them blame each other for their problems, but they were finally talking about their issues, and as I listened, I prayed that it was a new beginning for their marriage.

A few days and several emotional conversations later, I was in the kitchen preparing dinner at the sink. Behind me I heard some footsteps, and before I could ask who it was, I felt two arms wrap around me from behind. Nik leaned in to my ear and squeezed me tight.

"Mom, Krystal and I are going to give it another try." Then I heard Krystal by my side, and I began to cry so hard it made them laugh, which only made me cry harder. I grabbed both of them and hugged them as tight as I could, as if they had both just survived a tornado and I thought I'd lost them forever.

Recently Nik and Krystal celebrated their eighth wedding anniversary. After they returned to Alaska from our house in Dallas, they settled into a new rhythm. Nik quit drinking, Krystal stopped hiding her emotions, and their boys became the light of their lives.

To this day I'm not sure what exactly happened between them during their stay in Dallas, but I know with certainty it changed the trajectory of their lives. When I told a well-meaning friend the good news about Nik and Krystal, she suggested God planned Jody's death in order to save their relationship.

I don't think that is true. When I pray, I don't thank God that

Jody's life is ended. I thank him for the grace that allowed something good to come out of something bad. After all, isn't that what redemption is all about? And aren't we all in need of redemption from time to time?

DONNA MATTHEWS is a retired RN living in Wister, Oklahoma.

64

MARKED BY LOVE

SHARIE ROBBINS

I'll never forget my husband's face as he stood by my hospital bed, grinning ear to ear with joy as he held our youngest daughter for the first time. Our baby Justine, our third child, was healthy and happy in her father's arms.

I'll also never forget my husband's face as he told me about his own doctor's appointment. It had only been six months since we took Justine home, and we had just found our stride with our new family routine. Quinn explained that the doctors confirmed he had a genetic disease called Alport syndrome, and unfortunately there was no way to reverse it. They could provide medication and treatments, but eventually he would need a kidney transplant. When that time would come, we had no idea; it was anybody's guess. Fortunately Quinn's diagnosis was early, so his treatment was limited to dietary regulations and medication. He was healthy and strong enough to work, play with our children, and go to church with us on the weekends.

It was new for us as a family to attend a Sunday service, but

Quinn's health issues came with lots of questions about life and death. We found refuge in the story of God and comfort from the congregation members, and before long we had both accepted Christ and begun trusting him with our family, our careers, and yes, even our health.

Then it happened. Six years after we discovered his illness, Quinn could no longer survive without a transplant. The fears we had buried long ago about finding the right donor at the right time resurfaced. What if we couldn't find the right match? How long could he live without a transplant?

We were both very mindful that God was in control of our situation. And we had a sense of peace that surpassed all understanding of those around us. We drove to the hospital and met with the transplant team. "Quinn, you will be placed on a cadaver donor list," one doctor informed us. "Oftentimes it is a very long wait for a match, so we need to talk about other options." We held hands and listened to the suggestions. "First, do you know if any of Quinn's family members are able to donate? It's quite common for blood relatives to be identical organ matches, and it significantly speeds up the process." I could see Quinn shaking his head. His brother also had kidney disease, and his other family members could not donate due to their religious beliefs. Who else was there?

I looked back to the doctors. "I want to be tested!" The doctors looked at me in amazement. Quinn knew that I had talked about being tested, but in this moment he was still unsure if that was what he wanted me to do. It may have sounded liked a surprise, but truthfully it was far from it. Since the day Quinn was diagnosed, I had been harboring the hope that I would be able to donate one of my own kidneys.

"Test me," I insisted. "I might be a match." The doctors shuffled uncomfortably in their chairs. Clearly, they were convinced I hadn't been paying attention.

"The odds of a spouse being a successful donor are slim to none," said one doctor, speaking slowly so I was sure to understand him. I squeezed Quinn's hand and looked him in the eyes.

"I am sure that is true, but something in my heart won't rest until I am tested and I know for sure. God works best when the chances are slim to none." I looked back to the donor team. "Please, test me." Three days later our phone rang, and Quinn and I both were overcome with thankfulness when the doctor told us, "Not only are you a match; you're almost a perfect match!"

"Can you believe it?" Quinn shouted as he hung up the phone. He hugged me, and the phone calls started coming in from our family and friends, all doing their best to encourage us to reconsider our decision. Who would care for our children while we both recovered from major surgery? What if something went wrong, and they were left without a father? Or a mother? Or both?

We defended our decision, confident it was no accident that I was a donor match. Quinn and I were meant to be together. We knew it to be true the day we were married, and we believed it now more than ever. We would go through this ordeal together, side by side, sharing the surgery, the scars, and the outcome.

Two weeks before the surgery, I was asked to visit the psychologist at the hospital. He shared some of his experience from working with donors and asked me, "Are you aware that many donors end up resenting the recipient?"

"Resent Quinn? There is no way; he is my husband," I assured him.

"Yes, of course, but believe me: I have seen it before. This is a very difficult operation. The recovery is slow and painful, and there is a lot of time to think. There is also no guarantee his body will accept your kidney. If that is the case, there is no rewind. You won't get your kidney back. What you will have, whether the transplant is successful or not, is a long scar running up your back."

Suddenly I was uneasy. Why was he telling me these things? Where was the support? Did no one think this was a good decision? "I appreciate your concern," I told the psychologist, regaining my resolve, "but I have made up my mind. I'm going to do this for my husband."

Later that night after the kids were down and Quinn was out running errands, I drew a hot bath. As I soaked in the warm water, I started thinking about what the doctor had said earlier that day. I wondered how I would cope with the ugly scar that would be left on my body. *Am I making the right decision?* I began crying. *What if they are right? What if it doesn't work? What if Quinn sees my scar and thinks I'm ugly? Will he still look at me in the same way, or will we both see it as a reminder of a bad decision?*

My tears dripped into the water and rippled toward the porcelain tub. "Lord, I am going to do this, but I need strength. Take away my vanity. Please help me."

Two weeks later Quinn was healing brilliantly. My kidney was cooperating with his system, and it looked as though his disease would be a thing of the past for our family. Still, I went to my two-week post-op appointment heavily burdened. I would finally see the extent of the damage to my skin, which I had only been imagining since the surgery. As the doctor removed my bandage, he chirped, "That looks beautiful!"

"Oh, is it healing well?" I responded, assuming his sarcasm. "How ugly is it, Doctor?"

Looking at me strangely, he asked, "Don't you know?" When I said that I didn't know, a small smile played on his lips. "We were able to have a visiting plastic surgeon come in to finish your operation," he explained. "Your scar will hardly be noticeable in a year or so." I stood and walked to the mirror, gently twisting so I could see my back. The scar was a vertical line no wider than a pencil, and it stretched from my hip bone to the bottom of my bra strap. Just two weeks since my surgery, and already the angry red was fading—as if a gentle hand had traced a smooth line across my skin.

It was beautiful.

Fourteen years after the transplant, my husband remains perfectly healthy. I don't think about my scar every day anymore, but when I do, I take a moment to touch it with my fingertips. It is now a thin, pale line. In my scar I don't see pain or sacrifice. Instead I see a mark traced on my body by love, connecting Quinn and me and inviting us to trust that there will be even more goodness and grace in the years to come.

SHARIE ROBBINS lives in La Canada, California, with her husband, Quinn. They have three children: Anthony, twenty-three; Ashley, twenty-three; and Justine, twenty-one. Quinn and Sharie have been married for twenty-five years.

65

A DIVINE HAIR APPOINTMENT

AMY VON BORSTEL

They gave me thirty days' notice today at my job," my husband told me, his shoulders slouched forward and a despondent look in his eyes. It was the fourth time in twenty-two years that my husband had lost a job, and it wasn't getting any easier. It hurt every time, and I felt as if my heart were sinking into my stomach, fluttering for life as fear grabbed hold of my soul and tempted me to give up hope.

The economy was bad. I knew it—everyone was talking about it—but it didn't feel sufficient to blame the job market. I wasn't blaming God either, but I was questioning whether or not he had our lives in his hands. *Why, Lord? How can this be? Where did we go wrong?* Memories of bare cupboards played in my mind. Realizing we had no savings made matters worse. *Looking for another job? We can't do this alone*, my husband and I prayed. *Please, God, be with us.*

As my husband's last thirty days at work slowly passed by, we looked at our finances and the coming months. "It's going to be tight," Michael said, with a slightly anxious tone in his voice.

"It always is," I tried to comfort him, "but we always make it."

"I know," he said, sitting back in his chair, letting out a deep sigh. "I just don't want to work only to pay the mortgage anymore. You know?"

I nodded because I did know; we had talked several times while dating and after being married about following our dreams. Michael wanted to work in the medical field so he could use his training doing international missions. I, too, had a dream to work abroad with orphans in Africa. "Maybe this is the time to take it more seriously," I told him. "Michael, let's pray and ask God to lead us in the right direction, and I'll look for work."

I began searching on the Internet for job openings, wondering where or if I'd find a job before we spent my husband's last paycheck. An ad for a catering business caught my eye. The hours would fit in perfectly with my schedule as a homeschooling mom. The catering business would offer flexibility and allow me to choose the events I would work.

I sent in my résumé and was called back for an interview the following week. I was thrilled, and so was my husband, but my excitement quickly turned to feelings of uneasiness. It had been almost ten years since I'd needed to dress up for work. I looked through my wardrobe and then glanced in the mirror. "My hair," I sighed. I tried to remember the last time I was in a salon but quickly gave up. *It would be nice to get a few highlights and a trim*, I told myself, trying not to think of our budget for a moment. *I need to look professional.* Trying to think of a cost-saving solution, I leafed through my address book, looking for an old friend's number. She cut hair in her house at a fraction of the cost of a salon, but she didn't answer or call me back for several days.

Time was running out. The interview was now only four days away, so I took a friend's advice and called a hairdresser she had raved about. It was eight o'clock on a Saturday evening, and I didn't expect anyone to pick up, let alone set up an appointment. But a sweet lady named Tonia answered, listened to my situation, and booked me as her first Tuesday morning client.

"Thank you so much, Tonia. This is such a blessing."

"Of course, honey," she replied. "See you Tuesday." I sensed a warm spirit of relief wash through me as I hung up. Even knowing I'd have to borrow money from our grocery budget to pay for the appointment, I felt it would be worth every penny.

When I arrived at the salon Tuesday morning, I was nervous, but Tonia greeted me with a kind smile. "This way. Come on. Let's get started." she said, inviting me to sit down in her chair. She wrapped the cape around me and gently put her hands on my shoulders. "Now, I want you to tell me," she said, looking at me in the mirror, "if money were not an issue, what would you want to have done to your hair?" I sat back in shock, my mouth caught open and my eyebrows curled over my eyes.

"I don't know," I mumbled. "I guess I haven't really thought about it." But the truth was, I had thought about it. I had stood in front of the mirror the night before, imagining my hair dressed up like a movie star. Highlights, color, cut, styled.

"Well," Tonia smiled, "I've been praying about you since we talked on Saturday, and I want to do your hair at no charge." I can only imagine the look of shock on my face as I briefly looked away from her gaze. *Is she serious?* I asked myself. *There is no way.* I looked back to her, and the joy on her face was undeniable.

"Anything you want," she added, "color, highlights, a haircut— I can even do your eyebrows!" My face fell into my hands, and I began weeping. I couldn't contain myself; I was shocked. Why would a stranger bless me in such a huge way? How could she know exactly what I wanted?

"Yes," I said, with tears running down my face. "A total makeover!" Tonia began moving her fingers through my hair, talking about color options and different styles. She ran warm water through my hair and washed it with wonderful, scented shampoo. She combed, clipped, and cut while talking about her mission trip to Africa and the work she had done with orphans in other developing countries. She told me story after story, quoted some of my favorite scriptures from the Psalms and Ephesians, and then suddenly stopped and asked me, "What is your heart's desire?"

I couldn't answer; I was still crying too hard. How could a hair appointment feel so sacred? How did Tonia know exactly what to say? Why was I feeling so encouraged? *It's just a haircut*, I kept trying to tell myself, but it wasn't true. It was so much more. I had never experienced anything so surreal or life-giving or unexpected. Joy grabbed hold of my heart and pulled it back into the light, into hope. I felt at peace, as if each touch of Tonia's fingers were restoring my soul.

"Amy," she told me, somewhere in the third hour of my makeover, "God has given you his heart for Africa." I cried, and cried, and cried, and Tonia just kept smiling. "I can sense it in you."

How could a hairdresser know so much about me? I wondered. Then it hit me—Tonia wasn't just a hairdresser; she was a blessing, moved by God to serve me with her talent and her time but mostly with her spirit. It was a supernatural encounter, the kind you never believe can happen until it happens to you. By the time I left the salon, my hair had never looked so good, I had never stood quite as tall, and my soul had never been so refreshed.

I walked into my interview that week, feeling confident in the love of God, and received the job on the spot. A few months later my husband found a good program, was accepted, and began studying for his dream career. He graduated two and a half years later and was hired quickly by a wonderful company that specializes in medical diagnostics. They sponsor a medical train in South Africa that gives medical care to people in villages with limited resources. His company also assists employees with adoption fees.

It's no coincidence that Michael's company does medical missions in Africa and helps to support orphans through adoption. And it wasn't a coincidence all those years ago that led me to Tonia's salon. I don't believe in coincidence anymore. There are only divine appointments sent by God to reveal his extravagant love in amazing ways. My husband's job is just one example. Another is the son we are hoping to adopt from Africa. And so is my cherished friend Tonia, who came into my life as an unexpected gift at the exact right time and remains one of my dearest friends.

AMY VON BORSTEL is a wife and homeschooling mom, living her dream of being home with her family and writing the stories of God's faithfulness in her life. She lives in the suburbs of Atlanta, Georgia, with her husband and two children.

LEMON DROP

Two things needed to be in place for this divine moment to happen—Amy needed to be ready to receive, and Tonia needed to be ready to give. Sometimes we are in need of encouragement, and other times we are blessed to be able to encourage others. No matter where you are right now, I hope you are looking for the divine in the everyday—it's where it most often shows up.

—Don

66

CONNECTION

ANONYMOUS

I t's just after three o'clock in the morning, and my husband is drunk, again. I can hear him walking through the hallway, about to reach our apartment door.

Lord, please give me the strength. The door flies open, and he shouts my name. "Hey! Where are you?" I walk out of the bedroom and see him leaning over, hardly keeping his balance.

"It's late, and you're being too loud," I say, thinking maybe he'll reason with me and go to bed.

"I don't care!" he says, wobbling back and forth.

"Our son is sleeping and—"

"Shut up!" A quiet second passes between us, and I know it is coming. It always feels as though the air is escaping the room, as if there is nothing left to breathe and no place safe to stand. As if I am a dying star, sucking everything into myself, turning inside out, slowly dying. Then he erupts.

He stumbles across the room, shouting, spit flying from his mouth, and he pushes me back into the wall. His hands are on my shoulders, strong and firm, and I shout back. I don't even know what I'm saying or thinking, but I scream and try to pry his hands from me. His grip is unrelenting. He pushes me harder into the wall and raises his voice even louder.

He is swearing now. Every word is obscene and deafening, and he is screaming so loud, so close to me, I have to close my eyes. I feel his right hand loosen, then pull away. I close my eyes tighter and brace myself. His fist strikes me in the face, and the pain explodes through my head. As he reaches back again, I open my eyes and see him over me. My husband. The father of my son and our baby on the way. I cover my pregnant belly and take the second blow.

Then a voice I've never heard, loud and decisive, shouts inside me. *No!*

I look up to my husband, to his lips, and he is still swearing. He didn't hear it, but I hear it again.

No!

I push him back far enough to step around him and run across the room ahead of his drunken stumble. The phone is hanging on the wall, and I grab it.

9-1-1.

As my finger pushes the last button, he tears the phone from my hand and rips it out of the wall. Plaster and paint scatter across the room. We look each other in the eye, and I see his rage rising. He rushes toward me. I raise one hand to cover my head and lower the other to protect my unborn daughter.

I see a light, narrow and focused, searching around the room. Then there is a sound, in between my husband's frantic, enraged breaths; it comes from the door.

Bang! Bang! Bang! "Police, open up!"

My husband is suddenly gone, running into the next room. I race to the front door and turn the knob. The officer looks me in the eyes, then down to the welts on my shoulders, the bruises on my arms, my pregnant belly, then back up to my eyes.

"How did you know to come?" I ask, panting.

"You called 9-1-1."

"But my call never went through. My husband knocked the phone out of my hand and out of the wall. Which neighbor called you?"

"No," he says, shaking his head. "The call came from *you*." The officers walk through the apartment and find my husband on his hands and knees, trying to put the phone line back into the wall. One officer handcuffs and walks him down to the car. The other stays and asks me a few questions.

Then I ask my own question. "How did my call go through?"

"It's a new system," he answered. "Every 9-1-1 call registers instantly, regardless if it goes through or not. Now anytime anyone dials for help, we come." He finishes his questions and tells me they will contact me in the morning. I close the door behind him, and everything is quiet. I sit down on the sofa, safe from the words and fists that have hurt me so many times before.

I did it, I think to myself. *I asked for help. Finally. Thank you, Lord, for the strength!*

The weeks and months following my husband's arrest were not easy. I hadn't told anyone what was happening at home, so when they learned about the domestic violence, they were less than empathetic.

Several friends seemed to blame me, implying it wasn't fair for the kids to be without their father.

I began to feel anxious and alone. I started hearing noises at night and imagined someone was breaking into the apartment to take the children. I sought out a counselor to help me with the fear. She told me I needed to get up and identify unknown noises; otherwise, my imagination and anxiety would only get worse.

I was working on naming my fears, and one morning while I was preparing breakfast, a sudden noise from the living room terrified me. It was high-pitched and repetitive. Was someone breaking in? My heart was pounding. *What do I do?*

Identify the noise, I heard my counselor say. Cautiously I rounded the corner from the kitchen. On the floor, playing with his trucks, was my son. He was laughing. I walked around him, slowly. His head was thrown back behind his shaking shoulders, and his face was split by the widest smile I've ever seen. I sat down next to him, and tears poured down my cheeks as I realized *I had never heard my son laugh out loud.*

Our home had been so full of tension and fear that laughter was impossible. We kept our heads down, our mouths shut, and our emotions hidden. We had been walking on eggshells for so long that we had forgotten how to laugh. My son was the first to remember—I was the second.

I joined him, erupting with hope-filled, full-body laughter. We laughed until we were exhausted, and when we finally picked ourselves up off the floor, I knew I had rediscovered what it meant to be alive.

I told my priest the story of learning the sound of my son's laughter, and he smiled. "That is beautiful," he said. "God doesn't want you to suffer." I agreed with him, and since then I have thanked God a thousand times for the miracle call that saved my life. No matter the shape of our family or how dark the night, we have each other, and we have remembered how to laugh.

—Anonymous

67

A NEW SONG

JAY COOKINGHAM

Hope is her name, and she is just twelve weeks in the womb. She already has teeth, fingernails, nerves, and hiccups, and we already have the nursery paint picked out and old baby clothes pulled from the closet. But the technician at the ultrasound appointment turns from the machine with a ghastly look in her eye and heartache in her voice.

"Your baby is dead," she whispers.

Hope is gone. Before she ever drew a breath or felt her mother's touch; before her fingerprints ever stained the walls or her laugh filled the room; before she ever held her hand in mine, her life is over.

Even with four healthy children already born and growing, the loss of Hope is devastating. How am I supposed to tell them about their baby sister? What do I say? It's hard to be at home and feel the empty space where Hope should be.

At work I lock myself in my office three, four times a day so no one walks in and sees me sobbing. Sometimes when I'm walking down the hallway, I can feel the grief warming up and rising from my gut, like a rocket from a launchpad, blasting through the atmosphere until I'm floating in the endless black of grief. I duck into the nearest room and bury my face in my hands until I can feel my feet on the ground again. Sometimes it takes minutes; other times it takes hours.

My wife and I don't want people to call or come over—they just don't understand. But when no one calls or comes over, we get resentful. We are so hurt we don't know what to do or what to want or what to need; every hour is a different struggle.

There is no stopping, though. If we wait for the pain to go away before we get back to living, we will never live another day. We wake up and get the kids off to school. I drive to work, make my calls, sit through the meetings, and wonder what color her hair would have been or where she would have wanted to go for dinner on her birthday. I feel as though I need to mourn, but I have no memories of my daughter, only what I imagine, and my imagination is restless, always finding us in the park on the swings, on the doorstep the night of senior prom, or in the car, driving to a college campus.

Can a father bear the loss of a daughter? Can a marriage endure the grief? Can our family ever be complete?

Several months have passed since we drove home from the ultrasound in silence. The hurt is still there, but we are learning how to embrace the genuine love of our friends and family. We are also discovering we are not alone. Others are hurting too.

On a recent trip to Manhattan for a company-planning meeting, I walked into a conference room of somber stares.

"Is everything okay?" I asked.

A colleague at the end of the table spoke up. "Tim just found out his sister miscarried twins."

I looked around the room, searching for Tim's face. "Where is he now?"

"I think he is in the video room. He said he wanted to be alone."

I walked down the hallway to the video room and turned the doorknob. It was dark, and I could hear him before I could see him, his heavy breathing and the sound of his weight, rocking back and forth in the chair. When I sat down next to him and he looked at me, I was looking into a reflection of my own grief-stricken face.

"Do you want to talk about it?" I asked, and he didn't waste a second. The story poured out of him. Then my story poured out of me.

I spoke in short bursts, speaking through the tears. "It's the hardest, darkest thing I've ever gone through."

Tim wiped a tear away from his face and asked, "How do you deal with it? Do you still believe in God?"

"It was a struggle," I said, being as honest as I could. "But through it all, I kept believing two things: God is good, and he is holding on to me." I paused for a moment, then added, "I believe he is holding on to you, too, and your sister."

A few minutes later, when we had regained our composure, he pulled out his cell phone and called his sister. As I was leaving the room, I could hear him say, "I need to tell you something someone just shared with me."

As I drove home that day, I thought about the cage grief had built around me. When I wondered if I would ever escape, a bird called Hope came to perch on the iron bars. She sang her sweet song and set my soul free. Now she is in the dark room of another man's grief, sharing her song, lighting a way forward.

How many hopeless souls will Hope reach? We don't know,

but we are grateful every time God uses the story of our little girl to encourage another. She may never have taken a breath, but she endures—sharing the gift of life and healing with the world.

JAY COOKINGHAM is a freelance writer/poet as well as a graphic artist. He writes a blog (soulfari.blogspot.com) geared toward men and their role as fathers and husbands. He has been published in the following books: *God's Way for Fathers*, *God's Ways for Teachers*, *God's Way for Christmas*, *Smiles for Dads*, *Soul Matters for Men*, *The Rainy Day Book*, and *A Man of Honor*. A father of seven, Jay has been happily married to his wife, Christine, for twenty-nine years.

68

FRIDAY NIGHT LIGHTS

BECKY ALEXANDER

The girl performing her drill routine in front of me was flawless: energetic and beaming, high-stepping to every beat, the red shaker in her left hand mirroring the white shaker in her right. She spun her head from side to side, her wavy hair whipping back and forth like a stadium crowd doing the wave. She must have practiced for hours and hours to nail the performance so completely, and I should know. *She was me.*

I was dancing on the front porch of my house in rural Ohio, watching my reflection perform in the picture window. As I caught my breath at the end of the routine, I knew I was as ready as I could be for Friday night. To most people in my small town, Friday night was all about football, and even though I hadn't missed a game since starting high school three years ago, I didn't pay much attention to the game.

For me, Friday nights were about pulling on a pair of shiny Sheer

Energy panty hose and feeling as if I could be the star of Broadway's biggest show. They were about ironing my red-and-white uniform with the perfectly pleated skirt and thick, embroidered letters stitched across the chest. They were about lacing up my brilliant white boots adorned with red pom-poms. They were about getting to our stadium and seeing the towering lights creating halos in the dark sky, as hundreds of excited fans streamed toward the front gates.

Friday night was my time to shine as a member of the Madison High drill team, and I loved everything about it. Dancing like crazy on the sidelines while the band played "Louie, Louie" and "Tequila" as loud as it could; shivering under a plaid stadium blanket while drinking concession-stand hot chocolate out of a Styrofoam cup; hopping up into the stands to steal a few minutes with my current boyfriend—and maybe even a peck for good luck—before returning to the sidelines to prepare for our halftime drill routine. I'm sure football games happened too; it's just that I'd never bothered to see one.

I performed my routine that Friday night perfectly. As usual, no one in the stands even noticed my prosthetic left hand. I'd been born with only my right hand, so I'd had plenty of time to learn how to live without my left. I'd never let a drill routine get the best of me.

But the next week at practice, our captain, Beth, called us into a circle. "Girls, I have a *totally* big announcement. Are you ready?" Beth was bouncing up and down on the balls of her feet, and she had her hands hidden behind her back. "Well, for next week's game against the Cougars, we're going to use . . ." Beth paused and looked around the circle, making sure we were hanging on her every word. "New! Gloves!" She shouted each word, at the same time pulling her hands from behind her back for the big reveal. Her gloves were white on the back and red on the palm, and Beth quickly rotated her hands at the wrists to show us the possibility of flashing between the two colors.

"It's going to be *so* neat!" she gushed, clapping her hands together in a blur of red and white.

She was right. The gloves *were* so neat . . . and I was *so* not going to be able to use them. I knew right away that I could practice every hour of every day until the game, and it wouldn't make a difference. This wasn't a matter of hard work—it was simply a reality of my prosthetic hand. I could open and close it, but it didn't rotate at the wrist. And even if it did, the fingers were always curved, which allowed me to grip things. A flat hand didn't make any sense for my prosthetic hand. I tried to picture myself on the field with the drill team, but all I could see was a precise line of flat, flashing hands . . . and me at the end of the line, holding my prosthetic hand into the air, motionless, for all the crowd to see.

That night at dinner I told my father about the new gloves. "I'm going to have to sit on the bench this game," I said. Through no fault of my own, my four-year streak of performances was about to end. Dad put down his fork and laced his calloused fingers together. He looked at me, his forehead wrinkled with concern, and said, "Don't give up just yet. Let me think about it."

That night, when he went to his job at Armco Steel, he got his fellow machinists to think about my problem too. Meanwhile, I went to bed, convinced I would be forced to actually *watch* my first football game ever. The next day Dad told me he had something to show me. I followed his voice into the kitchen and saw him holding something. "Let's see if this might do the trick," he said, handing me a prosthetic hand I'd never seen.

He explained that he and his fellow workers at the mill had cut the rotating mechanism off an ice-cream scoop and attached it to the cabling on one of my prosthetic wrists. Next they'd fabricated extended "fingers" from strips of metal and surrounded them with a thin layer of padding. The new red-and-white glove pulled down over the padded fingers like a dream—from more than a few feet away, it looked just like a real hand. I removed my standard wrist and placed it on the counter; then I fitted on the new wrist. Holding my breath, I manipulated the cable, the same motion that normally opened and closed my curved prosthetic fingers. This time the fingers stayed where they were—extended inside the red-and-white glove—and, instead, the whole hand rotated, front to back and back to front. I looked up from my new hand in wide-eyed wonder and found Dad looking at me, a wide smile creasing his face.

All week I practiced with my new hand and new gloves until the motions were second nature. Come Friday night, the lights shone especially bright as I danced my heart out. My hands flashed back and forth between red and white, in sync with each other and the rest of the drill team. I have no idea who won the game that night or who was named Most Valuable Player. As always, I wasn't there for the football. That week I wasn't even there for the drill team and the fans—Dad was the real star, and I was there for him.

That night I performed for an audience of one, and I knew my father was watching every red-and-white spin of my hands with joy on his face. He was delighted to see me succeed, and his delight was equaled by my own—delighted because I wouldn't have been there without his love. My happiness could have lit the field.

BECKY ALEXANDER serves as executive pastor at Crosspoint Community Church in Decatur, Alabama. She is wife to Tim and mom to Cassie and Isaac. Her dad, Mark Selby, is still her hero, and her mom is pretty awesome too. You can catch what Becky is contemplating today on her blog at beckyalexander.tv.

LEMON DROP

The older I get, the more and more I'm convinced of God's fatherly love. Becky's story reminds me of the verse in Matthew 7, where Jesus says, "So if you sinful people know how to give good gifts to your children, how much more will your heavenly Father give good gifts to those who ask him" (v. 7). The love of Becky's dad is a glimpse into the heart of our heavenly Father, who cherishes us, fights for us, and gives us good gifts.

—Don

AFTERWORD

Sometimes I wonder if our world doesn't pay enough attention to hope.

Love can change the world, and faith can get us through tough times. But sometimes we act as though we can live without hope. I don't know about you, but the times I'm best at loving and being faithful are the times I'm also filled with a sense of hope. Reading these stories has filled me to overflowing—and made me even more grateful for those sweet moments in life.

Do these stories have you thinking about the lemonade moments in your life? Well, now is the chance to tell your story of unexpected sweetness in the midst of sour circumstances. We have already collected more stories than we could use in this book, and we are planning

to work on the When God Makes Lemonade™ series for a long time, so visit godmakeslemonade.com right now, and share your story.
We're looking forward to hearing from you.

Don Jacobson

If these stories encouraged you, you can
like us on Facebook at facebook.com/godmakeslemonade, or visit our
website, where you can tell us your story at
GodMakesLemonade.com.

ABOUT THE AUTHOR

Don Jacobson has served as president and owner of Multnomah Publishers, where he oversaw the production of more than one thousand titles and the sale of more than 100 million books. After twenty-eight years in the publishing industry and selling Multnomah to Random House in 2006, Don founded D. C. Jacobson & Associates (DCJA), an author management company, so he could continue working closely with authors—together dreaming about books that change the world by changing the church. That passion is still the heartbeat of Don's professional life as he guides DCJA.

A graduate of Multnomah University in Portland, Don lives with Brenda, his wife of thirty-five years, in Portland, Oregon. The couple has four amazing adult children, three of whom are married to equally amazing spouses.